Springer Proceedings in Business and Economics

Springer Proceedings in Business and Economics brings the most current research presented at conferences and workshops to a global readership. The series features volumes (in electronic and print formats) of selected contributions from conferences in all areas of economics, business, management, and finance. In addition to an overall evaluation by the publisher of the topical interest, scientific quality, and timeliness of each volume, each contribution is refereed to standards comparable to those of leading journals, resulting in authoritative contributions to the respective fields. Springer's production and distribution infrastructure ensures rapid publication and wide circulation of the latest developments in the most compelling and promising areas of research today.

The editorial development of volumes may be managed using Springer Nature's innovative EquinOCS, a proven online conference proceedings submission, management and review system. This system is designed to ensure an efficient timeline for your publication, making Springer Proceedings in Business and Economics the premier series to publish your workshop or conference volume.

This book series is indexed in SCOPUS.

Michael Lustenberger · Florian Spychiger ·
Lukas Küng
Editors

Decentralized Autonomous Organizations—Governance, Technology, and Legal Perspectives

Proceedings of the 2nd European DAO Workshop (DAWO), Zurich, Switzerland, 2025

Springer

Editors
Michael Lustenberger
ZHAW Zurich University of Applied Sciences
Winterthur, Switzerland

Florian Spychiger
ZHAW Zurich University of Applied Sciences
Winterthur, Switzerland

Lukas Küng
ZHAW Zurich University of Applied Sciences
Winterthur, Switzerland

University of Nicosia
School of Business
Institute for the Future
Nicosia, Cyprus

ISSN 2198-7246 ISSN 2198-7254 (electronic)
Springer Proceedings in Business and Economics
ISBN 978-3-032-03272-0 ISBN 978-3-032-03273-7 (eBook)
https://doi.org/10.1007/978-3-032-03273-7

This Springer imprint is published by the registered company Springer Nature Switzerland AG
The registered company address is: Gewerbestrasse 11, 6330 Cham, Switzerland

Preface

This volume contains the proceedings of the 2nd European DAO Workshop (DAWO 2025), held in Zürich, Switzerland, from June 23 to June 24, 2025. The event was hosted by ZHAW Zurich University of Applied Sciences and the University of Zurich, and brought together researchers, practitioners, and academics from around the world to discuss recent advances in research on Decentralized Autonomous Organizations (DAOs).

Following the success of the first European DAO Workshop in 2024, it was highly encouraging to see that the second edition was also very well received, drawing a vibrant and highly interdisciplinary group of participants. The event was marked by rich discussions and meaningful interactions across disciplinary boundaries, reinforcing the need for a dedicated forum to explore the complexities and potential of DAOs.

DAOs are a rapidly growing phenomenon, and the importance of these new organizational forms is expected to increase significantly with the continued adoption of blockchain and distributed ledger technologies. As interest in decentralized governance models grows, there is a pressing need for deeper research into how such systems can support inclusive, democratic, and cooperative values. DAWO was conceived as a testbed for this ongoing conversation, aiming to critically examine the potential of DAOs as transformative infrastructures for the digital age.

The two-day workshop fostered a culture of participation and open dialogue, encouraging interdisciplinary exchange and knowledge transfer between researchers across law, economics, computer science, and organizational theory. The objective is to support the development of DAO-related scholarship while laying the groundwork for sustained research collaboration. We anticipate that the discussions initiated at DAWO 2025 will lead to a variety of novel research directions and partnerships.

A total of 44 papers and abstracts by 88 authors from 25 different countries were submitted to the conference. Each submission was reviewed by two members of the Program Committee. After a thorough double-blind review process, nine papers were selected for publication in these proceedings. These papers span a diverse set of themes and reflect the interdisciplinary nature of DAO research, covering areas such as:

- DAO Concepts & Design
- DAO Economics
- Voting & Democracy
- Legal Analysis & Innovation

The selected papers in these proceedings reflect four major research themes that illuminate the multifaceted evolution of DAOs. A prominent focus is on **institutional innovation**, where contributions explore novel governance architectures that move beyond traditional firms or markets. This includes the conceptualization of contribution systems as programmable and adaptive institutions that coordinate participation and value creation (Paper 1), as well as re-examinations of Bitcoin as a foundational DAO model, highlighting both its democratic potential and governance challenges (Paper 2). Literature reviews further reveal opportunities and hurdles in implementing digital democracy within DAOs, particularly around power distribution and participatory mechanisms (Papers 3).

Another key theme centers on **community design and tokenomics**, which addresses socio-economic factors essential for fostering inclusion and cooperation. Research advocates integrating sociological principles into tokenomics to better support local communities and collaborative goals, moving beyond market-driven frameworks (Paper 4). Real-world experiments such as the Optimism Retroactive Public Goods Funding initiative provide insights into improving DAO governance by applying computational social choice methods that enhance fairness and strategyproofness in funding allocations (Papers 5).

The **dynamics of trust and governance** form a critical area of inquiry, where the interplay of token concentration, regulatory ambiguity, and conflicting incentives threatens to undermine legitimacy and participation. By applying social capital, public goods, and principal-agent theories, studies reveal how these challenges affect institutional confidence and grassroots engagement, prompting calls for tailored governance strategies that foster resilience and inclusiveness in DAO ecosystems (Paper 6).

Finally, the theme of **legal and regulatory transformation** explores how existing frameworks must evolve to accommodate the decentralized and autonomous nature of DAOs. Innovative regulatory concepts such as embedded supervision and polycentric co-regulation aim to reconcile decentralization with compliance, especially as artificial intelligence becomes integrated in governance processes (Paper 7). Comparative analyses identify gaps in current company laws and propose new liability regimes suited for decentralized entities (Paper 8). Moreover, the emergence of Lex Cryptographia as a new legal order challenges traditional jurisdictions and calls for updated taxation and valuation models in digital economies (Papers 9).

Together, these contributions delineate the multifaceted evolution of DAOs as emergent institutional, socio-technical, and legal phenomena. They highlight the significant potential of DAOs to reshape governance and economic organization in the digital age while acknowledging the complexity of the challenges ahead.

We would like to express our sincere appreciation to the Program Committee members for their diligence and expertise in evaluating the submissions. We also thank the keynote speakers, workshop moderators, panelists, session chairs, and all the authors whose contributions made the conference a success.

The Conference Committee deserves special thanks for their dedication and efforts in organizing the event. We are grateful to Springer for their continued support in publishing this volume as part of the book series Springer Proceedings in Business and Economics, and to ZHAW Zurich University of Applied Sciences for providing open access funding for this volume. We also extend our sincere thanks to the University of Zurich (UZH) and the Swiss National Science Foundation (SNSF) for their generous support—particularly through the SNSF-funded project *Decentralised Decision-Making in DAOs: Learnings for Digital Democracy* (project no. 10000911)—which made the conference and its proceedings possible.

We are confident that readers will find these proceedings both informative and inspiring, and that they will serve as a valuable resource for future research and collaboration in the field.

Winterthur, Switzerland

Michael Lustenberger
Florian Spychiger
Lukas Küng

Organization

DAWO25 Committees

Conference Chair

Michael Lustenberger	ZHAW Zurich University of Applied Sciences
Florian Spychiger	ZHAW Zurich University of Applied Sciences
Claudio J. Tessone	University of Zurich

Steering Committee

Javier Arroyo Gallardo	Universidad Complutense de Madrid
George M. Giaglis	University of Nicosia
Bruno Pasquier	FernUni Schweiz
Ellie Rennie	Royal Melbourne Institute of Technology
Uwe Serdült	Center for Democracy Studies Aarau

Organizing Committee

Lukas Küng	ZHAW Zurich University of Applied Sciences
Benjamin Kraner	University of Zurich

Program Committee

Anna Kasimati	Durham University

Benjamin Kraner	University of Zurich
Bruno Pasquier	FernUni Schweiz
Harald Bärtschi	ZHAW Zurich University of Applied Sciences
Irene Buller	Fachhochschule Nordwestschweiz
Jens Hunhevicz	ETH Zurich
Jens Martignoni	ZHAW Zurich University of Applied Sciences
Kelsie Nabben	Royal Melbourne Institute of Technology
Mark C. Ballandies	University of Zurich
Matija Piškorec	Ruđer Bošković Institute
Michael Schillig	Kings College London
Nathan Schneider	University of Colorado Boulder
Nils Augustin	University of Innsbruck
Parminder Kaur Makode	University of Zurich
Pascal Moriggl	Fachhochschule Nordwestschweiz
Pınar Çağlayan Aksoy	Bilkent University
Romain Rossello	HEC Paris
Stefanie Boss	University of Amsterdam
Stephan Meyer	University of Lucerne
Udi Shapiro	Weizmann Institute of Science
Vero Estrada	IEEE
Yann Vonlanthen	ETH Zurich

Sponsor

BlackVogel Consulting
Crypto Finance AG
DFINITY
DIZH
Innovation Booster Artificial Intelligence
Swiss National Science Foundation (SNSF)
UZH, Blockchain Center
ZHAW Zurich University of Applied Sciences

Contents

Design Principles for Contribution Systems

Ellie Rennie and Jason Potts

Abstract Contribution systems are emerging as a novel institutional form for coordinating value creation in decentralized communities. Unlike firms or markets, these systems structure participation, recognition, and value accumulation over time, relying on machine-readable contributions and computational governance. This paper develops a framework of design principles for contribution systems, drawing from empirical research on SourceCred, Protocol Guild, Regen Network, and Deep Funding. We build on Kealey and Ricketts' theory of contribution goods, which conceptualizes value as participation-excludable, in contrast to conventional public goods frameworks. A key governance challenge in contribution systems is achieving and sustaining critical mass—ensuring enough contributors participate for the system to become self-sustaining. Other core principles include tracking dependencies, ensuring continuous valuation, and structuring modular, adaptive governance mechanisms. Contribution systems do not merely reward contributions; they create futural institutions, where contributions persist and recompute dynamically over time. Their programmability allows for automated governance, AI-assisted valuation, and scalable incentive structures, distinguishing them from traditional commons governance. This paper positions contribution systems as an emerging institutional paradigm, offering a set of governance principles that will require further empirical research and testing.

Keywords Contribution systems · Institutions · Design principles

---

Present Address:
E. Rennie (✉) · J. Potts
RMIT University, Melbourne, VIC, Australia
e-mail: ellie.rennie@rmit.edu.au

M. Lustenberger et al. (eds.), *Decentralized Autonomous Organizations—Governance, Technology, and Legal Perspectives*, Springer Proceedings in Business and Economics,
https://doi.org/10.1007/978-3-032-03273-7_1

1 Introduction

The theory of *contribution systems* has recently been proposed by Rennie and Potts [1, 2] as a general analytic framework to explain detailed ethnographic observations on a range of permissionless organizations (see [3, 4]) through a combination of *New Institutional Economics* and the evolutionary game theory lens of *contribution goods* [5]. Rennie and Potts theorize that a contribution system is a new type of economic institution, made possible by new technologies (including blockchains and AI), that represents an evolution of the commons to enable computation over a new institutionally legible object—namely a *contribution*. Individuals make contributions (of resources, time and effort) toward a common joint project, and software turns those actions into computable objects that form the basis for subsequent claims of value as the project develops. A contribution system is the institutional mechanism by which distributed and permissionless contributions are processed into interobjective value.Please check and confirm if the authors and their respective affiliations have been correctly identified. Amend if necessary."?>

Contribution systems are a new class of economic institution that has evolved from the commons, but is also composed of properties of other economic institutions such as markets, networks, and hierarchies. It is a novel and still experimental institutional innovation. The significance of contribution systems is that they seem well adapted to digital production at internet scale, and especially where a particular problem to be solved involves joint production.

A theory of contribution systems has an additional purpose beyond explaining empirical observations (i.e. its scientific contribution over a range of early prototypes); it also provides a foundation for innovation and design improvements on next generation contribution systems. The challenge is how to design better contribution systems, which we see as a challenge of institutional design. This paper is a first attempt to develop a framework for design principles for contribution systems. Our goal is to articulate principles that address the unique challenges of contribution systems—a category of decentralized institutions that structure participation, recognition, and value creation in digital economies.

We adopt an abductive approach grounded in ethnographic and case study data, generating provisional principles from observed institutional regularities, following Ostrom's logic of theorizing from empirical design patterns. The core theoretical insight guiding this work is that contribution goods serve a similar function to common-pool resources (CPRs) in Ostrom's [6] Institutional Analysis and Design (IAD) framework: they define the governance challenge. Just as CPRs are difficult to exclude people from but require governance to prevent depletion [7], contribution goods require governance to sustain participation and prevent under-contribution. The governance challenges they pose are distinct: whereas commons governance focuses on preventing overuse (with positive-sum participation a necessary element of this), contribution systems must ensure ongoing contributions, participation-based exclusion, and dynamic value recognition over time. In this sense, contribution systems are not simply digital commons, they are machine-readable institutions designed to anchor contributions in ways that persist across time and scale. Inspired by the Ostrom framework of design principles for governing the commons (see [7, p. 90]), this paper seeks to develop design principles for contribution systems.

2 What Are Contribution Systems?

Unlike traditional institutions—such as firms, states, or markets—that rely on contracts, hierarchical enforcement, or pricing mechanisms to structure participation, contribution systems create continuous, decentralized records of contributions that endure beyond any single moment of exchange. The substantive novelty here is the creation of a new institutional object—a contribution, and a mechanism to which that object is legible—a contribution system. This means that rather than being time-bound to a contract, employment period, or immediate transaction, a contribution in these systems can accumulate value, recognition, or influence over extended time-frames. Contributions do not merely exist in the present; they persist and recompute, resurfacing as dependencies are activated in future contexts. This futural dimension positions contribution systems as a new class of institution, capable of structuring long-term cooperation in decentralized settings.

Additionally, machine-readability transforms governance itself. Because contributions can be tracked, computed, and re-weighted over time, they enable automated decision-making, dynamic incentives, and AI-assisted recognition of value in ways that traditional institutions cannot. This programmability allows for new forms of automated governance, real-time recalibration of incentives, and scalable contribution tracking, expanding the ways in which decentralized cooperation can be structured. Our intention here is to explore how contribution systems function as future institutions, structured around a set of core governance principles that emerge from both empirical cases and theoretical insights into contribution goods.

Contribution systems are emerging as a significant mechanism for coordinating value creation in distributed communities. A contribution system is generally defined as a system that recognizes, measures, and may reward contributions made by individuals or machines to a collective endeavour, even when participants are largely strangers. Unlike firms (which rely on hierarchical control) or markets (which rely on price signals), contribution systems use computational metrics and social feedback to attribute value to objects representing contributions. This allows them to incentivize activities that would otherwise remain untraced and unrewarded in a pure market setting.

The significance of contribution systems lies in their potential to coordinate resources and knowledge that are distributed across society, without requiring a centralized company or clear property rights. Early examples have existed in limited forms (for instance, social and technical protocols for academic citations), but they have become fundamental within blockchain protocols and decentralized autonomous organizations (DAOs). As we have argued elsewhere, Ethereum itself is a contribution system, where validators confirm or reject contributions (blocks) and are rewarded or penalized accordingly (Rennie [8, 9] (*under review*)). Contribution systems create value by computing relationships between contributions and upstream outcomes over a complex forward graph of dependencies, rather than by assigning prices to outputs from an accounting of exchange relations. In doing so, they can bring to light productive activities (such as open-source code maintenance or environmental stewardship) that markets often undervalue. A contribution system therefore builds from the activity of the commons, generating new forms of valued output (reputation, tokens, shared knowledge) that may help sustain communities and protocols.

Institutions are defined in New Institutional Economics as the "rules of the game in a society, or more formally, are the humanly designed constraints that shape human interaction" (North [10], p. 3). These refer to rules such as contracts, hierarchical enforcement, or pricing mechanisms that structure interaction and participation, and it is usually not even mentioned that this happens *in the present*. Institutions are persistent and legitimate rules *from the past*. However, we suggest that contribution systems are a "future institution". The way they coordinate and constrain human interaction is that they move actions in the present (contributions) into the future and compute them back, as value. Institutions persist and are selected for under economic evolution because they provide long-term structures, in the form of social technologies, for coordination, value recognition, and decision-making. Contribution systems are still institutions in the "rules of the game" sense, but they are fundamentally "futural" in their aspect. Contributions are valued by what they add to the future, rather than market and hierarchy mechanisms that value in the present (e.g. exchange value, or cost value). Contribution systems, though emerging from digital and decentralized contexts, are not just tools for managing interactions but foundational mechanisms for anchoring contributions in ways that persist across time and scale.

Contribution systems work by creating continuous, decentralized records of contributions that endure beyond any single moment of exchange. This means that rather than being time-bound to a contract, employment period, or immediate transaction, a contribution in these systems can accumulate value, recognition, or influence over extended timeframes. The ability to track, recompute, and resurface contributions long after they are made introduces a new way of organizing human cooperation, one where individual and collective efforts become legible over long time scales rather than being ephemeral or forgotten when the immediate context shifts.

This temporal (futural) dimension—the ability to make contributions visible and relevant across different moments in time through the creation of a new institutional object, a contribution record—is what positions contribution systems as a future institution. They do not merely record present activity; they create infrastructures that bind past, present, and future contributions into an evolving system of value recognition. They are what we elsewhere call "hyperinstitutions" (extending on Timothy Morton's "hyperobjects" [11]).

This is a significant departure from conventional institutional frameworks, where contributions are often constrained to finite windows of recognition (such as a wage). Instead, a contribution made today may gain recognition later when its dependencies are activated in another context, much as Deep Funding's dependency graph surfaces foundational Ethereum code contributions. Moreover, because contributions become machine-readable, they can be scaled, programmed, and recombined in ways that produce different outcomes than the rules and monitoring systems of traditional commons. This programmability allows for automated governance, dynamic incentive structures, and AI-assisted recognition of contributions, expanding the ways in which decentralized cooperation can be structured. This ability to compute and contextualize contributions dynamically over time suggests they could become powerful governance mechanisms for long-term collective endeavours.

3 Defining Contribution Goods

The term contribution goods, introduced by Terence Kealey and Martin Ricketts [5], describes goods—often knowledge-based—that are non-rivalrous (one person's use doesn't reduce availability to others) yet partly excludable in an unusual way. Unlike private goods (excludable via prices) or club goods (excludable via membership fees), contribution goods are effectively excludable through participation: one must contribute or have certain capabilities to fully benefit. The example they use is scientific knowledge: once discoveries are published, they are in principle open to all (no one's use diminishes another's), but *only those who become scientists and contribute to the field can truly understand and utilize those discoveries.* Outsiders may enjoy some spillover benefits, but the most valuable insights remain "clubbed" among contributors with the requisite expertise. This soft form of exclusion is not enforced by a paywall or patent (leaving aside the problems of scholarly publishing), but by the inherent cognitive/skill barrier—effectively an earned membership instead of a bought one.

By requiring contribution as the "ticket" to full benefits, contribution systems invert the usual incentive problems of public goods. In a pure public good, anyone can benefit regardless of whether they helped produce it, leading to classic free-rider incentives (why pay if you can enjoy it for free?). Contribution goods change this calculus. Because key benefits (like deep knowledge, skill, reputation) accrue mainly to those who participate in creating or understanding the good, non-contributors are naturally left behind. In essence, would-be free-riders exclude themselves by not contributing. The outcome is similar to a club good—a subset (the contributors) enjoys most of the benefits—but without formal exclusion mechanisms. This concept was developed to better explain knowledge-driven collective projects (science, open-source, etc.) that did not fit neatly into standard categories. For Kealey and Ricketts [5], it provides a new lens for examining how innovation communities organize and why they succeed or fail.

Because of these properties—and despite being used for so-called retroactive public goods funding [12]—contribution goods challenge the standard public/private/club good classification. Traditional economic models often treat collective innovation or knowledge production as a public goods problem modelled by a Prisoner's Dilemma: everyone would be better off if all contribute, but each individual is tempted to shirk and free-ride on others' efforts. Science and open knowledge projects, however, appear to defy this trap. Kealey and Ricketts [5] argue that science is not a Prisoner's Dilemma at all, but a coordination game. The reason is that spillover benefits in science are *asymmetrically greater for contributors* than for outsiders. A scientist who contributes to the knowledge pool gains early access to new findings, know-how, and reputation that a non-contributing observer does not. This tilts the payoff structure so that contributing becomes the best response when others are contributing. In game-theoretic terms, the "game of science" (p. 1014) shifts from a prisoner's dilemma to one of pure coordination. If enough peers are working at the research frontier, an individual's optimal choice is to join and contribute, so as not to be left behind. Conversely, if nobody is contributing yet, there is little to gain by being the lone contributor—hence the need for a critical mass to kick start the endeavour.

This leads to a crucial insight: the key collective action problem in contribution systems is not ongoing free-riding, but achieving critical mass. Early on, a contribution-based project faces a coordination challenge—how to attract a minimum viable group of contributors so that contributions become worthwhile for each other. Kealey and Ricketts call this initial core the "visible college", distinguishing it from the broader "invisible college" (p. 1015) of peripheral participants. Once a sufficient base of active contributors is established, each member has strong incentives to continue contributing, since they directly share in the fruits of the joint effort. In effect, contribution systems offer a built-in selective incentive for participation: contributors simply get more utility or value from the good than do non-contributors. Once the project is self-sustaining, members have much less incentive to free-ride in the usual sense, because opting out means losing access to significant benefits. The result is a more optimistic outlook for collective innovation: under the right conditions, individuals can coordinate to produce knowledge, software, or other shared goods without the situation devolving into a defection-heavy dilemma. The incentives are structured such that cooperation (contribution) begets more cooperation, as success breeds success.

The contribution good concept also refines our understanding of knowledge commons—resources like scientific knowledge, open data, or shared digital content that are managed by communities [13]. Ostrom's work on commons emphasized how communities can self-govern shared resources with the right norms and institutions. Knowledge commons scholars have noted that scientific communities function as self-governing commons, often relying on informal norms of sharing and credit rather than market or state control [14]. The contribution lens adds that these commons often have an intrinsic gating mechanism: one must *enter the community* to reap full benefits. This naturally encourages continued contribution, as seen in open collaboration projects.

As a result, contribution systems alter the incentive structure of collective action. They mitigate the free-rider problem by embedding selective incentives (access, knowledge, reputation) in the good itself, turning potential dilemmatic situations into problems of coordination and participation. This is not to say free-riding disappears—indeed, many people *do* consume open-source software without contributing.

However, those free-riders don't undermine production as they would in a pure public goods scenario, because the core contributors have sufficient private reasons to keep producing. A primary challenge is ensuring enough contributors exist and feel valued, rather than preventing outsiders from consuming for free.

4 The Need for Design Principles for Contribution Systems

Over almost thirty years Elinor Ostrom gathered thousands of empirical studies of successful and unsuccessful governance of common-pool resources and realized that despite the immense diversity of commons governance systems, it is both possible and necessary to identify generalizable patterns that underlie successful self-governance. She called these high-level theoretical summaries "design principles" (see [15]).

> The diversity of regularized social behaviour that we observe at multiple scales is constructed [...] from universal components organized in many layers. In other words, whenever interdependent individuals are thought to be acting in an organized fashion, several layers of universal components create the structure that affects their behaviour and the outcomes they achieve. [6, p. 6]

She observed that scholars and practitioners were often lost in case-specific details, making it hard to learn broader lessons. To overcome this, Ostrom asked whether we can dig below the immense diversity of social settings to find common *building blocks* of human cooperation. Her answer was yes—she believed there are underlying principles of organization shared by effective commons institutions, even if the surface rules differ from one community to another. Ostrom justified the search for general principles as a way to develop better theory and policy—by identifying common patterns, we can create a shared framework to understand how fallible humans nonetheless achieve and sustain self-governance in complex, varied environments. In her view, communities managing resources from forests to fisheries are not utterly unique; they often rely on analogous solutions (e.g. defining user boundaries or monitoring resource use) that can be distilled into core principles. Ostrom explicitly posited that a set of *universal components* or "grammar" of institutions exists beneath the particularities of real-world cases. This conviction laid the groundwork for her formulation of general design principles applicable to commons governance everywhere. At the same time, she acknowledged this was a conjecture open to challenge—her approach was to propose common principles and then test them against diverse evidence.

In *Governing the Commons* [7], Ostrom distilled insights from a "meta-analysis of a large number of existing case studies" [16, p. 641] to propose several core principles that successful commons institutions tend to exhibit. These came to be summarized as *eight design principles* (e.g. clearly defined user and resource boundaries, congruence between local conditions and rules, participatory collective-choice arrangements; effective monitoring of use; graduated sanctions for rule-breakers; cheap conflict-resolution forums; minimal recognition of the community's right to self-organize; and for larger systems, nested enterprises). Ostrom emphasized that these principles were *empirical patterns*, not mere theories—each was derived from multiple real-world cases of commons that had persisted or thrived over decades or centuries. For instance, in virtually all the enduring commons she studied, the user community had a clear sense of who had rights to the resource and what the boundaries were (Principle 1), in contrast to open-access situations that led to overuse. The repetition of such features across cultures—from Japanese farmer cooperatives to Swiss villagers—gave Ostrom confidence that these were generalizable "best practices" in commons governance. She defined a "design principle" as an "element or condition that helps to account for the success" [7, p. 90] of institutions in sustaining a resource over the long term. Notably, her empirical research was not limited to observational field studies. She also drew on history (e.g. colonial era records of communal resource management) and conducted laboratory experiments on collective action. The convergence of evidence from these varied methods reinforced the design principles.

The role of the design principles, therefore, is not to dictate rigid templates for institutions, but to provide adaptable guidelines that communities can use in crafting their own rules (one of Ostrom's design principles itself is that rules should be congruent with local needs and conditions, underscoring that there is no one-size-fits-all approach to governing a commons). The design principles we outline below likewise function as a diagnostic checklist or heuristic—a set of critical factors to consider—rather than a statutory code. They are intended to guide users, developers, and researchers in asking the right questions.

Our approach to understanding contribution systems began with empirical research, specifically an ethnographic study of SourceCred [3], supplemented by case studies of other decentralized contribution networks. Through this work, we identified recurring governance challenges and incentive structures that did not fully align with existing economic categories, such as public goods or club goods. During the SourceCred ethnography we realized that Kealey and Ricketts' [5] theory of contribution goods offered a useful framing for what we had already observed: that these systems function not by enforcing strict excludability, but by structuring participation in ways that make contributions the mechanism for accessing benefits. Rennie incorporated Kealey and Ricketts' contribution goods framework as a way to refine and interpret her findings.

In the principles presented below, contribution goods serve a similar function to common-pool resources in Ostrom's work, in that they define the core governance challenge of the system. Just as Ostrom identified design principles to sustain CPRs, we identify governance principles to ensure contribution systems remain viable and continue to generate value.

5 Principles for Governing Contribution Systems

Drawing on Kealey and Ricketts' work on contribution goods, alongside empirical research from Ethereum, SourceCred, Regen Network, and Deep Funding, we suggest the following set of principles for governing contribution systems. These principles ensure that contribution systems remain effective, fair, and self-sustaining.

5.1 High-Value Contributors Drive System Strength

Thesis: A contribution system is stronger the more high-value contributors it attracts. Systems should be designed to maximize long-term engagement and retention of high-impact participants. Contribution systems do not merely benefit from high-value contributors—they require them to function.

Corollary: Contributions are orderable by value (high-low), the ordinal distribution of that value matters to system performance.

Example: Ethereum's Protocol Guild ensures that long-term, high-value contributors receive pooled compensation and governance privileges, maintaining a self-sustaining cycle of expertise and contribution.

5.2 Contributions Are Prioritized Over Passive Participation

Thesis: A well-functioning contribution system ensures that contributors receive greater rewards than non-contributors. Unlike traditional public goods, where free-riders can enjoy the benefits of a shared resource without contributing, contribution systems tie access to participation. This means governance mechanisms should prioritize rewarding active contributors while ensuring passive participants do not disproportionately extract value.

Corollary: An effective contribution system mechanism must ensure that contributors have (some form of) priority over users.

Example: Ethereum's liquid staking issue allowed passive stakers to capture rewards without directly contributing to network security or governance, leading to the concentration of influence among large staking providers. Contribution systems must actively differentiate between high-value contributors and extractive participants.

5.3 Public Goods as Byproducts

Thesis: While public goods may emerge as a byproduct, the primary function of a contribution system is to create and sustain a contribution economy. Unlike public goods funding models, which focus on collective benefits without direct reciprocity, contribution systems function by incentivizing and sustaining continuous value creation. Contribution systems do not exist to fund open-access resources per se but to ensure the ongoing viability of contributor networks.

Corollary: Contribution systems produce new property rights objects as byproduct (consensus descriptions that are institutionally legible of new digital objects).

Example: Despite the fact that scientific discoveries can be public goods, science is best understood as contribution systems where reputation, governance power, and funding flow to high-value contributors.

5.4 Value Is Created Through Networks of Dependencies

Thesis: A contribution system should recognize, record, and reward dependencies between contributions, ensuring upstream work is valued. Components such as the knowledge graph function as an institutional ledger, tracking how past contributions support future work and ensuring contributors continue to derive value from prior efforts.

Corollary: Contribution systems enable distributed value to be modelled or visualized.

Example: Deep Funding explicitly maps dependencies between projects, ensuring credit is given to foundational work that enables later innovations. The governance mechanism must enforce rules that reward contributors proportionally to their downstream impact.

5.5 Dynamic and Continuous Valuation

Thesis: Contributions should gain value over time as they interact with new contributions, rather than being valued only at the moment of action. Since machine-readable contributions enable automated governance and incentive recalibration, valuation in contribution systems should be an ongoing, adaptive process. Note that instead of speculative forecasting, futural valuation here refers to the way contribution systems recompute past inputs based on observable dependencies. This allows systems to increase or decrease attribution dynamically rather than external market speculation.

Corollary: Contribution systems are recursive and cumulative.

Example: Citation networks in academia: A paper's value is not determined upon publication but increases as others reference and build on it. Similarly, contribution systems must design mechanisms to reassess past contributions and update their importance over time. Citations can fail at this through behaviours like citing research to highlight its problems as opposed to value.

5.6 *Legibility in Value Recognition*

Thesis: Contributors should be able to trace how their contributions are valued, weighted, and rewarded. Contribution systems do not just make contributions visible; they structure how contributions are programmed and computed.

Corollary: Contribution systems increase the computational complexity of a social order.

Example: In SourceCred, contributors were initially expected to view and challenge weightings. The system became problematic when this feature was hidden to non-developers. Contribution systems should have open valuation models that allow for audits and adjustments.

5.7 *Adaptive Governance*

Thesis: Contributors should be able to adapt contribution rules to their local needs while maintaining system-wide coherence (see also terraforming in [3]).

Corollary: Contribution systems facilitate the use of local knowledge into system-wide coordination an adaptation.

Example: Regen Network uses localized ecological contribution tracking, nested within a broader blockchain-based credit system, ensuring different ecological zones can develop their own governance models while maintaining interoperability.

5.8 *Critical Mass for Network Activation*

Thesis: Contribution systems do not primarily struggle with free-riding, but with achieving critical mass. The biggest risk is not that too many users extract value, but that too few contribute early on to reach sustainability. Early contributors must be incentivized enough to bootstrap participation and establish a viable contributor network. This aligns with research on complementary currencies, which similarly depend on reaching a user base where both contributors and consumers derive meaningful value [17].

Corollary: Contribution systems create a new incentive mechanism to direct rewards from the future to early adopters and developers. This creates intertemporal arbitrage.

Examples: SourceCred discussed this in their Trust Levels (ref). Protocol Guild was explicitly designed to address early-stage contributor retention for Ethereum core developers.

5.9 *Machine-Readable Contributions Enable Scalability and Automation*

Thesis: Contribution systems are not just evolving commons—they are programmable governance systems. Contributions should be machine-readable so they may be scaled, recomputed, and adapted dynamically, enabling automation and AI-assisted decision-making.

Corollary: Contribution systems facilitate digital cybernetic development of autonomous digital systems.

Example: Deep Funding's AI-augmented juries and agent-based evaluations illustrate how contribution evaluation can be automated while still allowing for human intervention, ensuring scalability without losing accountability.

6 Next Steps for Empirical Research

Ostrom's confidence in general principles was rooted in extensive empirical research. She and colleagues amassed a remarkable body of evidence on how real communities manage common-pool resources (see, e.g. [18, 19]). These studies were drawn from fieldwork, archival records, and collaborations with other researchers, producing a rich comparative dataset. Crucially, the cases included both successes and failures, allowing Ostrom to identify which institutional arrangements tended to sustain the resource and community over time. By comparing these diverse cases, Ostrom looked for shared factors present in the enduring, successful regimes and often absent in the failed ones. As we have only a small body of empirical work to date, the draft principles outlined above will require refinement and testing.

How such empirical research should proceed is a key concern of our current work. Studying contribution systems empirically presents new challenges for researchers, as these systems are often distributed, technical, and rapidly changing. We are exploring Actor-Network Theory (ANT) as it is useful for mapping how systems recognize, structure, and sustain value [20]. This approach helps reveal value as an emergent property of networks that include both human and non-human actors. In the context of contribution systems, the relevant actors include not only the contributors (people) but also algorithms, data structures, sensors, tokens, and even natural entities (in the case of systems like Regen Network). According to ANT, each of these entities can be seen as an actant that influences the state of the network. Value is not a static attribute, but is continuously co-constructed through interactions among the actors. A contribution system essentially formalizes these interactions into a "valuemeter"—a concept borrowed from Latour and Lépinay's [21] essay on the work of Gabriel Tarde to describe devices that materialize collective value.

The task of empirical research is to reveal how meaning (or value) is inscribed in material forms and how those inscriptions stabilize social order. In contribution systems, the inscriptions are things like commits in a repository, transactions on a blockchain, or entries in a cred ledger—these are the traces or footprints of contributions. The system aggregates and interprets these traces, effectively translating subjective appreciations into objective data. In ANT terms, the value of the contribution is enacted by the network: it comes into being when a chain of actors acknowledges and incorporates that contribution. While traditional ethnographic methods—participant observation, interviews, qualitative coding—remain valuable, they do not always transfer easily to the types of field sites where contribution systems are observable (discord servers, governance forums), or to the technical dimensions (smart contracts, etc.). To address this, we have been developing tools for investigating contribution systems. This approach blends immersive qualitative research with computational tools, including custom software like Telescope, knowledge management systems like Obsidian (see [4, 22]).

7 Conclusion

Contribution systems represent a fundamental shift in institutional design, offering an alternative to firms, markets, and traditional commons governance. Unlike conventional institutions that rely on excludability through property rights or state enforcement, contribution systems introduce participation-based exclusion, where access to value is determined by contribution rather than ownership. This inversion of traditional governance logics demands new design principles—ones that ensure high-value contributors remain engaged, contributions are dynamically valued, and governance structures adapt over time.

In this paper, we have proposed draft principles for contribution systems that address the unique incentive structures, valuation mechanisms, and scalability challenges these systems present. These have been developed from our deep observations of SourceCred, and initial observations of Protocol Guild, Regen Network, and Deep Funding. The governance principles developed here emphasize the need to attract critical mass, track and reward dependencies, and structure adaptive, modular governance frameworks that can evolve alongside the systems they support.

However, this is only a starting point. As contribution systems continue to develop, there is a need for further empirical research to test these governance models, refine valuation mechanisms, and explore how AI and automation will shape future contributions. By developing a robust institutional theory of contribution systems, we can better understand how decentralized communities coordinate and sustain long-term collaboration. As these systems continue to evolve, they may become a primary governance mechanism for structuring cooperation and managing shared knowledge—in other words, future institutions.

References

1. Rennie, E., Potts, J.: Contribution systems: a new theory of value. Available at SSRN https://doi.org/10.2139/ssrn.4754267 (2024)
2. Rennie, E., Potts, J.: Contribution Systems. Available at SSRN https://doi.org/10.2139/ssrn.5018758 (2024)
3. Rennie, E.: The CredSperiment: an ethnography of a contributions system (SSRN Scholarly Paper 4570035). https://doi.org/10.2139/ssrn.4570035 (2023)
4. Rennie, E., Zargham, M., Tan, J., Miller, L., Abbott, J., Nabben, K., De Filippi, P.: Toward a participatory digital ethnography of blockchain governance. Qual. Inq. **28**(7), 837–847 (2022). https://doi.org/10.1177/10778004221097056
5. Kealey, T., Ricketts, M.: Modelling science as a contribution good. Res. Policy **43**(6), 1014–1024 (2014)
6. Ostrom, E.: Understanding Institutional Diversity. Princeton University Press, Princeton (2005)
7. Ostrom, E.: Governing the commons: the evolution of institutions for collective action. Cambridge University Press, Cambridge (1990)
8. Rennie. E.: Machine politics: the cultural science of permissionless systems. Cult. Sci. **14**(1), 56–62 (2022). https://doi.org/10.2478/csj-2022-0008
9. Rennie. E.: Value through contribution systems. Plat. Soc. **2** (2025). https://doi.org/10.1177/29768624251358683
10. North, D. C.: Institutions, institutional change and economic performance. Cambridge, Cambridge University Press (1990)
11. Morton, T.: Hyperobjects: Philosophy and Ecology After the End of the World. Minneapolis, University of Minnesota Press (2013)
12. Buterin, V.: AI as the engine, humans as the steering wheel. Vitalik Buterin's Website. https://vitalik.eth.limo/general/2025/02/28/aihumans.html, February 28, 2025
13. Potts, J.: Innovation Commons. Oxford University Press, Oxford (2019)
14. Frischman, B.M., Madison, M.J., Strandburg, K.J.: Governing knowledge commons, pp. 1–44. Oxford University Press (2014)
15. Earl, P., Potts, J.: A Nobel prize for governance and institutions: Oliver Williamson and Elinor Ostrom. Rev. Polit. Econ. **23**(1), 1–24 (2011)
16. Ostrom, E.: Beyond markets and states: polycentric governance of complex economic systems. Am. Econ. Rev. **100**(3), 641–672 (2010)
17. Desquilbet, J.-B., Farvaque, E.: "As one dies, so dies the other"? On local complementary currencies as two-sided platforms. HAL Open Science (2022). halshs-03518592
18. McGinnis, M., Ostrom, E.: Design principles for local and global commons. Int. Polit. Econ. Int. Instit. **2**, 465–493 (1996)
19. Cox, M., Arnold, G., Tomás, S.V.: A review of design principles for community-based natural resource management. Ecol. Soc. **15**(4) (2010). https://doi.org/10.5751/ES-03704-150438
20. Law, J.: Actor network theory and material semiotics. In: Turner, B. (ed.) The New Blackwell Companion to Social Theory, pp. 141–158. Blackwell. https://www.admscentre.org.au/wp-content/uploads/2025/02/Law2007ANTandMaterialSemiotics.pdf (2009)
21. Latour, B., Antonin Lépinay, V.: The science of passionate interests: an introduction to gabriel tarde's economic anthropology. Chicago. Prickly Paradigm Press (2009)
22. Nabben, K., Zargham, M., Rennie, E.: 'Computer-Aided Ethnography' (CAE): Ethnography using computational methods in the field of Web3. BlockScience Blog. https://medium.com/block-science/computer-aided-ethnography-cae-ethnography-using-computational-methods-in-the-field-of-web3-f3e8495ec20b, February 20, 2023

Bitcoin, a DAO?

Mark C. Ballandies, Guangyao Li, and Claudio J. Tessone

Abstract This paper investigates whether Bitcoin can be regarded as a decentralized autonomous organization (DAO), what insights it may offer for the broader DAO ecosystem, and how Bitcoin governance can be improved. First, a quantitative literature analysis reveals that Bitcoin is increasingly overlooked in DAO research, even though early works often classified it as a DAO. Next, the paper applies a DAO viability framework, centering on collective intelligence, digital democracy, and adaptation, to examine Bitcoin's organizational and governance mechanisms. Findings suggest that Bitcoin instantiates key DAO principles by enabling open participation and employing decentralized decision-making through Bitcoin Improvement Proposals (BIPs), miner signaling, and user-activated soft forks. However, this governance carries potential risks, including reduced clarity on who truly "votes" due to the concentration of economic power among large stakeholders. The paper concludes by highlighting opportunities to refine Bitcoin's deliberation process and reflecting on broader implications for DAO design, such as the absence of a legal entity. In doing so, it underscores Bitcoin's continued relevance as an archetype for decentralized governance, offering important findings for future DAO implementations.

Keywords DAO · Bitcoin · Cryptoeconomics · Digital democracy · Complex systems · Blockchain

1 Introduction

Decentralization is on the rise in society [1–9] and blockchain-based decentralized autonomous organizations (DAOs) accelerate this broader shift [10–12]. Governed democratically through participatory algorithms, they transcend geographical, cultural, and traditional boundaries, often engaging thousands of members worldwide [13, 14]. By removing clear distinctions between internal and external stakeholders,

---

M. C. Ballandies (✉) · G. Li · C. J. Tessone
University of Zurich, Zurich, Switzerland
e-mail: markchristopher.ballandies@uzh.ch

M. Lustenberger et al. (eds.), *Decentralized Autonomous Organizations—Governance, Technology, and Legal Perspectives*, Springer Proceedings in Business and Economics,
https://doi.org/10.1007/978-3-032-03273-7_2

DAOs allow anyone to quickly influence decision-making and contribute to tasks [11].

DAOs have demonstrated their effectiveness through the management of substantial assets, sometimes exceeding $500 million, and rapid capital deployment [13]. In addition to pooling capital, they streamline operations via algorithmic systems and blockchain tools, resulting in more efficient and cost-effective voting mechanisms [13, 14]. Regular, ongoing voting replaces traditional periodic voting, making active participation more feasible [13]. Also, smart contracts can further facilitate liquid democracy, reducing complexity and costs in proxy-based voting while enhancing transparency and lowering the risk of fraud [13]. Nonetheless, DAOs face notable challenges [10], including declining participation [13, 15, 16], increasing centralization [17], adaptation difficulties [17], and balancing potentially conflicting values [21].

As the first blockchain, Bitcoin demonstrated the potential of a decentralized network of peers operating without a central authority or legal entity. Several definitions have since been proposed for what constitutes a DAO (see Sect. 2.1), with some viewing Bitcoin as a DAO and others not [18]. This paper argues that Bitcoin, when positioned within the DAO viability framework (Table 1), can be considered a DAO. Recognizing Bitcoin in this way would help researchers address the above-mentioned challenges facing DAOs, as Bitcoin's distinctive approach to digital democracy and adaptation, rooted in permissionlessness and transparency, broadens the design space for DAO development. In particular, the limited ability of many DAOs to adapt to changing conditions [10] could be addressed, which Bitcoin tackles through its focus on individual autonomy (Table 1).

Hence, given Bitcoin's success, we encourage and, with this work, provide the foundations for researchers to examine the advantages and disadvantages of its governance and organizational structure to derive insights for other DAOs. And for Bitcoin practitioners, this work offers a foundation for conceptual discussions on improving Bitcoin's governance, a topic that continues to resurface within the community. In particular, the following contributions are made in this work:

- Quantitative Analysis of related work and their sentiment toward Bitcoin being a DAO, illustrating a change in perception over time (Sect. 2).
- Analysis of Bitcoin's governance and organizational mechanism via the DAO viability framework [10], illustrating Bitcoin's unique approach to Digital Democracy by using Bitcoin Improvement Proposals (BIP) for deliberation as well as hash power signaling and code forking for decision-making.
- Discussion of important design decisions in Bitcoin, such as the lack of a legal entity or the permissionless entry into the organization, put into the context of recent developments, e.g., Bitcoin ETFs.
- Proposals to improve Bitcoin's governance, such as its deliberation mechanism.

In Sect. 2 we quantitatively analyze related work on DAOs and identify their sentiment toward Bitcoin and provide an introduction to the DAO viability framework. We then describe Bitcoin's organizational mechanisms in Sect. 3 and analyze them by applying the DAO viability framework. This is followed by a discussion, among others informing improvements to the Bitcoin's governance mechanisms (Sect. 4). In Sect. 5 we conclude and give an outlook on future work.

2 Background

2.1 Bitcoin, a DAO? A Quantitative Analysis

See Fig. 1.

As early as 2013, leading blockchain practitioners recognized Bitcoin as an example of a decentralized corporation [19], and it has since been identified in academic works as a DAO [20]. In particular, Bitcoin depicts characteristics of an organization: Bitcoin is a multi-agent system, with established boundaries, a clear purpose, and coordinated actions [20]. Notably, it even operates with a kind of marketing department [19], aligning with characteristics typical of an *organization* [21]. Unlike traditional organizations though, Bitcoin is distinctive for its *decentralized* governance, emerging from the complex interdependencies among its diverse

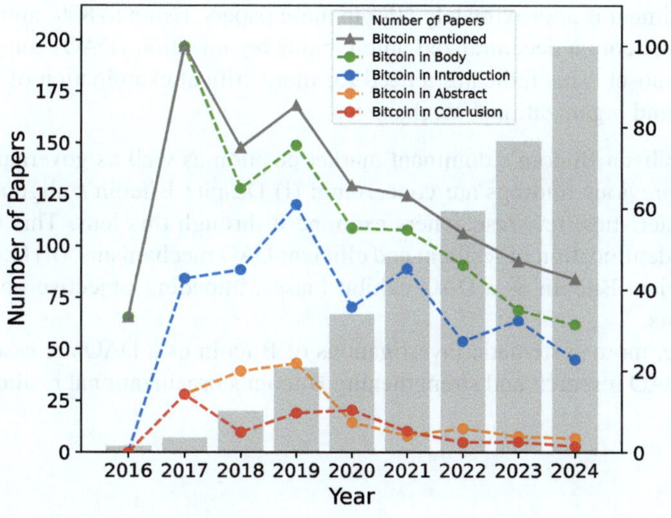

Fig. 1 Total numbers of DAO papers published (*bar chart*), the proportion of Bitcoin being mentioned in those papers (*solid line*), and the proportion of papers mentioning Bitcoin in different parts of the paper (*dashed lines*)

stakeholders [22]. Also, its permissionless structure enables individuals to independently act on behalf of Bitcoin, ensuring its *autonomy* which is backed and mediated by a set of self-executing rules on-chain (e.g., Nakamoto Consensus). This aligns Bitcoin to be classified as a DAO according to the definition given by Hassan and De Filippi [23].

Nevertheless, a common definition of DAOs often restricts them to entities that explicitly use smart contracts for decision-making or manage collective treasuries, thus excluding Bitcoin as a DAO [18]. This view is gaining traction within the DAO research community, as shown in Fig. 1. The figure displays the number of papers indexed in Elseviers ScienceDirect database found with the search terms ("Decentralized Autonomous Organizations" OR DAO) AND (Blockchain OR Distributed Ledger). Over time, there has been a marked increase in DAO-related publications (gray bars in Fig. 1), in total 826 works have been published. However, an analysis of Bitcoin mentioned within these papers reveals a decreasing trend in discussions of Bitcoin, e.g., in 2017 all papers discussed Bitcoin, whereas in 2024 this number decreased to 42%. Given Bitcoin's ongoing success, this decline suggests it is increasingly viewed as something other than a DAO, as its mechanisms would otherwise be more frequently examined in that context. Analyzing this further, we used ChatGPT on the articles that mention Bitcoin to identify if the works consider Bitcoin as a DAO (Figure 2a). For this, we used the prompt as illustrated in Appendix. Over time, only 22 papers identify Bitcoin as a DAO, representing 6% of papers discussing Bitcoin in the context of a DAO and 3% of all papers.

Figure 2b presents the average sentiment of authors toward the statement "Bitcoin has great potential" in papers discussing Bitcoin as identified by ChatGPT. The average sentiment is approximately 60% in these papers, rising to 80% among those considering Bitcoin a decentralized autonomous organization (DAO), suggesting a bias in this subset. This indicates a need for more critical examination of Bitcoin's governance and organizational mechanisms.

Summary: Given Bitcoin's dominant market position as well as governance challenges, the previous findings are concerning: (i) Despite Bitcoin's alignment with DAO characteristics, few researchers examine it through this lens. This oversight hinders the identification of resilient and efficient DAO mechanisms. (ii) Conversely, those who view Bitcoin as a DAO exhibit biases, impeding objective governance improvements.

Therefore, more systematic investigations of Bitcoin as a DAO are essential for advancing DAO research and strengthening Bitcoin's organizational resilience.

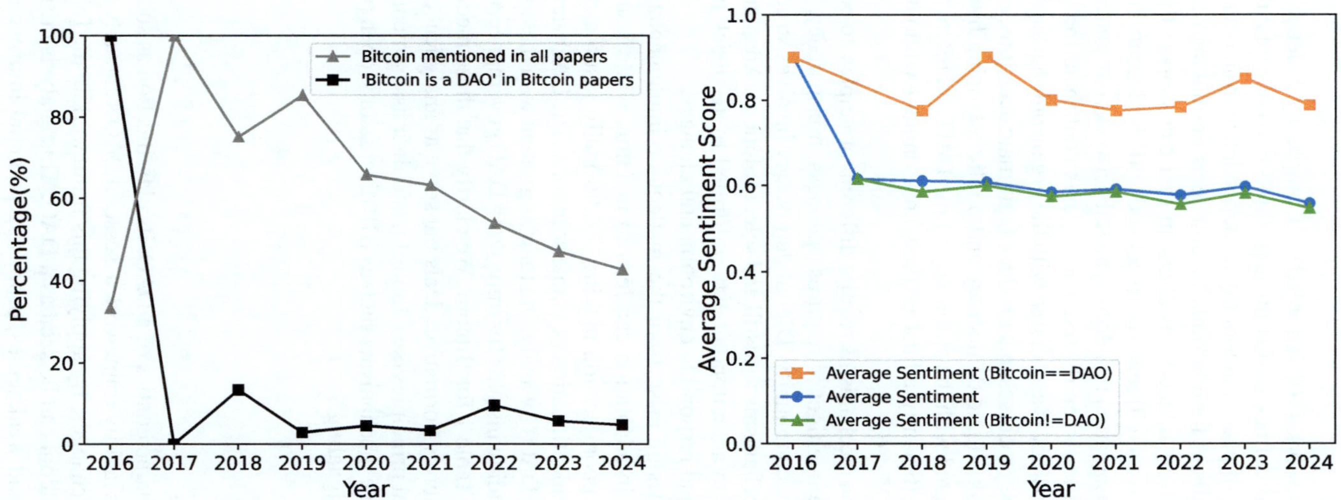

Fig. 2 **Left:** Proportion of academic papers discussing Bitcoin, and within that subset, the proportion considering Bitcoin as a DAO. **Right:** Average sentiment toward the statement "Bitcoin has great potential" across papers discussing Bitcoin, comparing those that explicitly consider Bitcoin as a DAO (Bitcoin == DAO) and those that do not (Bitcoin == False)

2.2 DAO Viability Framework

The DAO viability framework [10] is rooted in Complexity Science and Digital Democracy literature and defines DAOs through three key concepts: decentralization (a broad community of peers), autonomy (independence from coercive forces), and organization (mechanisms for coordination and decision-making). Each of these concepts facilitates a self-organization mechanism that can support the well functioning of a DAO: Collective intelligence is associated with the decentralization of the DAO and draws on the observation that decentralized networks can generate superior problem-solving capabilities when diverse participants contribute freely and transparently [8]. Digital democracy is associated with the organizational aspect of a DAO and illustrates deliberative processes that produce legitimate decisions, exemplifying democratic innovations like liquid democracy and public reasoning frameworks [2, 24]. Adaptation is associated with the autonomy of the DAO and refers to the ability of complex systems to efficiently adjust to their environment without centralized coordination or control [25, 26].

These self-organization mechanisms require different principles do be manifested in DAOs [10]. Collective intelligence requires openness, transparency, privacy, and free expression within the community. Digital democracy involves structured deliberation and fair voting mechanisms to distill and select solutions. Adaptation depends on community members to act autonomously, informed by feedback mechanisms, to implement decisions and respond to environmental changes.

Challenges in DAO design arise from the inadequate implementation of these principles [10]. Failures in adaptation can lead to inaction, while issues in digital democracy may result in poor decision-making. Additionally, insufficient collective intelligence can skew the identification of viable solutions. The DAO viability framework supports evaluating DAOs by analyzing their alignment with these mechanisms and their principles, providing insights for improving DAO governance and functionality, as demonstrated in Table 1 for Bitcoin. We clarify that these mechanisms and their principles are not merely normative ideals but serve as analytical criteria: each is grounded in operational principles (see Table 1), and their assessment in Bitcoin's case is based on observable mechanisms such as BIP discussions, open participation, and decentralized node signaling.

2.3 Summary

While Bitcoin exhibits characteristics of a DAO, its classification as such is increasingly debated. The DAO viability framework assesses a DAO's capacity to adapt efficiently to environmental changes. By applying this framework in the following onto Bitcoin, we show that Bitcoin can be seen as a DAO. This analysis critically examines Bitcoin's strengths and weaknesses, proposing potential improvements. Given

Table 1 Bitcoin's accomplishment of the eight DAO viability principles [10] (last column)

	Princip.	Goal	Bitcoin accomplishment
Collective Intelligence	Openness	Permeable borders for entering and leaving the organization	Medium-high
	Transp.	Information related to the organization can be accessed by all community members	High
	Privacy	Community members can independently/unmanipulated explore and experiment with solutions	Medium-high
	Free express	Community members can freely express their thoughts and opinions	High
Digital Democ.	Delib.	Processes are in place that effectively and thoughtfully distill options for decision-making from the collective intelligence	Medium
	Voting	Choosing (desired) system states, goals and approaches to attain them fairly from the options of the deliberation process	Medium
Adaptation	Autonomy	Community members can act as they think is best for the organization	High
	Feedback	(unsolicited real-time) feedback mechanisms are in place	High

Bitcoin's success, this approach may identify resilient and efficient mechanisms for DAO instantiation.

3 Bitcoin's Decentralized Organization

Table 1 illustrates Bitcoin's organizational mechanisms within the DAO viability framework. In the following, these are illustrated in greater detail.

3.1 Collective Intelligence

Bitcoin's debate processes are intertwined across multiple online and offline platforms, ranging from specialized developer forums to mainstream social media, and offline venues such as conferences and local meetups. This mix ensures that different segments of the Bitcoin ecosystem can participate, collaborate, and influence the protocol's evolution, all without the oversight of a centralized authority [22], which can facilitate collective intelligence to emerge [8]. In the following, the collective intelligence principles of *openness, transparency, privacy and freedom of expression* are analyzed in greater detail.

Openness Bitcoin has no legal entity that decides on the entry into the organization or expulsion of community members facilitating open boundaries to enter the organization, potentially being open to anyone wanting to contribute. Nevertheless, different roles within the organization exists, such as Bitcoin holders, node operators, or Bitcoin core developer, which add (explicit) restrictions for entering or leaving. For instance, being a node operator implies having a particular technical skill set, and no formal processes exist to apply or enter the Bitcoin core developer group.

Table 2 provides an overview of the different communication channels, virtual and physical, that the Bitcoin community uses to come together to discuss all aspects of Bitcoin, from the very technical protocol discussions to more educational fora for a wider group of interested people. None of the channels has formal barriers erected by the Bitcoin community.

Table 2 Communication channels and events used by the Bitcoin community

Channel/Event	Type	Key characteristics
bitcoin-dev mailing list, GitHub	Virtual	Debates on technical proposals and reviews (BIPs)
bitcointalk.org	Virtual	Original forum for all Bitcoin discourse in the early days
Twitter/X, Telegram, Reddit, Discord	Virtual	Dynamic platforms for community interaction and real-time updates
Specialized Channels (IRC, Slack, Mattermost)	Virtual	Real-time discussions among developers and stakeholders
YouTube, Podcasts	Virtual	Interviews, tutorials, and capturing community sentiment
Onboarding programs	Virtual	Geared to onboard developers to Bitcoin core or related projects, eg bitcoindevs.xyz
Workshops	Physical	Smaller developer gatherings around protocol upgrades (eg Scaling workshops)
Conferences	Physical	Organized larger-scale educational gatherings about economic, regulatory, industry topics
Local Meetups	Physical	Knowledge sharing and networking within regional Bitcoin communities
Coding Workshops, Hackathons	Physical	Hands-on collaboration and innovation for developers
University Seminars, Research Symposia	Physical	Academic rigor, research findings, and theoretical advancements in Bitcoin

Transparency Transparent access to the information concerning the organization is made available via various online and offline channels, as illustrated in Table 2.

The Bitcoin community employs online forums to collaboratively develop and discuss protocol modifications. Technical proposals and reviews primarily occur on the bitcoin-dev mailing list and GitHub, where Bitcoin Improvement Proposals (BIPs) (see Sect. 3.2) are introduced, debated, and refined. Long-established platforms such as Bitcointalk and Reddit facilitate broader discourse, covering everything from scaling debates to general news, while Twitter (X), Telegram, and Discord serve as more dynamic locations for community interaction and real-time updates. In parallel, specialized channels like IRC, Slack, or Mattermost host real-time discussions among developers and stakeholders, and YouTube/podcasts provide venues for interviews, tutorials, and community sentiment.

Face-to-face engagements complement digital interaction by convening stakeholders in formal and informal settings. Prominent conferences (e.g., in Miami, Amsterdam, or El Salvador) bring together developers, miners, entrepreneurs, and investors to address protocol upgrades, regulatory shifts, and market dynamics. Local meetups in cities worldwide encourage knowledge sharing and networking, while coding workshops and hackathons offer opportunities for hands-on collaboration and innovation. Furthermore, university seminars and research symposia introduce academic rigor to Bitcoin's development, enabling researchers to present findings, debate theoretical advancements, and shape the community's technical direction.

Collectively, these digital and physical spaces foster transparent participation, peer review, and consensus-building across diverse audiences. In particular, suggestion to the Bitcoin protocol is made early accessible to a broad audience. The largest challenge might be to keep an overview and to know *how* to interact meaningfully with the community.

Privacy No identity provision is required by Bitcoin, neither on-chain nor off-chain. Users of the Bitcoin protocol can create new identities in a permissionless way; nevertheless, these identities can be linked [27]. In particular, no inherent privacy mechanisms exist, making the exposure of identities possible. Joining the digital discussion spaces usually requires an online identity that can also be created anew. Also physical events usually do not require identification. In particular, there is no official identity to be part of the Bitcoin organization or not.

Freedom of Expression The Bitcoin community engages in open, public discussions that embrace a wide range of viewpoints and communication styles. The debate over Bitcoin maximalism, particularly regarding its toxicity or benefits, highlights this diversity, featuring opinions from support to opposition and discourse ranging from harsh disputes to neutral, nuanced exchanges [28, 29] (Table 3).

Table 3 Bitcoin's digital governance mechanisms

Princip.	Mechanism	Who	Locat.	How
Deliberation	Bitcoin Improvement Proposal (BIP)	Core Developers	Off-chain	Proposals are introduced, debated, and refined through a public and structured process
Voting	Hash Power Voting	Miners	On-chain	Miners signal support for changes by embedding markers (e.g., version bits) in mined blocks and eventually (not) upgrading their clients
Voting	User-Activated Soft Fork (UASF)	Full Nodes	On-chain	Full nodes enforce new rules by rejecting blocks that don't comply after a specified date

3.2 Digital Democracy: Decision-making

The digital democracy component of a DAO consists of (i) *deliberation*, methods to find voteable options, and (ii) *voting*, methods to agree within the community on these options [10].

Deliberation: Central to Bitcoin's deliberation is the Bitcoin Improvement Proposal (BIP) process, moderated by the Bitcoin core developers on GitHub. It is the only formal mechanism for its deliberation. Stakeholders wishing to modify Bitcoin's source code draft BIPs, which outline potential protocol changes, technical details, and implementation strategies. These proposals are typically reviewed by the wider development community on public forums (e.g., mailing lists, GitHub, see Table 2) to solicit feedback. While Bitcoin core developers maintain the reference implementation, they do not unilaterally decide on proposals; rather, extensive peer review and consensus-building shape the evolution of each BIP. Nevertheless, core developers have a veto right [22], as they ultimately decide on integrating code into the code base.

Voting: Two voting mechanisms can be identified within the Bitcoin community.

Hashpower voting is executed by consensus participants ("miners") via their contributed hashpower: After a new feature is integrated into Bitcoin core, the network's miners individually choose whether to upgrade. If a majority of the network adopts a particular change, it becomes the de facto rule set. Conversely, if the network fragments over a contentious proposal, a "fork" may emerge, leading to separate blockchains adhering to different consensus rules. Several upgrade mechanisms have been utilized in the past by the miners [22]:

– Flag day: All miners upgrade their nodes on a particular block height.

- BIP34: Bitcoin miners indicate support for a BIP by adding a version bit to its produced block
- BIP9: followed BIP34 and introduced the ability for miners to signal readiness for multiple upgrades with version bits in the block header

User voting: UASF and URSF. Beyond the miners, the so-called economic majority[1] maintaining full nodes that independently from miners verify the blockchain's state—exchanges, payment processors, merchants, and large-scale holders—wields significant influence. These entities often shape decisions by signaling which version of Bitcoin software they support, since their adoption patterns can influence user confidence and liquidity. As a result, even if miners favor a change, that change may fail if influential economic actors do not upgrade or recognize the new rules, or vice versa, make miners upgrade to new rules that they otherwise would oppose. The former is referred to as User Resisted Soft Fork (URSF) and the latter as User-Activated Soft Fork (UASF) [22].

3.3 Adaptation

The two principles of *autonomy* and *feedback* enable a DAO to adapt effectively to changing environmental conditions [10].

Autonomy: Bitcoin has no legal entity or central authority such as a vocal founder that could dictate members of the organization how to act [20]. Instead, Bitcoin is permissionless, meaning anyone can join and act for Bitcoin without permission. For instance, anyone is enabled to maintain a miner, hold Bitcoins, or perform any other action on behalf of Bitcoin. In particular, any individual in the network decides in a case of a fork which chain is considered to be the main chain, which is ultimatively decided by the collective action of these individuals. This voting by the feet characterizes also federal democracies [30]. It is even argued by leading practitioners that this form of decision-making is the superior form when compared to token-based votings [31].

Feedback: Blockchain-based tokens function as a feedback mechanisms facilitating self-organization in decentralized systems [32–34]. Bitcoin directly utilizes token units to incentivize the desirable behavior of mining. Also, the Bitcoin price can be seen as a further signal to the community on their overall performance. In particular, the recent stagnation of the Ethereum price is considered as an underperformance of its ecosystem, which initiated a change in the governance of the Ethereum foundation.[2]

[1] https://en.bitcoin.it/wiki/Economic_majority, last accessed: 2025-01-18.

[2] https://cointelegraph.com/news/ethereum-foundation-infighting-and-drop-in-dapp-volumes-put-cloud-over-eth-price.

Another feedback mechanism is the adoption of new software clients by miners [22] and users, eventually providing feedback on which is the right implementation via the longest blockchain rule.

4 Discussion

A fundamental value of Bitcoin lies in its permissionless nature, exemplified by the absence of a legal entity or organization that owns it and could impose restrictions on the participation of community members. Given Bitcoin's success, this observation could serve as a starting point for discussions on whether DAOs should operate without legal entities in general. Specifically, the establishment of a legal entity can bind a DAO to a legal jurisdiction, potentially compromising its decentralized character and the autonomy of its participating members (Autonomy in Table 1). However, adapting to changing environments in a decentralized manner relies on individual actors responding quickly to local conditions [10]. Without a governing body capable of censoring, directing, or manipulating such responses, one could argue, based on Bitcoin's success, that this decentralized adaptability was instrumental in its growth and resilience. However, recent work on DAO legal frameworks (e.g., DAO Model Law [35]) reflects a discussion that DAOs must navigate legal ambiguity to engage in real-world operations. While Bitcoin's governance is enabled by the absence of a legal entity, ensuring high autonomy, other DAOs may benefit from limited liability structures or legal wrappers to interface with institutions. This raises a question: is the absence of a legal form a feature or a limitation? We argue that Bitcoin's model expands the design space for DAOs by illustrating that meaningful coordination and value accrual can occur entirely outside of legal personhood. Nonetheless, future DAO designs may adopt hybrid forms, balancing legal interoperability with permissionless organizations.

Bitcoin utilizes a basic deliberation mechanism through its Bitcoin Improvement Proposals (BIPs) that has been adopted by many (smart contract-based) DAOs. In contrast, digital democracy initiatives, such as those in Taiwan, have developed advanced deliberation tools that enhance reasoning, feedback, and sentiment analysis, thereby improving consensus-building and the identification of actionable options [2, 8]. However, considering the discussion on Bitcoin maximalism (Sect. 3.1), it remains questionable whether the Bitcoin community is willing to adopt new mechanisms. Nonetheless, introducing voluntary deliberation mechanisms in sub-communities of Bitcoin would not alter the underlying Bitcoin protocol; thus, a minority could initiate and experiment with them, potentially influencing the larger ecosystem if proven effective. According to the DAO viability framework, this would enhance the DAO's viability through more effective deliberation.

Also, how to vote and who the deciding parties are in Bitcoin is not clearly defined, which can raise confusion on who is the decisive party. In particular, the user-activated-soft-fork voting mechanism poses the risk of major economic actors unidirectionally changing Bitcoin. For instance, Blackrock is by now one of the largest Bitcoin holders. In their service agreement for their iShares trust, they specify that it is up to them to decide which Bitcoin chain will function as underlying to their ETFs in case of a Fork.[3] In case, Blackrock and some other major actors like Microstrategy decide to go for a chain that does not align with the larger Bitcoin ecosystem, this could pose a significant risk to the value of Bitcoin and subsequently its security [27]. In particular, there is a significant risk that such major economic actors support values that do not align with the larger community of Bitcoin holders.

4.1 Limitations

Elinor Ostrom's design principles for successfully governing the commons [36] have been applied to illustrate DAOs [12]. Taking such a commons view on DAOs, the DAO viability framework could be extended with those principles to illustrate in how far a DAO is viable to govern a commons. In particular, it would provide a more differentiated view into the openness aspect of collective intelligence (Table 1), as a commons needs to have clear boundaries and sanctioning mechanisms defined [36]. Bitcoin seems to fulfill this differentiated view on the boundaries, as people can enter and leave freely the organization, but entering the inner circles is less transmissive (e.g., becoming a core developer).

Also, the performed literature analysis could be extended to involve further scientific databases. In particular, investigating the sentiment toward Bitcoin being a DAO in social science-related databases would provide a greater nuanced view on the perception of Bitcoin being a DAO, as a significant amount of research on DAOs is performed in these fields [18]. Moreover, the quantitative analysis could be strengthened by adding further sentiment analysis methods besides ChatGPT.

[3] "In the event of a hard fork of the Bitcoin network, the Sponsor [iShares Delaware Trust Sponsor LLC] will, if permitted by the terms of the Trust Agreement, use its discretion to determine which network should be considered the appropriate network for the Trust's purposes, and in doing so may adversely affect the value of the Shares.", page 24, https://www.sec.gov/Archives/edgar/data/1980994/000143774923028549/bit20231017_s1a.htm, last accessed: 2025-01-21.

5 Conclusion and Outlook

This work demonstrates that Bitcoin can be regarded as a decentralized autonomous organization, instantiating the three self-organization mechanisms of the DAO viability framework, collective intelligence, digital democracy, and adaptation (Table 1), through novel methods such as decentralized node signaling for voting. Given its economic success and the ongoing governance debate within the Bitcoin community, the DAO research community would benefit from analyzing Bitcoin's DAO mechanisms to derive insights into successful DAO instantiation. In turn, practitioners could draw on these scholarly insights to inform their discussions.

For instance, applying the DAO viability framework, we identified several mechanisms supporting Bitcoin's viability, such as the absence of a legal entity, that stem from its core value of permissionlessness. We also found that Bitcoin governance could be enhanced by improving deliberation, potentially initiated by a sub-group within the ecosystem integrating recent findings from digital democracy research.

In general, Bitcoin was described early on as a decentralized corporation exhibiting core DAO features such as open participation and rule enforcement via code. That the term "DAO" emerged later does not diminish Bitcoin's alignment with the concept—in fact, Bitcoin helped shape it. While smart contract-based DAOs emphasize programmable governance, Bitcoin represents an alternative archetype of a DAO focused on social consensus and permissionless actions. Recognizing this divergence broadens the DAO design space and affirms Bitcoin's continued relevance as a living, functional DAO.

Beyond refining the DAO viability framework through Ostrom's work (Sect. 4.1), two further research directions emerge. First, Bitcoin's on-chain miner signaling remains understudied; network science could reveal key governance dynamics. Second, quantitative methods could assess adherence to the eight viability principles, potentially using machine learning or network analysis methodologies. This would lay the foundation for quantitatively accessing the viability of a DAO.

Acknowledgements We thank Marcus M. Dapp for his valuable feedback on this manuscript.

Appendix: ChatGPT Prompt

```
PROMPT_TEMPLATE = """As an expert in blockchain research, you are analyzing a paper mentioning Bitcoin and Decentralized Autonomous Organizations (DAOs).

Your task is to:
1. Determine whether the paper supports or opposes the idea that "Bitcoin is a DAO."
2. Determine the author's overall sentiment toward 'Bitcoin is a DAO', give true or false. In addition, give a sentiment score.
3. Give a general sentiment score. If the author likes bitcoin or think bitcoin has great potential, the score should be high.
3. Provide supporting reasoning for 'bitcoin is a DAO', including cases where both supporting and opposing arguments are present.

Content
{text}

Output requirements
Format: JSON
Fields:
"dao_relation": A boolean (true or false) indicating whether the author ultimately supports (true) or opposes (false) the idea that Bitcoin is a DAO.
"sentiment_score": A float between 0 and 1, representing the author's overall sentiment toward 'Bitcoin is a DAO' (0 = very negative, 1 = very positive).
"general_sentiment_score": A float between 0 and 1, representing the author's overall sentiment toward bitcoin (0 = very negative, 1 = very positive).
"reasoning": A concise summary of the author's stance, highlighting supporting and opposing arguments if both exist.
"citations": A list of locations where relevant arguments appear.

Example output
{{"dao_relation": true, "sentiment_score": 0.85, "general_sentiment_score": 0.4, "reasoning": "The author explicitly states that 'bitcoin is a DAO' in paragraph 3. "citation": ["paragraph 3", "bitcoin can be considered a DAO due to its decentralized nature"]}}

Important Notes:
If the paper presents both supporting and opposing arguments, determine whether the overall stance leans more towards supporting (true) or opposing (false) and classify "dao_relation" accordingly.
If mixed arguments exist, explicitly mention both views in "reasoning" and cite them in "citations".
"""
```

References

1. Welling, T., Heravan, F.B., Sharma, A., Gelauff, L., Haenggli, R., Pournaras, E.: Fair and inclusive participatory budgeting: voter experience with cumulative and quadratic voting interfaces. arXiv preprint arXiv:2308.04345 (2023)
2. Yang, J.C., Hausladen, C.I., Peters, D., Pournaras, E., Fricker, R.H., Helbing, D.: Designing digital voting systems for citizens: achieving fairness and legitimacy in digital participatory budgeting. arXiv preprint arXiv:2310.03501 (2023)
3. Hoda, R., Murugesan, L.K.: Multi-level agile project management challenges: a self-organizing team perspective. J. Syst. Softw. **117**, 245–257 (2016)
4. Hoda, R., Noble, J., Marshall, S.: Organizing self-organizing teams. In: Proceedings of the 32nd ACM/IEEE International Conference on Software Engineering, vol. 1, pp. 285–294 (2010)
5. Laloux, F.: Reinventing Organizations, vol. 58. Nelson Parker Brussels (2014)
6. Wyrzykowska, B.: Teal organizations: literature reviewand future research directions. Cent. Eur. Manage. J. **27**(4), 124–141 (2019)
7. Majumdar, S., Pournaras, E.: Consensus-based participatory budgeting for legitimacy: decision support via multi-agent reinforcement learning. In: International Conference on Machine Learning, Optimization, and Data Science, pp. 1–14. Springer (2023)
8. Helbing, D., Mahajan, S., Fricker, R.H., Musso, A., Hausladen, C.I., Carissimo, C., Carpentras, D., Stockinger, E., Sanchez-Vaquerizo, J.A., Yang, J.C., et al.: Democracy by design: perspectives for digitally assisted, participatory upgrades of society. J. Comput. Sci. **71**, 102061 (2023)
9. Ballandies, M.C., Wang, H., Law, A.C.C., Yang, J.C., Gösken, C., Andrew, M.: A taxonomy for blockchain-based decentralized physical infrastructure networks (depin). In: 2023 IEEE 9th World Forum on Internet of Things (WF-IoT), pp. 1–6. IEEE (2023)
10. Ballandies, M.C., Carpentras, D., Pournaras, E.: Daos of collective intelligence? unraveling the complexity of blockchain governance in decentralized autonomous organizations. arXiv preprint arXiv:2409.01823 (2024)
11. Spychiger, F., Lustenberger, M., Martignoni, J., Schädler, L., Lehner, P.: Organizing projects with blockchain through a decentralized autonomous organization. Project Leadersh. Soc. **4**, 100102 (2023)
12. Hunhevicz, J.J., Hall, D.M., Brasey, P.A., Bonanomi, M.M., Fischer, M.: Decentralized project delivery on the crypto commons: conceptualization, governance mechanisms, and future research directions. Project Leadersh. Soc. **5**, 100132 (2024)
13. Wright, A.J.: The rise of decentralized autonomous organizations: opportunities and challenges (2021)
14. Pournaras, E.: Proof of witness presence: blockchain consensus for augmented democracy in smart cities. J. Parallel Distrib. Comput. **145**, 160–175 (2020)
15. Rikken, O., Janssen, M., Kwee, Z.: Governance challenges of blockchain and decentralized autonomous organizations. Inf. Polity **24**(4), 397–417 (2019)
16. Faqir-Rhazoui, Y., Arroyo, J., Hassan, S.: a comparative analysis of the platforms for decentralized autonomous organizations in the ethereum blockchain. J. Internet Serv. Appl. **12**, 1–20 (2021)
17. Santana, C., Albareda, L.: Blockchain and the emergence of decentralized autonomous organizations (DAOs): an integrative model and research agenda. Technol. Forecast. Soc. Chang. **182**, 121806 (2022)
18. Name, A.: A conceptual framework on decentralized autonomous organizations. under submission (2025)
19. Buterin, V.: Bootstrapping a decentralized autonomous corporation: Part I (2013). https://bitcoinmagazine.com/technical/bootstrapping-a-decentralized-autonomous-corporation-part-i-1379644274
20. Hsieh, Y.Y., Vergne, J.P., Anderson, P., Lakhani, K., Reitzig, M.: Bitcoin and the rise of decentralized autonomous organizations. J. Organ. Des. **7**(1), 1–16 (2018)

21. Puranam, P., Alexy, O., Reitzig, M.: What's "new" about new forms of organizing? Acad. Manage. Rev. **39**(2), 162–180 (2014)
22. Crypto Fish, R., Lee, S., Alden, L.: Analyzing bitcoin consensus: risks in protocol upgrades (2024). https://bitcoinnews.ch/wp-content/uploads/2024/11/bcap_v1.0.pdf
23. Hassan, S., De Filippi, P.: Decentralized autonomous organization. Internet Policy Rev. **10**(2) (2021). 10.14763/2021.2.1556
24. Yang, J.C., Bachmann, F.: Bridging voting and deliberation with algorithms: field insights from vtaiwan and kultur komitee. arXiv preprint arXiv:2502.05017 (2025)
25. Heylighen, F., et al.: The science of self-organization and adaptivity. Encycl. Life Support Syst. **5**(3), 253–280 (2001)
26. The vision of autonomic computing: Computer **36**(1), 41–50 (2003)
27. Ballandies, M.C., Dapp, M.M., Pournaras, E.: Decrypting distributed ledger design-taxonomy, classification and blockchain community evaluation. Cluster Comput. **25**(3), 1817–1838 (2022)
28. Boomer: A newcomer's perspective on toxic bitcoin maximalism (2022). https://bitcoinmagazine.com/culture/what-toxic-bitcoin-maximalism-means-to-onlookers
29. Buterin, V.: In defense of bitcoin maximalism (2022). https://vitalik.eth.limo/general/2022/04/01/maximalist.html
30. Frey, B.S., Bohnet, I.: The Swiss experience with referenda and federalism. Idioma **6**, 147–160 (1994)
31. Buterin, V.: Moving beyond coin voting governance (2021). https://vitalik.eth.limo/general/2021/08/16/voting3.html
32. Kleineberg, K.K., Helbing, D.: A "social bitcoin" could sustain a democratic digital world. In: Finance 4.0-Towards a Socio-Ecological Finance System: A Participatory Framework to Promote Sustainability, pp. 39–51. Springer International Publishing, Cham (2021)
33. Dapp, M.M., Helbing, D., Klauser, S.: Finance 4.0-Towards a Socio-ecological Finance System: A Participatory Framework to Promote Sustainability. Springer Nature (2021)
34. Ballandies, M.C.: To incentivize or not: impact of blockchain-based cryptoeconomic tokens on human information sharing behavior. IEEE Access **10**, 74111–74130 (2022)
35. Choi, C., De Filippi, P., Dudley, R., Elrifai, S.N., Fannizadeh, F., Guillaume, F., Leiter, A., Mannan, M., McMullen, G., Riva, S., et al.: Model law for decentralized autonomous organizations (DAOs). Coalition of Automated Legal Applications (2021)
36. Ostrom, E.: Governing the Commons: The Evolution of Institutions for Collective Action. Cambridge University Press (1990)

Digital Democracy in Decentralised Autonomous Organisations

Theodor Beutel, Parminder Kaur Makode, Claudio J. Tessone, and Uwe Serdült

Abstract Decentralised autonomous organisations (DAOs) are institutional technologies that enable democratic governance innovation. They inherit key democratic principles such as procedural transparency and immutable records from being based on blockchain technology. This paper conducts a systematic literature review to examine governance mechanisms and challenges of digital democracy in DAOs. While issues like power concentration and coordination failures exist in current implementations, we argue that the concept of DAOs offers new opportunities for transparent governance and participatory decision-making. As testbeds for governance experiments, we find that DAOs have the potential to reshape democratic processes and foster innovative governance models in the digital era. Calling for interdisciplinary collaboration, further research is needed around Sybil-resistant voting mechanisms, ideological path dependencies and deliberation mechanisms.

Keywords Digital governance · Literature review · Voting mechanisms · Blockchain technology

---

T. Beutel · U. Serdült (✉)
Center for Democracy Studies Aarau (ZDA), University of Zurich, Zurich, Switzerland
e-mail: uwe.serdult@uzh.ch

T. Beutel
e-mail: theodor.beutel@uzh.ch

T. Beutel
Ethereum Foundation, Zug, Switzerland

P. K. Makode · C. J. Tessone
UZH Blockchain Center, University of Zurich, Zurich, Switzerland
e-mail: parminderkaur.makode@uzh.ch

C. J. Tessone
e-mail: claudio.tessone@uzh.ch

U. Serdült
College of Information Science and Engineering, Ritsumeikan University, Kyoto, Japan

M. Lustenberger et al. (eds.), *Decentralized Autonomous Organizations—Governance, Technology, and Legal Perspectives*, Springer Proceedings in Business and Economics,
https://doi.org/10.1007/978-3-032-03273-7_3

1 Introduction

For the past decade, decentralised autonomous organisations (DAOs) have been explored and experimented with, risen and fallen many times [1]. The ability of "self-infrastructuring" [2] and user innovation on an institutional level [3] resulted in rapid prototyping around novel governance systems. The rich variety of DAOs across blockchain (sub-)ecosystems including decentralised finance (DeFi), layer 2 solutions (L2s), non-fungible token (NFT) communities, "social DAOs" and many more resulted in a vast natural experiment in coordination, based on the "confidence machine" [4] of blockchain technology.

De Filippi and Hassan [5] define a DAO as a "blockchain-based system that enables people to coordinate and govern themselves mediated by a set of self-executing rules deployed on a public blockchain, and whose governance is decentralised (i.e. independent from central control)" [p. 2]. Most definitions in academic literature characterise a DAO through rules being enshrined in smart contracts, whose code is deployed on a public blockchain. However, controversies remain around each of the dimension "decentralised", "autonomous" and "organisation" [ibid., p. 6]. In practice, however, the term *DAO*tends to be used rather inflationary and is an "incredibly broad term whose meaning has evolved a lot over the years" [6]. Reports from Asia where DAOs are not always considered a technology per se but framed as an "enabling philosophy"[1] suggest that DAOs are subject to cultural variations.

The term "DAO", it seems, can serve as a mantra for change of—"often still emergent and yet to be refined"— governance. Being aware of such perspectives on DAOs is arguably important to fully grasp the reality of DAOs (real of self-proclaimed) when they are "complex, socio-technical, algorithmic system[s]" [7, p. 75]. Diverse use cases and individual perspectives to what constitutes trust and confidence in their respective communities [8] stress the importance of complementing technical system analyses with research methods of the social sciences, such as ethnography.

While the technologies behind DAOs in principle allow to them "radically advance democratic ownership and governance", Schneider argues that much more attention has been given to securing property rights, while the technological potential of implementing and maintaining digital democracy is "missing from the crypto-optimist culture" [9]. Even if attention is given to democratic values, Nabben and Zargham argue that "software developer ontologies are shaping governance infrastructures, with ideals of *digital democracy* manifesting as paradigms of plutocratic token voting, rather than *inclusion*" [7]. As a result, the distribution of voting rights can be highly unequal—"with more inequality in some DAOs compared to the general distribution of wealth in the world" [10].

[1] Reports from Metagov (https://github.com/metagov/daostar/tree/main/Reports) describe DAOs in Japan which don't use smart contracts nor on-chain voting systems, while South Korean examples are paradoxically described as "off-chain DAOs". A report on Taiwan points out that the term DAO is often used as part of civic engagement by communities innovating around local culture and society's needs, without necessarily making use of blockchain and on-chain voting at all. Similarly, a Singaporean perspective suggests to move beyond a "tech-centric view of DAOs".

Previous research has described extensively how blockchain-based governance in DAOs adopts decision-making mechanisms, such as token-weighted voting [11–14] which tends to result in plutocracy, reputation-weighted voting [11, 13, 15] which can resemble a meritocracy, quadratic voting [11, 12, 16–18] and conviction voting [11, 12]. Even though they are clearly alternatives to classical majority voting, they should not be declared as non-democratic. In modern liberal democracies, and increasingly in a digital democracy setting, they can provide for useful solutions in more complex settings. Complex preference aggregation problems appear, for example, when we have a setting of not only individuals but also organisations, or a mix thereof. However, a number of empirical studies have shown a significant concentration of voting power amongst major DAOs in DeFi and elsewhere [10, 19, 20]. On the other hand, some authors described democratic governance as the original ethos of crypto yet, while contributing valuable perspective to the discourse, they are mostly works of conceptual [12] or essayistic [9] nature. Little attention has been devoted to analysing implementations of democratic mechanisms in DAOs specifically.

Through a systematic review of the literature on DAOs, we seek to find out: Does the short history of DAOs provide novel insights for the notion of democracy? Or are DAOs merely a wishful projection, a "narrative of democracy done right?" [7]

The objective of this paper is therefore to explore implementations of digital democracy DAOs, focusing on *mechanisms* and *challenges*:

1. Which *mechanisms* are discussed around digital democracy in DAOs?
2. Which *challenges* are associated with these mechanisms?

In line with the UN E-Government Survey, we define digital democracy as a process that involves citizens in the design, decision-making and implementation of policies with the help of information and communication technologies, with the aim of making this process participatory, inclusive and deliberative [21].

This paper is structured as follows. After this brief introduction to digital democracy in DAOs, we describe the methodology of a systematic literature review in Sect. 2. Section 3 summarises our findings, which we continue to discuss in Sect. 4. We conclude by summarising our findings in Sect. 5, pointing to limitations and presenting avenues for future research at the intersection of "DAO science"[2] and democracy research.

2 Methodology

This systematic literature review on digital democracy in DAOs employs the PRISMA 2020 Statement developed by Page et al. [22]. The PRISMA 2020 methodology is designed to enhance the transparency, completeness and reproducibility

[2] https://daoscience.org/ curates a 29-author-paper of "Open Problems in DAOs".

of systematic reviews. It facilitates a rigorous and structured approach to identifying, selecting, appraising and synthesising relevant studies. By adhering to this methodology, we ensure that the selection process for literature is systematic, unbiased and comprehensive, thereby enabling the identification of the most relevant and high-quality studies for this review (see Fig. 1).

The objective of this paper is to explore the implementations of digital democracy in DAOs, with a specific focus on the mechanisms employed and the challenges encountered. The research questions mentioned above aim to provide a comprehensive overview of the key aspects of digital democracy as reflected in the existing literature, promoting an understanding of both the theoretical frameworks and practical implementations within the context of DAOs. The research questions were formulated to capture a broad understanding of the current academic discourse, laying the groundwork for further explorations around digital democracy within DAOs.

To ensure a comprehensive collection of the relevant literature, searches were conducted across four major academic databases: *Elsevier, Scopus, Web of Science and EBSCOhost*. These databases were selected for their extensive coverage of peer-reviewed articles, particularly within the fields of blockchain, governance and digital democracy. The search strategy was designed to capture studies focusing on digital democracy within the context of DAOs and blockchain governance. This resulted in the following search string:

("digital democracy" AND ("blockchain" OR "DAO" OR "DAOs")) OR (("decentralized autonomous organization" OR "decentralised autonomous organisation" OR (("DAO" OR "DAOs") AND "blockchain" AND "governance")) AND ("democracy" OR "democratic" OR "edemocratic" OR "edemocracy" OR "e-democratic" OR "e-democracy" OR "vote" OR "voter" OR "voters" OR "voting" OR "voted" OR "democratic decision-making" OR "participatory governance"))

The search was conducted using the following fields: *Article Title, Abstract, and Keywords*. This approach ensured that included studies explicitly address digital democracy in DAOs, either theoretically or empirically.

Grey Literature, including technical reports and preprints, was sourced from *Google Scholar* to capture recent developments in DAOs and digital democracy. This approach of including emerging perspectives not yet reflected in peer-reviewed research accounts for an academic lag due to the particularly face-paced nature of the field.

Before screening, the database searches yielded a total of **2137 articles** before removing duplicates, distributed as follows: Elsevier (1944), Scopus (82), Web of Science (59), EBSCOhost (18) and Google Scholar (34).

As part of the screening process, duplicate records were identified and removed using Mendeley and Zotero, both reference management tools. This step helped eliminate redundant entries that appeared across multiple databases. After the removal of duplicates, the intermediate count of articles was reduced to **599**.

Next, titles and abstracts of the remaining articles were screened to assess their relevance to the research objectives. To ensure the selection of high-quality, relevant studies, this screening was conducted based on the following, pre-defined inclusion and exclusion criteria. Studies were included if they were relevant to

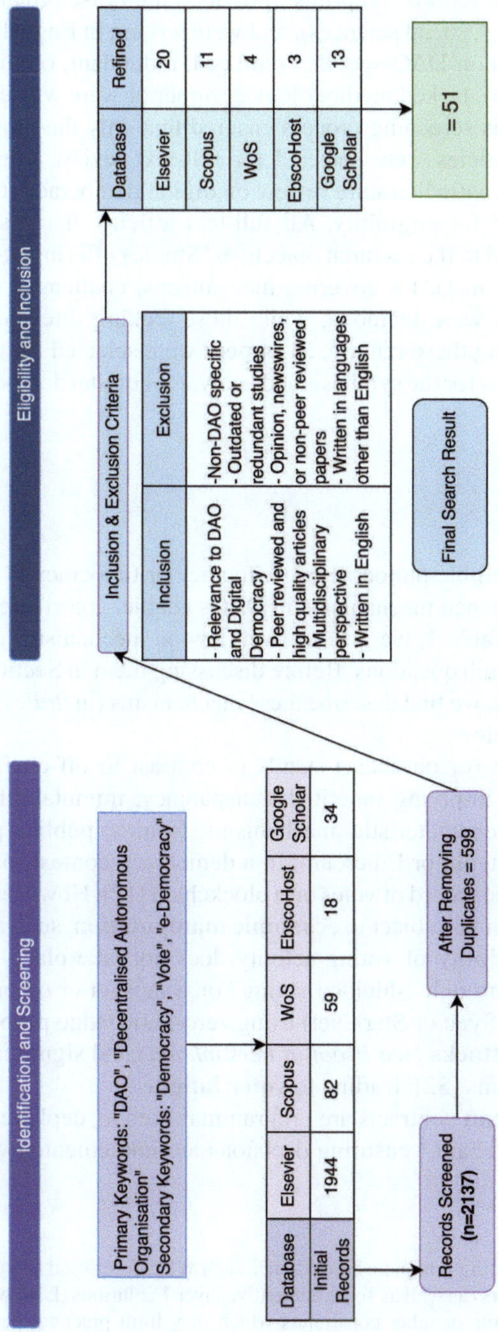

Fig. 1 PRISMA flow diagram

DAOs and Digital Democracy, high-quality peer-reviewed articles or credible grey literature (e.g. technical reports, preprints), provided multidisciplinary perspectives (governance, technology, social sciences), and were written in English. Studies were excluded if they were non-DAO-specific, outdated, redundant, opinion-based (e.g. news articles, editorials), lacked methodological rigour or were written in languages other than English. This screening process ensured that only the most relevant and academically sound articles were selected for full-text review, aligning with the objectives of this systematic literature review on digital democracy in DAOs.

Lastly, we screened for eligibility. All full-text articles that passed the initial screening were assessed to the research objectives. Studies offering in-depth insights into digital democracy in DAOs covering mechanisms, challenges, and empirical or theoretical analyses were included, while those lacking direct relevance were excluded. After applying these criteria, **51 papers** were selected for this systematic review, forming the basis for the synthesis and analysis of digital democracy in DAOs.

3 Results

While DAOs often resemble plutocracy, meritocracy or timocracy [11, 23], we find that a variety of governance mechanisms in DAOs enable, contribute to or result in digital democracy. In Table 1, we give an overview on mechanisms and challenges in response to the research questions. Before discussing them in Section 4 based on a broader range of papers, we first describe these mechanisms (in *italic*) and associated challenges (in **bold**) below:

On-chain: On-chain (or on-chain) stands in contrast to off-chain [31–33] and is used as a qualifier, implying inherited transparency, immutability, censorship-resistance and other characteristic mechanisms from a public, permissionless blockchain, such as Bitcoin or Ethereum. In a democracy context, on-chain voting systems provide a public record of votes on a blockchain [12]. However, in pseudonymous settings, votes can be subject to **economic manipulation**, such as vote buying. Currently, the vast majority of voting activity does not take place in anonymous settings[3] as provided through "shielded voting" on Snapshot or on privacy-focused L2s (such as Scroll, zkSync or StarkNet) using zero-knowledge proofs. Other challenges include **Sybil attacks** (see *Proof of Personhood*) and significant transaction fees on some blockchains [32], leading to **voter fatigue**.

Smart contracts: Smart contracts are programmable code, deployed on a (quasi-) Turing-complete blockchain,[4] ensuring decisions are implemented without human

[3] According to https://deepdao.io/.

[4] Smart contracts run on Turing-complete blockchains, such as Ethereum and L2s (Base, Optimism, Arbitrum, zkSync and others) as well as some alternative layer 1 solutions (L1s) with the exception of Bitcoin. Due to gas limits or other constraints which may limit practical performance, some blockchains are sometimes referred to as quasi-Turing complete, even if they are Turing complete in theory.

Table 1 Overview of mechanisms in DAOs and challenges in a democracy context

Mechanisms in DAOs	References	Challenges in a democracy context
On-chain (public blockchains, public ledger)	[11, 12, 14, 15, 17, 18, 24–33]	Sybil attacks, economic manipulation, voter fatigue
Smart contracts	[11, 12, 15, 17, 18, 24–30, 33–37]	Exploits and hacks, rule of code
Branches of governance	[12, 15, 17, 28]	Rule of code, coordination failures, centralisation of power, economic manipulation
Proof of Personhood (Sybil resistance)	[11–13, 17, 29, 37–39]	Sybil attacks
Delegation and liquid democracy	[7, 11–13, 15, 17, 23, 24, 28–30, 35, 40–44]	Voter fatigue, centralisation of power
Pluralism and polycentricity	[25, 43, 45]	Centralisation of power, coordination failures
Subsidiarity	[7, 28]	Coordination failures
Dynamic quorum	[11–13, 17]	Voter fatigue
Temporality	[11, 18, 32]	Coordination failures, exploits and hacks
Incentives	[13–15, 17, 18, 27–30, 37, 46, 47]	Economic manipulation, centralisation of power, voter fatigue
Constitutions	[7, 17, 25, 26, 48]	Rule of code
Exiting (fork, ragequitting)	[11–14, 24, 29, 40]	Coordination failures

intervention. They are autonomous entities with a publicly verifiable *if-this-then-that-*logic of self-execution [12, 34–36] and can be designed to process proposal submissions, voting processes and resource allocations. While some DAOs partially govern themselves off-chain, on-chain execution through governance smart contracts, such as OpenZeppelin's Governor, is considered the gold standard for DAO governance. However, when "code is law" [49], their feature of the "**rule of code**" [50] results in rigidity and may become problematic in certain democratic contexts, unless embedded in metagovernance (or the absence thereof) ratified by the demos [35, 37]. A smart contract's executive abilities are constrained by its pre-defined code—and more generally by the capabilities of its blockchain as well as the (reverse) oracle problem[5]—including potential bugs which can lead to **exploits and hacks** [37]. Code audits of smart contracts are necessary but cannot ever be sufficient to avoid exploits [1], partially due to smart contracts being incomplete [51].

[5] The oracle problem refers to sourcing data from off-chain to on-chain in a trustless and verifiable manner, or from on-chain to off-chain respectively in reverse.

Branches of governance: Most DAOs are not embedded in the three classical functions of executive, legislative and judicative. This can be explained partially through the opposing design goal of a **rule of code**, and due to immature governance frameworks and overall complexity [24], leading to some **centralisation of power**. However, there are similarities. Proposal-based DAO governance frameworks with deliberation mechanisms can resemble a legislative function. As described above, *smart contracts* and *on-chain* execution of elections can eliminate principal-agent problems between the legislative and the executive. However, DAOs are not free of principal-agent problems (see *Delegation*). As for judicative functions, only a few DAOs make use of dispute resolution mechanisms or decentralised arbitration services [15, 29], such as Kleros or Aragon Court. Moreover, checks and balances through political or legal constitutionalism are rare (e.g. Optimism's Citizens' House keeping its Token House in check) and generally seen through the lens of economic constitutionalism, specifically cryptoeconomic and game-theoretical incentive design. In democratic contexts, these characteristics may result in **economic manipulation** and may be considered **coordination failures**.

Proof of Personhood [52]: While most nation state democracies have long-standing routines to organise one-person, one-vote elections, blockchains don't. On the Internet, nobody knows you're a dog. Likewise, on the blockchain, nobody knows you're a bot. In a blockchain context, agents are usually only identifiable to the level of an account address. As it is generally unclear whether that agent is human or not, blockchains are prone to **Sybil attacks**. These occur when, for instance, a single actor controls a large number of accounts, indistinguishable from other accounts of honest actors [53]. The related concept of vote buying, or "bribing", is common in some DAOs and can occur at scale on "marketplaces for votes" [12]. Dotan et al. show that this goes as far as governance participants holding "governance tokens for the duration of a single proposal which they created and voted for with a majority of the voting power" [54]. Flash loans can amplify this issue further [11]. While such attacks can undermine the legitimacy of a system [7], Sybil attacks are technically not an issue in plutocratic, token-based voting where governance tokens are transferable by design and vote buying is a feature, not a bug. This may be a reason why so many DAOs fall back to this mechanism, as it "just works". However, Ohlhaver et al. argue that vote buying can always move from on-chain to off-chain [52], which can affect DAOs with democratic governance mechanisms, too. Sybil-resistant governance mechanisms are an essential prerequisite for one-person, one-vote governance on the blockchain. They are closely intertwined with blockchain-based universal basic income (UBI) projects. So-called Proof of Personhood mechanisms [55], a kind of decentralised identity system (DID), attempt to solve this issue in a blockchain context [17, 26, 29], known as Proof of Humanity, BrightID, Idena, Circles or more recently, World. World, formerly known as Worldcoin, is using biometric data and zero-knowledge proofs [38, 39]. They aim at uniquely identifying a human and may allocate them "Soulbound" tokens [37, 56], but struggle to distinguish honest humans from bot-like humans and are subject to **economic manipulation**, too [52]. Ethical concerns also arise from the risk of centralisation inherent in some proof-of-personhood systems, which can conflict with the core DAO principle of decentralisation. Furthermore, maintaining robust fraud prevention measures without compromising user privacy adds another layer of difficulty. Ensuring the authenticity of identities while safeguarding personal data is a delicate balance [39]. As such implementations remain controversial and each individual solution may scale towards a "global oligopoly", Olhaver et al. call for a "plurality of identity games" [52].

Delegation and liquid democracy: While delegating votes in DAOs is a common practice, that is mostly in the context of token-weighted voting. Best practices of delegation in democratic DAOs are scarce but technically feasible. Liquid democracy, implemented through nested smart contracts, could result in more dynamic and equitable governance mechanisms [15] and might blur the boundaries between engaged voters and professional politicians [40]. Delegation was widely regarded as a way to tackle **voter fatigue**, which many early DAOs struggled with. Actively taking part in DAO governance comes with high opportunity costs [30] and participation rates are even lower when transaction fees are higher [54], especially with many early DAOs running on Ethereum mainnet. As DAOs such as ENS and Gitcoin required users to delegate their governance tokens before being able to claim "airdropped", i.e. allocated tokens, delegation became increasingly common practice across DAOs. However, this also fueled a **centralisation of power** amongst just a few delegates [23, 35, 42–44, 54]. These patterns can be structurally more similar to shareholder meetings than to democracies [10] and subject to voter coalitions [57]. Moreover, professional and institutional participants tend to dilute the influence by ordinary "retail" users [19]. Fernandez et al. show that, even if the initial distribution of a project's governance tokens is "fair", voting power will become concentrated over time as long as the corresponding governance token is tradable [20], confirming Barbereau's et al. [23] findings. In a similar vein, Goldberg et al. [58] argue that "a blockchain-based governance system and ownership layer constitute a necessary but not a sufficient condition for neutral metaverse infrastructure".

Pluralism: As DAOs usually operate globally, across cultures, jurisdictions and political affiliations, some explicitly stress the importance of pluralistic governance or polycentricity. Yet, they often struggle with **coordination failures** and particularly **centralisation of power** (see above), when their governance mechanisms do not appropriately represent the plurality of their members. DAOs appear to be "following the 'iron law of oligarchy' – larger DAOs also correlate with greater inequality" [43]. Moreover, as noted by Han and Lee [11], it is common practice in at least some DAOs that individuals with a high degree of voting power, such as founding team members of major investors, refrain from voting. This can imply that the concentration of power is even greater than any analyses of cast votes suggest. Furthermore, the use of special admin keys stretches self-proclaimed definitions of decentralisation [59]. Such "decentralisation theatre" or "fake decentralisation" not only contributes negatively to the long-term viability of such DAOs compared to democratically governed DAOs [60], but also poses the risk of the DAO being considered centralised by regulators and being regulated as such [61]. Some DAOs apply principles of polycentricity, with elements of *subsidiarity* (see below), as multiple autonomous units operate at different scales while remaining interconnected. However, polycentric governance faces challenges such as coordination difficulties and conflicting objectives amongst different units. Addressing these issues requires effective communication and coordination mechanisms to maintain alignment [45].

Subsidiarity: In some DAOs, we observe geographical/time zone-based clusters, informal topic-specific working groups [28] and other kinds of bottom-up governance. Related on-chain governance mechanisms include pods (Metropolis), hats (Hats Protocol), multisigs (Safe), sub-spaces (Snapshot with SafeSnap/oSnap) or even the emerging field of AI agents in DAOs [28]. Such implementations allow for nested, tree-like dependencies, which can be part of an overarching democratic governance process. All of the former contribute to preventing **coordination failures**. However, best practices have yet to emerge. Subsidiarity in DAOs is related to polycentricity, as well as Ostrom's eighth principle of governing the commons of nested enterprises [62], and is still underexplored in literature.

Dynamic quorum: Many DAOs apply stricter quorum requirements for higher-impact proposals, while allowing lower (or no) quorums for lower-impact proposals [11]. Similarly, Alon et al. suggest that strategically important proposals requiring more deliberation should be subject to a higher quorum, while a lower quorum with more operational proposals accounts for **voter fatigue** and allows the DAO to operate more efficiently [13].

Temporality: Similar to dynamic quorums, some DAOs allow for longer voting periods with high-impact proposals. Even though Alon et al. do not observe adjustable voting durations in their sample of DAOs, they proceed to recommend voting durations to be dynamic—longer for strategic and shorter for operational proposals [13]. Related mechanisms include time-locks, grace periods and cooldowns. These mechanisms are used, for example, to avoid governance tokens being transferred during an ongoing vote and counted twice; to allow time for review before a passed proposal is executed; or to allow time to *rage-quit* before a passed proposal is executed. Non-traditional voting mechanisms such as conviction voting [12] or Curve Finance's vote-escrow system [11] grant the more voting power, the longer a member locks their governance tokens. This is similar to tenure-based voting mechanisms. A variety of time-related **coordination failures** can occur. Examples include the necessity to fix a critical **exploit or hack** immediately, but immutable rules only allow to do so through a week-long governance process [32]. Some DAOs implemented emergency procedures for that reason or fall back on other mechanisms which retain control and, in turn, become centralisation vectors [59]. Another challenge, though often a legitimate voting procedure, is the phenomenon of flipping a vote shortly before the voting period ends. Some DAO platforms, such as Aragon and DAOstack [63], designed for that through automatically extending the voting period if a vote is cast at the last minute and if it changes the result of the vote, but most DAO toolings do not.

Incentives: Besides staking rewards that are allocated unrelated from voting activity, few DAOs directly or indirectly remunerate voters to incentivise participation. For instance, Safe has a loyalty programme for its governance token holders, Tally and

Arbitrum reward delegates monthly with up to 5.000 ARB (approx. 2.000 CHF as of Feb '25), and—an example of indirect incentive mechanisms—past airdrops by Optimism (RetroPGF) and BanklessDAO have retroactively rewarded governance participants. Jurors in Klero's decentralised arbitration mechanisms are financially rewarded, too, or financially penalised if they appear to act maliciously [29]. However, studies evaluating financial rewards for voting are inconclusive whether they should be considered **economic manipulation**, or a legitimate means to tackle **voter fatigue**. While Rikken et al. suggest that the absence of incentives is beneficial for long-term viability [60], others describe financial incentives for delegates as a "good direction for future work" [54]. An underexplored theme is the dichotomy between governance tokens and security tokens. While the former cannot pay out dividends and have been tolerated in many jurisdictions, the latter are heavily regulated globally and only very few cryptocurrencies are officially marketed as a security. This led to a Cambrian explosion of governance tokens and creative ways of more or less indirectly financially rewarding its holders, e.g. through the value of the governance token itself appreciating in price. Securities, obfuscated as governance tokens, are one example of how DAO governance design is influenced by conflicting interests which do not primarily optimise for good governance. As previously mentioned, other examples include "decentralisation theatre" due to **centralisation of voting power** and preferring unincorporated DAOs over legal wrappers as a purported regulatory shield [37, 46, 47, 61].

Constitutions: Some DAOs make use of constitutions [64, 65], but unlike nation states, some DAOs refer to them as community covenant, charter, manifesto, code of conduct, voting principles, process document or lore [66]. While overall deliberation is less pronounced in most DAOs than in most democracies, DAO constitutions can limit **coordination failures** through better alignment when members previously agreed more or less explicitly on values and a vision [7, 65, 66]. Enforceability of constitutions remains a challenge, as DAO constitutions are often written in prose and subject to interpretation, which is in contrast to the "**rule of code**" of smart contracts. Unless they are enshrined in on-chain governance and receive objectively true information through a trustless oracle, the formal role of DAO constitutions is merely a signalling one, yet their informal role of community alignment remains an essential one [7, 48].

Exiting: A low-cost option of exit is another defining characteristic of polycentricity in DAOs [4]. While exiting is a rather uncommon option in traditional democracies of nation states and often rather inconvenient, it is common in DAOs. "Ragequitting" was coined by MolochDAO which makes use of plutocratic, token-weighted voting. It describes the process of withdrawing from MolochDAO (or any deployment based on its open-source code) by giving up a member's seat and receiving a proportional payout of the funds the member had originally contributed. While the concept of ragequitting does not apply to democratically governed DAOs, the concept of forking does. A (hard) fork describes a DAO (or a blockchain) splitting into two or more parts and adopting non-backwards compatible design choices. In some ways, forking is a feature to avoid capture and advance evolution. In other ways, it is the ultima ratio of a **coordination failure** when cooperation has come to an end. Famously, an attack in 2016 on one of the first DAOs, "The DAO", resulted in Ethereum (ETH) pursuing a hard fork from Ethereum Classic (ETC). In the case of Proof of Humanity DAO, the lack of a preamble in a constitution (and the lack of a debate thereof at an early stage of the project) led to not having an aligned vision. Ultimately, this resulted in a fork of the project, as the mere ability to fork fueled polarisation and an increasingly escalating discourse [17].

4 Discussion

This study investigated the mechanisms and challenges associated with digital democracy in DAOs. In line with [11, 23], we find there is a wide range of governance mechanisms used in DAOs, such as token-weighted voting with governance tokens that are transferable and usually traded on decentralised exchanges (DEXs). Plutocratic governance mechanisms continue to dominate the DAO space, as several studies showed before [10, 20, 43]. While Barbereau et al. [23] describe DeFi's governance as timocratic and call for a "philosophical intervention" to "dispel spurious, platitudinous notions of 'democracy'" [p. 12], Nadler and Schär show that most studies severely overestimate the actual concentration of voting power [67]. Nabben et al. [7] explain the lack of widely used democratic governance models by both meritocracy and plutocracy holding "pre-eminent value and respect in the [blockchain] space" [p. 84]. Allen and Nabben [12] remind of blockchain's pseudonymous, token-based participation system and the lack of permissioned structures—common in democratic governance systems of nation states—and conclude that blockchain is not naturally conform to democratic processes.

However, we identified several governance mechanisms that are in fact democratic or complement governance designs of democracy (see Table 1). In line with Ballandies et al. [24] who describe the two phases of deliberation and voting, we observe that the vast majority of mechanisms relate to the phase of voting, while few best practices and more challenges are associated with the preceding phase of deliberation. We identify challenges, namely Sybil attacks, economic manipulation, rule of code, economic manipulation, exploits and hacks, centralisation of power and coordination failures. That is in line with Merk, who suggests that governance minimisation and token voting were a result of the motto "don't trust, verify", common in Bitcoin and other blockchain communities, which "may have inadvertently led to some of the issues currently experienced by DAOs, such as a lack of participation and voter apathy" [8].

Yet, the practical feasibility and success in fostering truly democratic governance in DAOs remain highly uncertain. Shapiro et al. see "immense" [26] challenges for democratic DAOs, particularly given the challenges around Sybil-resistant mechanism design on blockchains where subjects are identifiable through pseodonymous account addresses and public keys [11–13, 17, 29] not as in nation state democracies with identity cards and voter registries. Attempts to uniquely verify humans on blockchains through "Proof of Personhood" remain a challenge and subject to controversies [52]. For instance, World has surpassed 11 million registered users across 160 countries, while users and policymakers globally look sceptically at World's iris-scanning technology. Key elements of democratic decision-making remain a challenge in a blockchain context, such as Sybil resistance, private voting or appropriate space for deliberation.

Moreover, blockchain-based smart contracts and DAOs are institutional technologies [68] which raise conceptual and normative questions around the creation of money and a democratisation thereof. Vatanparast [25] calls for "monetary pluralism of digital currencies [...] that are not driven by profit and extractive motives but rather driven by democratic aims to serve diverse publics' interests" [p. 195], echoed by [69]. While practitioners contemplate how to have "more good memecoins than bad ones" [70], the launch of the current US president's own memecoin TRUMP left observers perplexed by the absurdity, as Trump's own cryptocurrency could "serve as a vehicle for bribery" [71] and erode democracy itself.

However, we find that the contribution of DAOs to democracy research may be *more profound* than apparent by just looking at single instances at the level of implementation.

Traditionally, research on institutional design, democracy research and other governance-related topics has mostly been constrained to either theoretical modelling or quasi-experiments. DAOs come with a historically unique potential, as they offer a vast solution space (a blockchain as a "world computer"), operate globally across jurisdictions and remain relatively unaffected by geopolitical constraints (censorship-resistant "code is law"), are inherently inclusive (permissionless user innovation) and are digital-first. These properties enable anyone with Internet access to experiment with governance mechanisms, coordinate with others on a level playing field and reconstruct democratic systems from the ground up.

This is in line with Allen and Nabben [12] who go even further, stating that "the role of blockchain may not be to transform existing democratic governance institutions (at least in the short term), but in enabling novel forms of collective action that exist alongside traditional governance systems" [p. 12]. Exemplary design spaces include polycentric governance for global communities in a multipolar world of geopolitical instability, as well as liquid democracy for complex, domain-specific preference aggregation for more direct democracy even in democracies larger than, for instance, Switzerland. A common theme in DAO communities is the notion of metagovernance, when two DAOs exchange governance tokens with one another. As complex systems of polycentricity and subsidiarity emerge over time, metagovernance means "trying to comprehend a condition of bewildering integration" [p. 175], with DAOs as a form of "governable spaces" [72].

5 Conclusion

Through a systematic literature review we show that DAOs enable digital democracy by utilising a wide range of decision-making processes and governance mechanisms. While DAOs can and initially were thought to be designed following democratic ideals [9], popular DAOs and their underlying smart contract architecture are currently heavily influenced by plutocratic or meritocratic ideals [12]. We discuss that bribery, vote buying and other forms of economic manipulation remain a challenge in DAOs like in all forms of democracy. However, on-chain governance of DAOs creates an immutable record, enabling after-the-fact accountability mechanisms of voter fraud detection and thus disincentivising corruption beforehand.

Moreover, we suggest that the design space of DAOs is vast and offers tremendous potential for digital democracy. When DAOs are based on public, permissionless blockchains with strong characteristics of decentralisation, they inherit features of transparency, immutability and censorship-resistance. Beyond the technical dimension, subcultures have emerged where the term "DAO" stands for societal progress and techno-utopian futures. These use the digital realm of DAOs to experiment with bottom-up governance and to build new institutions, irrespective of geopolitical tensions or monetary policy. This goes as far as DarkFi, a "democratic economic experiment" and "operating system for society" [73], using zero-knowledge proofs to confront totalitarianism to defend a cypherpunk vision of privacy as a digital human right. However, similar "dark DAOs" can also be used for vote buying [1] and privacy-preserving architectures can both strengthen and destabilise democracy, e.g. through terrorism financing. This dual-use dilemma stresses the importance of further research exploring these emerging phenomena in democratic contexts as well as ethical debates amongst practitioners and the general public.

Our contribution to theory is twofold, contributing to research on blockchain and DAOs as well as to democracy research. Firstly, we discuss the prevalent issues in research on DAOs, including voter apathy, economic manipulation and concentration of power. We describe novel perspectives on DAOs as a means for digital democracy, explaining the significance of decision-making mechanisms used in DAOs in a democratic context. Secondly, we contribute to research on democracy by discussing DAOs as a means of user innovation [74] for democracy, enabling grassroots communities to explore new democratic governance mechanisms and allowing researchers to go beyond theoretical and simulation-based approaches and conduct empirical studies on governance mechanisms in practice.

This study faces several limitations that may affect its validity. The reliance on academic literature and grey literature introduces selection bias, potentially overlooking industry insights or unpublished studies. Survivorship bias is also a concern, as the academic literature may focus on active DAOs and may exclude failed projects that could provide valuable lessons. Additionally, the interpretation of governance mechanisms and challenges is subjective, despite efforts to maintain objectivity. The rapidly evolving nature of DAOs presents a temporal limitation, as governance structures and regulations continue to shift. Generalisability is another challenge, as DAO

An Interdisciplinary Approach to the Coordination Layer of DAOs and the Design of Token Economies

Irene Domenicale, Cristina Toti, Sowelu Avanzo, Cristina Viano, and Claudio Schifanella

Abstract This study explores blockchain applications designed for local communities, emphasizing tokenization as a tool to foster socio-economic participation, social inclusion, and collective action. Unlike market-driven cryptocurrencies, these applications require governance and token systems tailored to collaborative objectives. We propose a preliminary method that integrates sociological principles into tokenomics design, moving beyond traditional market-oriented models. This interdisciplinary approach not only enhances the accessibility of blockchain toolkits for developers and community members alike but also provides a robust methodological foundation for implementing effective tokenized systems at the DAO coordination layer.

Keywords Blockchain for local communities · DAO coordination layer · Token economy · Web3 toolkit

1 Introduction

This proposal is situated within a broader research aimed at identifying the principles and conditions that facilitate redistribution and recognition processes through blockchain-based applications and tokenized systems. By examining the suitability properties of participatory and collaborative economies, the objective is to develop a framework for designing, modeling, and implementing a tokenized system that supports community-based initiatives.

The motivation for this research is based on the increasing interest in utilizing blockchain technology for social good and non-speculative applications [1]. By exploring these areas, the aim is to enhance the accessibility of blockchain and

I. Domenicale (✉)
International School of Advanced Studies, University of Camerino, Camerino, Italy
e-mail: irene.domenicale@unicam.it

I. Domenicale · C. Toti · S. Avanzo · C. Viano · C. Schifanella
University of Turin, Torino, Italy

M. Lustenberger et al. (eds.), *Decentralized Autonomous Organizations—Governance, Technology, and Legal Perspectives*, Springer Proceedings in Business and Economics,
https://doi.org/10.1007/978-3-032-03273-7_4

tokenized systems, facilitating new value creation processes [2]. This has the potential to generate significant economic and social impacts, fostering more inclusive and collaborative economies [3].

In recent years, there has been a rise in blockchain-enabled systems aimed at sustainable development and social impact. However, only a few literature reviews and surveys have studied these initiatives [4, 5]. While the literature highlights the potential positive impacts of these applications, it also addresses the inherent constraints [6]. Indeed, there are critical perspectives on the concept of social good in the blockchain domain [7, 8] and concerns about techno-solutionist approaches that may sustain the status quo of speculative development perspectives [9]. This raises the question of how to rethink the mechanisms regulating blockchain functioning, highlighting the need to reorient these mechanisms toward collaborative and social purposes, which often differ from the logic behind mainstream cryptocurrencies. Redesigning these mechanisms effectively requires a comprehensive examination of the elements of the token economy and the underlying processes of participation. A central question in our research is: What happens when we move beyond orthodox economic paradigms to explore alternative frameworks for tokenized systems? Tokenomics brings to the forefront fundamental issues that have remained peripheral in economic thought, particularly the role of currency (and tokens) as social and governance technologies. The history of currency demonstrates that its function has never been neutral; rather, it has always been intertwined with values, norms, and political choices reflective of the society in which it operates. Tokens represent a continuation of this historical dynamic, offering mechanisms that not only facilitate exchange but also redefine governance structures and participation models, potentially enabling the emergence of *diverse* economic systems [10, 11]. For this reason, we explore the frameworks necessary to systematize blockchain-based applications oriented to collaborative economies, ensuring they are designed in alignment with the principles outlined above. There remains a significant gap in practitioner-oriented models that provide concrete guidelines for designing these systems. This study seeks to address that gap by exploring approaches that facilitate the design of blockchain-based solutions collaborative practices in social domain.

- RQ1 What theoretical and methodological frameworks can be used to analyze design and modeling tools for DAOs and tokenized systems?
- RQ2 What interdisciplinary principles and methodological steps are necessary for designing tokenized systems that support local communities and collaborative economies?

This proposal addresses the outlined questions by making two contributions. First, we consider the toolkit theory framework applied to the Web3 stack as proposed by Allen et al. [12], and use it as an analytical lens to examine a blockchain-based application and a modeling language used in real-world experiments with blockchain for local communities. By classifying these artifacts as toolkits of different types, we enhance the understanding of their potential, strengths, and limitations, providing insights into their applicability. Furthermore, this approach informs the design process of blockchain toolkits, ensuring they are not only accessible to developer-innovators but also to end-users within communities.

Second, we adopt an interdisciplinary perspective to token economy design. We introduce a preliminary method that integrates sociological principles into tokenomics design, moving beyond purely market-driven economic models. This approach provides a methodological foundation for practitioners, expanding the scope of existing toolkits. It enhances accessibility not only at the software level but also in the fundamental design principles required for implementing tokenized systems. The research methodology of this study follows the standard approach of a position paper. We first articulate our position by presenting an innovative hypothesis, positioning it as a basis for discussion. Subsequently, we provide relevant background information to contextualize our perspective. Finally, we examine two artifacts as toolkits and propose an interdisciplinary approach that expands their scope of application. Based on this analysis, we outline a course of action for developing tokenized systems for collaborative economies and introduce key enabling concepts to support this development.

2 DAOs, Token Economy, and Sociology

2.1 Socio-technical Perspectives on DAOs

Within the domain of Decentralized Applications (DApps), Decentralized Autonomous Organizations (DAOs) have emerged as a key technological framework for decentralized community governance. DAOs have been applied across various domains, including education, science, and social networks, and more recently, they have been explored as governance mechanisms for commons-oriented economic models [13, 14].

A comprehensive literature review on DAOs [15] highlights the growing interest of social scientists in their potential to challenge traditional governance and organizational theories. Despite increasing academic attention, DAOs remain a relatively new topic, lacking established theoretical frameworks. This contribution highlights several key issues: DAOs exhibit an inherent asymmetry of power and information, particularly favoring software developers, which raises concerns about the practical application of *code as law* [16, 17]. Moreover, DAOs rely on their design and coding, which are inherently subjective and not free from biases [18]. Important governance changes, implemented through improvement proposals, are often controlled by a small group of core developers. Some researchers advocate for hybrid governance models, where smart contracts automate certain processes while human intervention remains possible [19]. These challenges underscore the need for more robust theoretical frameworks and governance mechanisms to ensure that DAOs can respond to the real needs of the addressed community.

DAO governance is deeply reliant on incentive mechanisms and token economies, introducing further complexities in ensuring that participant behavior aligns with collective objectives [20, 21].

Addressing these challenges necessitates a more comprehensive exploration of DAO design principles, particularly in relation to community-driven governance and sustainable token economies. Despite the limited number of case studies exploring DAOs for commons management, existing research has begun to analyze the design requirements for DAOs in this context. DAOs offer a particularly suitable governance structure for managing commons and participatory processes, as they enable stakeholder participation in rule-making and activity monitoring [22]. Van Vulpen and Jansen [22]'s framework identifies three key governance areas: governance structure, enabling technology, and community governance. Among the governance mechanisms considered, community currencies play a crucial role in structuring internal economic relations. Hence, the token economy facilitates economic exchanges [23], enables collective decision-making through liquid voting [24], and regulates access to shared resources [25]. However, over-quantification of contributions may negatively impact community dynamics, underscoring the need for alternative economic models. While the proposed framework acknowledges the importance of token economy aspects, it does not provide a comprehensive exploration of their implications.

2.2 *Cross-disciplinary Domain of Tokenomics*

This proposal adopts an interdisciplinary approach to tokenomics, recognizing that the concept itself has been inherently interdisciplinary since its emergence. The terms cryptoeconomics and tokenomics are frequently used interchangeably or without precise definitions, leading to conceptual ambiguity [26].

These concepts and their definitions underscore the evolving and multifaceted nature of cryptoeconomics, which integrates several key dimensions [27]:

- Microeconomics: The study of optimal resource allocation within society.
- Game Theory: The analysis of decision-making among interdependent rational actors.
- Mechanism Design: The development of institutional structures (e.g., auctions, matching algorithms, voting systems) to autonomously achieve desired resource allocations.

Over time, tokenomics has expanded to include cryptoeconomics as a subset, reflecting its evolution into a more comprehensive discipline [28]. It draws extensively from neoclassical economics, particularly the interaction between supply-side value (marginal cost) and demand-side utility (marginal utility). These principles, traditionally applied to monetary systems, securities, and stocks, provide insights into blockchain-based monetary policies and digital currencies, particularly within mainstream blockchain applications [29].

Among literature on methods to design token economy [30–33] is particularly relevant the proposal of [34]: a five-step tokenomics goal model is presented that focuses on determining the number of tokens to release, deciding whether tokens should be allocated pre- or post-listing, choosing between a public and private token release, ensuring that tokens possess inherent value, and establishing an appropriate price management mechanism. This method aims to guide the design of successful tokenomics by addressing critical questions, such as the aspects of designing a token release schedule, the mechanisms for token distribution, and the strategies for ensuring token price sustainability. While this approach provides fundamental insights for constructing a sustainable and stable tokenomics framework—emphasizing the importance of monetary theory—it is primarily oriented toward market-based economic models.

To identify the principles necessary for fostering collaborative economies, an interdisciplinary approach that incorporates assumptions beyond those of neoclassical economics is required.

2.3 Coordination Layer and Socio-economic Concepts

The theoretical model proposed in [35] and refined in [20] and [21] conceptualizes DAO architectures as comprising five distinct layers, three of which are specific to DAO systems and define their organizational, coordination, and execution structures. The organization layer establishes the DAO's governance framework, shaping its structure in alignment with its long-term objectives. The coordination layer focuses on decision-making processes, such as voting mechanisms, and plays a crucial role in the design of the token economy, incorporating incentive structures to encourage desired behaviors. Lastly, the execution layer operationalizes the tasks defined in the upper layers, utilizing both on-chain functions executed through smart contracts and off-chain mechanisms [21]. In the present proposal, we focus specifically on the token economy dimension, situated within the coordination layer, as it directly influences governance, participation, and incentive structures within DAO ecosystems.

This research aims to examine how concepts derived from social economics can be systematically designed and implemented through technological frameworks such as blockchain. Central to this process is the development of a shared conceptual framework that enhances communication and alignment among stakeholders, communities, and developers, thereby bridging the gap between social-economic theory and decentralized technological infrastructures.

In this context, reference is made to the works of Zelizer and Polanyi [36, 37], both of whom contribute to the sociological-anthropological discourse on economic exchanges as relational practices.

Zelizer focuses on the micro-social and cultural dynamics of monetary circuits, conceptualizing them as intricate spaces of social and cultural interaction. Her analysis highlights how economic transactions are embedded within broader social relationships, challenging the notion of money as a neutral medium of exchange [37].

Polanyi, on the other hand, adopts a systemic perspective to examine these dynamics, aiming to historicize the concepts of economy and market. His work emphasizes the embeddedness of economic systems within social structures, illustrating how market economies are shaped by historical, political, and cultural forces [36].

3 Toolkits: A Theoretical Framework and Practical Applications

3.1 Web3 Toolkit Theory

In order to answer to RQ1, we find particularly interesting consider the perspective of [12], which frames Web3 stack as toolkits. This framework offers a valuable lens for conceptualizing the technical infrastructures employed in case studies and projects that leverage blockchain technologies to enable civic and collaborative processes. A first relevant aspect of this approach is its connection to open innovation theory, which aligns with the notion of toolkits. Toolkits are described as "coordinated sets of user-friendly design tools that enable users to develop new product innovations for themselves" [38]. The primary objective of toolkits is to reorganize the innovation process by facilitating the integration of specialized technical expertise with context-specific knowledge held by users—such as information about local conditions, user needs, cost constraints, and operational limitations [12].

This framework proposes viewing Web3 infrastructures as toolkits, offering valuable insights for the design of tokenized systems. According to this view, toolkits represent an intermediate evolutionary step between centralized industrial innovation and decentralized user innovation. They facilitate decentralized innovation by encoding centralized expertise into technical rules embedded in software and interfaces, allowing users to configure systems according to their needs. Web3 technologies can be understood as a stack of digital infrastructures with toolkit-like features.

A notable example are Decentralized Autonomous Organizations (DAOs). In DAO systems, users can customize various parameters—such as token supply, voting mechanisms, and wallet authorizations—to suit their local needs. This composability makes DAOs manifestations of toolkits that embed sticky local information—knowledge that is difficult to extract or formalize but is best applied within the community itself. Rather than following the industrial model of mass-producing DAO software, Web3 development tends to prioritize modular, user-friendly, and modifiable tools—that is, toolkits.

Another valuable insight from this framework is the distinction between two types of Web3 tools. The first type consists of

- *End-user products*, such as cryptocurrencies, NFT collections, or DAOs, which are designed to deliver final applications directly to users.
- *Toolkits for user innovators*, such as layer 1 blockchains, DeFi primitives, or governance frameworks, which provide foundational infrastructures for communities to create their own applications.

This distinction is particularly relevant for understanding which toolkits serve as infrastructural components and which act as final applications within the context of blockchain for collaborative economies. The following sections will provide examples of each approach, illustrating how these toolkits can enable decentralized governance and participatory economic systems.

3.2 *CommonsHood, End-User Product Toolkit*

The CommonsHood project [39, 40] exemplifies a blockchain-based approach to fostering local economies and civic engagement by providing a user-friendly wallet application that enables communities to create and circulate digital tokens. Through a graphical interface that requires no prior coding knowledge, participants can deploy various token types, each accompanied by a human-readable document specifying its intended purpose and conditions of use. Typical use cases include digital coupons, event tickets, local currencies, and NFTs designed for ownership traceability.

The platform supports the deployment of DAOs as a service, primarily used by associations for governance purposes. These DAOs incorporate role-based access control mechanisms and are integrated with FirstLife, a geo-referenced social network that enhances local interactions among individuals, social-economy organizations, and community-driven collectives [41]. This integration enables CommonsHood to align token-based transactions with neighborhood-level needs, such as crowdfunding campaigns and community-specific loyalty programs, ensuring transparency and trust through blockchain execution. CommonsHood is an Ethereum-based dApp that enables user-driven tokenization through predefined smart contract templates. Unlike traditional ERC-20 tokenization platforms, it supports different token types, including discount vouchers, complementary currencies, digital collectibles, and resource-sharing rights. It also facilitates purpose-driven tokenization to incentivize community-aligned behaviors. Beyond token issuance, CommonsHood offers crowdfunding, marketplace exchanges, and non-fungible asset management, fostering a dynamic multi-token ecosystem [42].

From the perspective of toolkit theory, CommonsHood can be classified as an end-user product toolkit that empowers individuals to develop tokenized systems tailored to local needs. It aligns with key toolkit attributes—usability, modularity, and adaptability—by allowing communities to modify and customize their token ecosystems based on localized knowledge and specific socio-economic conditions. In this way, CommonsHood acts as a decentralized innovation enabler, leveraging blockchain to facilitate grassroots economic experimentation and community-driven governance. Currently classified as a TRL 7 application, CommonsHood is actively deployed in real-world experiments, demonstrating its viability as a tool for fostering collaborative economies through blockchain technology [43].

While this app serves as a compelling example of a toolkit designed as an end-user product, its technological infrastructure and application require a complementary design framework to facilitate the structured development of tokenized systems. While the app provides the necessary digital tools for token issuance and management, an additional toolkit is needed to offer methodological guidance on how to effectively design, integrate, and utilize these tools within a cohesive token economy. This supplementary framework would enable users to conceptualize and implement tokenized systems that align with their specific economic, social, and governance objectives, ensuring that the technical affordances of CommonsHood translate into meaningful and context-sensitive applications.

3.3 DAOMod, Toolkit for User Innovators

DAOMod presents a holistic modeling methodology for Decentralized Autonomous Organizations (DAOs), developed through a rigorous investigation of both functional and non-functional requirements identified in the literature [20]. Building on these reference requirements, the DAOMod ontology formalizes the three key perspectives of DAO architecture—Organization, Coordination, and Execution—by integrating and extending existing models. The DAOMod approach consists of three core contributions.

- First, it develops an ontology that unifies governance structures, decision-making protocols, and token economies, ensuring that DAOs are modeled with relevant suitability properties.
- Second, it extends graphical modeling notations to support DAO-specific concepts, including permission assignment logic, tokenized resource specification, voting protocols, and smart contract primitives, thereby establishing the DAOMod modeling language.
- Third, it introduces step-by-step methodological guidelines to assist developers in selecting appropriate design features based on non-functional requirements, enabling platform-independent DAO design.

The effectiveness of DAOMod is demonstrated through in vivo case studies, showcasing its applicability across diverse real-world scenarios. By integrating reference requirements into a structured metamodel, DAOMod provides a systematic and adaptable framework for DAO development, significantly advancing the state of the art in governance modeling and decentralized system design.

DAOMod can be considered as a *toolkit for user innovators*, enabling the formalization of system configurations into technical rules and user interfaces that align with specific community needs. By providing a modeling language, DAOMod serves innovators including both *developers* and *community stakeholders*, allowing them to collaboratively design and develop decentralized applications. This facilitates the creation of tailored organizational structures and operational frameworks that reflect the requirements of each community.

4 Toward the Design of a Tokenized Collaborative Economy

This proposal extends the DAOMod methodology by refining the Tokenomics Design step, present in the method concerning this modeling language. For a comprehensive overview of the full methodology, we refer to the corresponding technical report [44]. While DAOMod adopts a holistic approach to DAO design, its Tokenomics Design step primarily focuses on mechanisms that reflect the interaction between supply-side value (determined by marginal cost) and demand-side utility (determined by marginal utility). In contrast, this proposal introduces an interdisciplinary perspective on token economy design that prioritizes non-market economic models, expanding the scope beyond conventional market-driven approaches (Fig. 1).

4.1 An Interdisciplinary Proposal for a Method

First step involves formulating what can be regarded as a manifesto for the tokenized economy. This manifesto situates itself within the broader constitutional framework referenced by [22], integrating a tokenomics layer into the foundational principles governing Decentralized Autonomous Organizations (DAOs). As a preliminary stage in the design process, the manifesto precedes the on-chain implementation and it serves as a foundational document that articulates the underlying values, principles,

Step	*Indicator*	*Description*	*Sociological Concept*
First	Shared Meanings	Moral and normative framework	Manifesto
	Needs Addressed	Value proposition	
	Values of Resources	Goods and services exchaged	
Second	Token Function	Interactions and relations enabled by the token	Integration Forms
Third	Token Type and Underlying Value	Distinctive medium of exchange Value capture mechanisms	Circuit of Commerce
	Token Behavior	Boundaries of the circuit of commerce (burnable, expirable, spendable)	
	Incentive Mechanisms	Monetary and non-monetary incentives promoting desired behaviors	
Fourth	Token Standard	Fungible, non-fungible, or semi-fungible	Monetary architecture
	Token Issuance	Deflationistic or Inflationistic model	
	Token Circulation	Distribution and circulation	

Fig. 1 Interdisciplinary proposal for a method for the design of a tokenized collaborative economy

and objectives of the token economy. Specifically, the manifesto encompasses the following key elements:

- **Shared Meanings**: Establishing the moral and normative framework within which transactions occur. Economic exchanges are inherently embedded in social relationships, giving rise to practices that are not only financial but also communicative and value driven.
- **Needs Addressed** (Value Proposition): Defining the core purpose of the token economy. The "value proposition" [45] refers to the primary benefits the token economy seeks to provide, such as enabling value transfer, fostering participatory processes, and supporting self-organization.
- **Values of Resources**: Identifying the goods and services included within the exchange system and determining the criteria for their valuation within the tokenized economy.

This manifesto serves as a conceptual foundation for the subsequent design phases, ensuring that the development of the token economy remains aligned with its intended social, economic, and ethical objectives.

Second step focuses on delineating the **Token Function** within the economic system. This step involves determining what kind of relationship and interactions the token is designed for, so its function may include

- serving as a medium of exchange
- providing access to resources
- facilitating voting mechanisms

The token's function is intrinsically linked to the broader economic model that the community seeks to implement. Karl Polanyi's framework on economic integration offers a valuable analytical perspective [36]. He identifies three primary modes of economic organization: *reciprocity*, based on mutual support within communities; *redistribution*, where a central authority allocates resources to maintain social cohesion; and *exchange*, involving transactions that, in pre-capitalist societies, were regulated by social norms rather than market forces.

Understanding the token's function through this perspective allows for a more nuanced approach to designing tokenized economies. By considering the interplay of reciprocity, redistribution, and exchange, the tokenomics framework can be tailored to align with the intended social and economic dynamics of the community.

Third step focuses on defining the *circuit of commerce*, a concept introduced by Zelizer [37], which states that monetary circuits are complex spaces shaped by social and cultural relationships. Within the tokenomics framework, this step involves determining the fundamental characteristics of the economic interactions within the system. Key aspects to be defined include:

- **Token Type and Underlying Value** The selection of a token type is closely tied to the economic model and medium of exchange a community aims to implement. *Utility tokens*, particularly suited for local communities, were originally designed

to support community-driven ecosystems by granting holders access to specific services and resources rather than serving as a medium for exchange. According to the tokenomics design framework [34], four primary mechanisms of value capture can be mentioned: *governance rights*, where tokens enable participation in system governance; *asset representation*, linking token value to real-world assets; *network value*, which grows with user trust and adoption; and *claim to earnings*, where tokens represent a share of ecosystem-generated revenue. The decision regarding token type is informed by the *distinctive medium of exchange* [37] (e.g., a community currency, a credit clearing system, time as unite of value) that the community seeks to establish, reflecting its intended usage and significance within the system.
- **Token Behavior**: This involves defining the boundaries of the circuit of commerce including whether tokens will have transferability limitations (e.g., burnable, expirable, spendable) [46] and whether specific transaction constraints will be imposed based on roles defined within a DAO.
- **Incentive Mechanisms**: These mechanisms are designed to promote behaviors that align with the overarching objectives of the token economy. The development of incentive structures must account for the various environmental factors that shape economic decision-making [45]. Incentives play an important role in mutually shaping transactions and participants; the question is how transactions influence participants' behavior and how participants' motivations shape the exchange system [47, 48].

By integrating these considerations, the circuit of commerce is structured not as a mere market mechanism but as a socially embedded system, where economic transactions are influenced by broader relational and normative frameworks.

Fourth step focuses on the monetary design of the token economy, which involves establishing the structural and functional parameters of the token system. This includes:

- **Token Standard Definition**: Determining whether the token will be fungible, non-fungible, or semi-fungible, based on the requirements identified in the previous design phases. The choice of token standard directly influences its role within the ecosystem, shaping its usability, interchangeability, and potential applications.
- **Token Issuance and Circulation**: Establishing the mechanisms governing token creation, distribution, and flow within the system. These processes are inherently linked to the boundaries of the circuit of commerce, as defined in the preceding step. The issuance model must align with the broader economic framework, ensuring that token distribution supports the intended economic interactions while maintaining the system's stability and integrity.

By defining these monetary parameters, the design process ensures that the token economy operates within a structured framework that balances technological feasibility with economic and social objectives. The level of tokenomics is part of the broader design of the DAO as a whole, all design decisions made during the steps described will be interdependent with the governance design and roles defined within the DAO.

4.2 CO.R.PU.S. Project

We aim to evaluate the proposed framework through in vivo case studies, one of which is the Corpus Project. As the research is currently in an ongoing phase of analysis and experimentation, the evaluation will be conducted at a later stage. At this point, we present preliminary directions emerging from the participatory research phase.

Corpus Project[1] is a EU-funded research project that investigates how Urban Living Labs (ULLs) [49] can foster tangible changes in public spaces through innovative material use, with an emphasis on material circularity and community engagement enabled by emerging civic technologies. Two case studies will assess the revitalization of neglected urban areas by leveraging participatory processes, upcycling techniques, and digitally enabled systems such as civic blockchain. In both cases, a system will be designed and implemented to promote reuse, repair, and upcycling within community-based initiatives.

- **First case: Turin, Italy.** In this case the focus is on establishing a sharing economy that connects local demand for items with the availability of unused resources, thereby fostering the exchange or lending of goods within the community.
- **Second case: Egaleo, Greece**. Here the project emphasizes the recovery and upcycling of materials with the goal of regenerating a public park through active collaboration between neighborhood residents and municipal authorities.

In this context, the proposed toolkit serves as an analytical framework to evaluate existing projects of similar community-based initiatives, systematizing the key elements required to design tokenized systems, while identifying technical feasibility, emerging field practices, and gaps between community needs and technological solutions. In this phase of the project, analysis was conducted across multiple dimensions and indicators, including digital tools, participation, geography, economy, and tokenization [50, 51].

Building on this broader analytical framework, a specific focus was placed on tokenization. The method proposed in 4.1 is intended to facilitate community-driven co-design sessions, enabling the translation of local stakeholders' inputs into concrete token requirements and governance models essential for implementing circular urban economies. The co-design phase with the community emerges as a critical component of the project. This phase is supported by a *toolkit user innovators* and is operationalized through workshop sessions that facilitate active engagement with community stakeholders.

[1] CORPUS. Phygital Models of Cooperation in the Retrofitting of Public Space. EUROPEAN PARTNERSHIP "DRIVING URBAN TRANSITIONS" DUT Call 2022 Co-funded by the European Commission (Grant N° 101069506) 2024–2026. https://corpusproject.eu/.

The first session focuses on the socio-economic system and aims to collaboratively map actors, resources, and needs within the community. This mapping helps identify collective priorities, understand relationships among stakeholders, assess what is already in place or missing, and define the flows of goods, services, and ownership. Particular attention is given to forms of economic integration, circular practices (such as reuse and upcycling), and the openness or closure of the value circuit. Tangible outputs of this phase include visual tools: cards representing actors and resources, post-its for community needs, and a poster framework summarizing the project's principles and vision. In the second session, the community co-designs the tokenomics model, building on the outcomes of the previous workshop. This includes defining what to tokenize, why, and how, ensuring token functions align with community values, behaviors, and incentive structures. Participants collaboratively shape token types, governance rules, and symbolic elements (such as logos and visual identity), ultimately creating a shared manifesto that anchors the system in collective goals and principles. During these sessions, participants collaborate to co-design the tokenized system model and establish the necessary requirements for adapting the CommonsHood app.

Following this collaborative phase, the project transitions into the implementation phase, where the *end-user toolkit* takes center stage. This toolkit is informed by the insights gained during the co-design process, ensuring that the final design aligns with stakeholder needs. The implementation phase is marked by a rigorous testing phase and a subsequent period of experimentation, allowing for iterative refinement and validation of the model.

5 Conclusion

In conclusion, this position paper presents an innovative, interdisciplinary approach for designing and implementing tokenized collaborative economies. By addressing RQ1, we apply toolkit theory as a framework to analyze the CommonsHood application and the DAOMod modeling language. Classifying these as toolkits, we provide insights into their synergistic use, ensuring that blockchain toolkits are accessible to developer-innovators and community end-users. In addressing RQ2, we introduce a preliminary method that integrates sociological principles into tokenomics, thereby transcending conventional market-driven models and expanding the scope of existing toolkits to support co-design processes. The Corpus Project serves as a case study for ongoing experimentation, where the proposed method is tested by co-designing a tokenized system to enable circular urban economies. Future work will focus on further refining the methodological steps and developing a comprehensive framework with operational guidelines for developers and communities. Additionally, we plan to evaluate the approach through use cases, proposing DAOs in community-based contexts—akin to those targeted by the Corpus Project—by employing the DAOMod modeling language and CommonsHood toolkit to test the accessibility and usability of the design processes and implementation. Adopting a participatory research approach and toolkit, as outlined in this work, entails recognizing digital platforms and tokenized value exchange systems not only as enablers of participatory tokenized systems but also as outcomes of participatory design. In this process, community members actively engage in discussions about the goals, logic, and value of tokens and incentives, shaping these systems collaboratively to align with their needs.

References

1. Mhlanga, D.: Block chain technology for digital financial inclusion in the industry 4.0, towards sustainable development? Front. Blockchain **6**, 1035405 (2023)
2. Viano, C., Avanzo, S., Cerutti, M., Cordero, A., Schifanella, C., Boella, G.: Blockchain tools for socio-economic interactions in local communities. Policy Soc. **41**(3), 373–385 (2022)
3. Voshmgir, S.: Token Economy: How the Web3 Reinvents the Internet, vol. 2. Token Kitchen (2020)
4. Bartoletti, M., Cimoli, T., Pompianu, L., Serusi, S.: Blockchain for social good: a quantitative analysis. In: Proceedings of the 4th EAI international conference on smart objects and technologies for social good, pp. 37–42 (2018)
5. Cunha, P.R.D., Soja, P., Themistocleous, M.: Blockchain for development: a guiding framework (2021)
6. Diniz, E.H., Cernev, A.K., Rodrigues, D.A., Daneluzzi, F.: Solidarity cryptocurrencies as digital community platforms. Inf. Technol. Dev. **27**(3), 524–538 (2021)
7. Semenzin, S.: 'Blockchain for good': exploring the notion of social good inside the blockchain scene. Big Data & Society **10**(2), 20539517231205480 (2023)
8. Sotoudehnia, M.: 'Making blockchain real': regulatory discourses of blockchains as a smart, civic service. Reg. Stud. **55**(12), 1857–1867 (2021)
9. Tomlinson, B., Boberg, J., Cranefield, J., Johnstone, D., Luczak-Roesch, M., Patterson, D.J., Kapoor, S.: Analyzing the sustainability of 28 'blockchain for good'projects via affordances and constraints. Inf. Technol. Dev. **27**(3), 439–469 (2021)
10. Toti, C.: La questione della moneta: riappropriazione del senso di un'istituzione (2024)
11. Cameron, J., Gibson-Graham, J.K.: The diverse economies approach. In: Handbook of alternative theories of political economy, (pp. 329–342). Edward Elgar Publishing. (2022)
12. Allen, D.W., Potts, J.: Web3 toolkits: a user innovation theory of crypto development. J. Open Innov. Technol. Mark. Complexity **9**(2), 100050 (2023)
13. Ding, W., Hou, J., Li, J., Guo, C., Qin, J., Kozma, R., Wang, F.Y.: Desci based on web3 and dao: a comprehensive overview and reference model. IEEE Trans. Comput. Soc. Syst. **9**(5), 1563–1573 (2022)
14. Zichichi, M., Ferretti, S., Rodríguez-Doncel, V.: Decentralized personal data marketplaces: how participation in a dao can support the production of citizen-generated data. Sensors **22**(16), 6260 (2022)
15. Bonnet, S., Teuteberg, F.: Decentralized autonomous organizations: a systematic literature review and research agenda. Int. J. Innov. Technol. Manag. **21**(4), 2450026 (2024)
16. Fritsch, R., Müller, M., Wattenhofer, R.: Analyzing voting power in decentralized governance: who controls daos? Blockchain Res. Appl. **5**(3), 100208 (2024)
17. Wright, A., De Filippi, P.: Decentralized blockchain technology and the rise of lex cryptographia. Available at SSRN 2580664 (2015)
18. Miscione, G.: Blockchain as organizational technology (2019)
19. Murray, A., Kuban, S., Josefy, M., Anderson, J.: Contracting in the smart era: the implications of blockchain and decentralized autonomous organizations for contracting and corporate governance. Acad. Manage. Perspect. **35**(4), 622–641 (2021)

20. Avanzo, S., Norta, A., Linares, J., Schifanella, C., Hattingh, M.: Dao-ml: A modelling language for the specification of decentralized autonomous organization governance. Methods **13**, 16 (2024)
21. Avanzo, S., Norta, A., Linares, J., Schifanella, C., Hattingh, M.: Extending trusted dapp modeling for decentralized autonomous organization development. In: International Congress on Blockchain and Applications, pp. 140–149. Springer (2024)
22. Van Vulpen, P., Jansen, S.: Decentralized autonomous organization design for the commons and the common good. Front. Blockchain **6**, 1287249 (2023)
23. Cila, N., Ferri, G., De Waal, M., Gloerich, I., Karpinski, T.: The blockchain and the commons: dilemmas in the design of local platforms. In: Proceedings of the 2020 CHI conference on human factors in computing systems, pp. 1–14 (2020)
24. Rozas, D., Tenorio-Fornés, A., Díaz-Molina, S., Hassan, S.: When ostrom meets blockchain: exploring the potentials of blockchain for commons governance. Sage Open **11**(1), 21582440211002530 (2021)
25. Hunhevicz, J.J., Brasey, P.A., Bonanomi, M.M., Hall, D.M., Fischer, M.: Applications of blockchain for the governance of integrated project delivery: a crypto commons approach. arXiv preprint arXiv:2207.07002 (2022)
26. Voshmgir, S., Zargham, M., et al.: Foundations of cryptoeconomic systems. Research Institute for Cryptoeconomics, Vienna, Working Paper Series/Institute for Cryptoeconomics/ Interdisciplinary Research **1** (2019)
27. Au, S., Power, T.: Tokenomics: The Crypto Shift of Blockchains, ICOs, and Tokens. Packt Publishing Ltd (2018)
28. Kampakis, S.: Auditing tokenomics: a case study and lessons from auditing a stablecoin project. J. British Blockchain Association (2022)
29. Kensuke, I.: Cryptoeconomics and tokenomics as economics: a survey with opinions. In: 2024 IEEE International Conference on Blockchain and Cryptocurrency (ICBC), pp. 729–746. IEEE (2024)
30. Kaal, W.A.: Crypto economics-the top 100 token models compared. BANKING & FIN. SER. POL. REP. (2018), U of St. Thomas (Minnesota) Legal Studies Research Paper (18-29) (2018)
31. Lage, O., Saiz-Santos, M., Zarzuelo, J.M.: Decentralized platform economy: emerging blockchain-based decentralized platform business models. Electronic Mark. **32**(3), 1707–1723 (2022)
32. Lommers, K., Xu, J., Xu, T.A.: a framework for dao token valuation. Available at SSRN 4309744 (2022)
33. Oliveira, L., Zavolokina, L., Bauer, I., Schwabe, G.: To token or not to token: tools for understanding blockchain tokens. ICIS (2018)
34. Kivilo, S., Norta, A., Hattingh, M.: A tokenomics conceptual goal model. In: International Congress on Blockchain and Applications, pp. 3–12. Springer (2024)
35. Qin, R., Ding, W., Li, J., Guan, S., Wang, G., Ren, Y., Qu, Z.: Web3-based decentralized autonomous organizations and operations: architectures, models, and mechanisms. IEEE Trans. Syst. Man, and Cybernetics: Syst. **53**(4), 2073–2082 (2022)
36. Polanyi, K.: The great transformation: The political and economic origins of our time. Beacon Press (2001)
37. Zelizer, V.A.: The social meaning of money: pin money, paychecks, poor relief, and other currencies. Princeton University Press, Princeton (2021)
38. Von Hippel, E., Katz, R.: Shifting innovation to users via toolkits. Management Sci. **48**(7), 821–833 (2002)
39. Avanzo, S., Boella, G., Schifanella, C., Viano: Commonshood: Participatory design of token economies in local communities. In: Titolo volume non avvalorato. CINI-Consorzio interuniversitario nazionale per l'informatica (2023)
40. Balbo, S., Boella, G., Busacchi, P., Cordero, A., De Carne, L., Di Caro, D., Guffanti, A., Mioli, M., Sanino, A., Schifanella, C.: Commonshood: a blockchain-based wallet app for local communities. In: 2020 IEEE International Conference on Decentralized Applications and Infrastructures (DAPPS), pp. 139–144. IEEE (2020). https://doi.org/10.1109/DAPPS49028.2020.00018

41. Boella, G., Calafiore, A., Grassi, E., Rapp, A., Sanasi, L., Schifanella, C.: Firstlife: Combining social networking and vgi to create an urban coordination and collaboration platform. IEEE Access **7**, 63230–63246 (2019)
42. Viano, C., Avanzo, S., Cerutti, M., Cordero, A., Schifanella, C., Boella, G., et al.: Commonshood: Blockchain tools for socio-economic interactions in local communities. Policy Soc. **41**(3), 373–385 (2022)
43. Viano, C., Avanzo, S., Boella, G., Schifanella, C., Giorgino, V.: Civic blockchain: making blockchains accessible for social collaborative economies. J. Responsible Technol. **15**, 100066 (2023). https://doi.org/10.1016/j.jrt.2023.100066
44. Avanzo, S., Pautasso, D., Domenicale, I., Norta, A., Linares, J., Schifanella, C., Hattingh, M.: [Name Removed for Anonymity]: a modeling method for decentralized autonomous organization development. Tech. rep. (2025), available at https://www.researchgate.net/publication/386019556_DAOMod_A_Modeling_Method_for_Decentralized_Autonomous_Organization_Development
45. Barrera, C., Hurder, S.: Cryptoeconomics: designing effective incentives and governance models for blockchain networks using insights from economics. In: Blockchains and the Token Economy: Theory and Practice, pp. 87–111. Springer (2022)
46. Freni, P., Ferro, E., Moncada, R.: Tokenomics and blockchain tokens: a design-oriented morphological framework. Blockchain Res. Appl. **3**(1), 100069 (2022). https://doi.org/10.1016/j.bcra.2022.100069
47. Domenicale, I., Fredda, F., Spadaro, E., Schifanella, C.: Participation by design: designing incentives for collaborative economies in local communities. Presented at the 7th Distributed Ledger Technologies Workshop (DLT2025). (2025)
48. Ballandies, M. C.: To incentivize or not: Impact of blockchain-based cryptoeconomic tokens on human information sharing behavior. **10**, 74111–74130. IEEE Access. (2022)
49. Innella, C., Ansanelli, G., Barberio, G., Brunori, C., Cappellaro, F., Civita, R., Fiorentino, G., Mancuso, E., Pentassuglia, R., Sciubba, L., et al.: A methodological framework for the implementation of urban living lab on circular economy co-design activities. Front. Sustainable Cities **6**, 1400914 (2024)
50. Confalone, F., Domenicale, I., Viano, C.: Circular economies and digital platforms for sustainability in urban local communities. In: Proceedings of the 7th Biennial RAMICS International Congress. Rome, Italy (November 6–8 2024), to appear
51. Viano, C., Sanchez, L.M., Cenere, S., Fenu, N., Giaccaria, P., Confalone, F.: Transformative hope: Blockchains and civic digital platforms for circular urban economies. In: Urbanism of Hope - Multi-city Online Conference, 16th Conference of the International Forum on Urbanism (IFoU). Online (December 12–14 2024), paper presented

A Social Choice Analysis of Optimism's Retroactive Project Funding

Eyal Briman, Nimrod Talmon, Angela Kreitenweis, and Muhammad Idrees

Abstract The Optimism Retroactive Project Funding (RetroPGF) is a key initiative within the blockchain ecosystem that retroactively rewards projects deemed valuable to the Ethereum and Optimism communities. Managed by the Optimism Collective, a decentralized autonomous organization (DAO), RetroPGF represents a large-scale experiment in decentralized governance. Funding rewards are distributed in OP tokens, the native digital currency of the ecosystem. As of this writing, four funding rounds have been completed, collectively allocating over \$100M, with an additional \$1.3B reserved for future rounds. However, we identify significant shortcomings in the current allocation system, underscoring the need for improved governance mechanisms given the scale of funds involved. Leveraging computational social choice techniques and insights from multiagent systems, we propose improvements to the voting process by recommending the adoption of a utilitarian moving phantoms mechanism [1]. This mechanism was originally introduced by Freeman et al. [1], is designed to enhance social welfare (using the ℓ_1 norm) while satisfying strategyproofness–two key properties aligned with the application's governance requirements. Our analysis provides a formal framework for designing improved funding mechanisms for DAOs, contributing to the broader discourse on decentralized governance and public goods allocation.

E. Briman (✉) · N. Talmon
Ben-Gurion University, Beersheba, Israel
e-mail: briman@post.bgu.ac.il

GovXS, Jerusalem, Israel

N. Talmon
e-mail: nimrodtalmon77@gmail.com

A. Kreitenweis
GovXS, Berlin, Germany
e-mail: angela@tokenengineering.net

M. Idrees
GovXS, Islamabad, Pakistan
e-mail: idrees535@gmail.com

M. Lustenberger et al. (eds.), *Decentralized Autonomous Organizations—Governance, Technology, and Legal Perspectives*, Springer Proceedings in Business and Economics,
https://doi.org/10.1007/978-3-032-03273-7_5

Keywords DAOs · Computational Social Choice · Voting Mechanisms · Simulations

1 Introduction

The Optimism Retroactive Public Goods Funding (RetroPGF) initiative, managed by the Optimism Collective–a decentralized autonomous organization (DAO)–is a prominent funding mechanism within the blockchain ecosystem.[1] It operates within a broader economic framework designed to incentivize innovation and retroactively reward projects that have demonstrably contributed to the Ethereum and Optimism ecosystems. The initiative has undergone four funding rounds [2–5], with this study conducted in the context of the ongoing fifth round [6]. Unlike forward-looking grant systems, RetroPGF distributes funds *ex post*, rewarding projects based on their verified impact rather than projected outcomes. This approach, increasingly adopted in decentralized ecosystems, addresses challenges in evaluating contributions in real time.

To date, RetroPGF has distributed over $100M, with $1.3B earmarked for future rounds.[2] Given the scale of resources involved, the governance structure of the funding process plays a crucial role in ensuring fair and effective allocation. However, we identify several limitations in the election system currently used, motivating the need for improved voting mechanisms.

Research Approach. In this work, we employ computational social choice to analyze and enhance the RetroPGF voting system. Specifically, based on formalized governance requirements derived from public discussions and direct engagement with the Optimism Collective, we propose a theoretically grounded and empirically tested improvement. Our analysis conceptualizes RetroPGF as a majority-based, ground-truth revealing, token-based allocation process, incorporating domain-specific constraints from blockchain governance.

To address observed inefficiencies, we propose adopting the utilitarian moving phantoms mechanism [1], which balances strategyproofness with social welfare maximization under the ℓ_1 norm. Our study consists of two primary components:

- A theoretical analysis of both the voting rules used in past RetroPGF rounds and the proposed alternative voting rules, along with their formal properties.
- A simulation-based evaluation of previous rules and an alternative rule to assess their practical performance under realistic voter behavior models.

[1] https://retrofunding.optimism.io/.

[2] https://optimism.mirror.xyz/nz5II2tucf3k8tJ76O6HWwvidLB6TLQXszmMnlnhxWU.

1.1 Our Contributions

This paper advances the study of decentralized funding mechanisms, with a focus on the RetroPGF process in Optimism. Our key contributions are as follows:

- **Formalization of Governance Requirements:** We provide the first formal mapping of Optimism's ideological and practical desiderata into social choice criteria, encompassing both qualitative and quantitative dimensions.
- **Comparative Analysis of Voting Mechanisms:** We conduct a rigorous theoretical and empirical evaluation of existing and proposed voting rules within the RetroPGF framework.
- **Proposal for an Improved Voting Rule:** We introduce and analyze the moving phantoms mechanism, demonstrating its advantages in strategyproofness, fairness, and social welfare maximization.

1.2 Paper Structure

The paper is structured as follows: We begin with a discussion on the informal requirements by Optimism, given by their forums and from personal communication (Sect. 2). We then discuss related work (Sect. 3). We continue to describe a formal model of RetroPGF (Sect. 4). Then, we discuss voting rules used for RetroPGF (Sect. 5). Concrete evaluation metrics are discussed in Sect. 6. We then report on our theoretical analysis (Sect. 7) and on our simulation-based analysis (Sects. 8 and 9). We conclude with a discussion (Sect. 10).

2 Application Requirements

Based on discussions from Optimism's public forums and direct communication with key stakeholders, we identified the specific application requirements for the RetroPGF process. The primary goal is to compare and evaluate the behavior of different voting rules in the context of these requirements. Our analysis is framed around key dimensions outlined in Optimism's governance documentation[3] and tailored to the unique characteristics of this decentralized funding mechanism.

We note that these requirements reflect a blend of common-value elements—where all voters aim to reward impactful projects—and private-value elements, stemming from heterogeneity in voters' domain expertise, interpretation of "impact," and strategic considerations. As a benchmark, we highlight that if all badgeholders had fully aligned beliefs and no individual bias, a symmetric preference profile would emerge, resulting in unanimous allocations. We return to this benchmark in later discussion.

[3] https://gov.optimism.io/t/the-future-of-optimism-governance/6471.

- **Badgeholder (voter) Responsibility**: A key feature of the RetroPGF process is the delegation of fund allocation to a small group of certified badgeholders (voters). These individuals possess a reputation within the ecosystem and are selected by the collective to distribute tokens to projects based on assessed needs. Badgeholders are expected to represent the broader interests of the community while maintaining impartiality through a strict code of conduct, including conflict of interest protocols. Each funding round is targeted at a specific context. For example, in Round 6, badgeholders evaluated governance-oriented projects such as Delegation Analytics and Agora, while in Round 4 the focus included infrastructure and public goods more broadly.
- **Majoritarian Decision-Making**: The RetroPGF process emphasizes a majority-based voting approach. The goal is to capture the "ground truth" of which projects have contributed the most value to the ecosystem. Badgeholders play a pivotal role in aligning their token distribution decisions with collective goals. For instance, projects that receive broad support across badgeholders are presumed to reflect shared community values.
- **Iterative Decentralization**: A core principle of the system is its ability to adapt and improve through iteration. As the RetroPGF process evolves, decentralization becomes more prominent. This iterative learning mechanism resembles adaptive systems in social choice theory, where feedback loops (such as post-round reports, retrospective debates, and proposal design changes) help refine collective decisions over time.
- **Equity and Balance**: Optimism seeks to balance governance power, ensuring that financial influence does not overshadow community input. In Retroactive Project Funding, one person—or more precisely, a pseudonymous wallet holding a badgeholder token—equals one vote, with equal voting power for all voters. This design aligns with social choice concepts of fairness, aiming to avoid plutocratic control and to promote outcomes that serve the ecosystem as a whole. For example, the cap on the number of badgeholders per funding round reinforces equal voice in decision-making.
- **Impact = Profit**: The RetroPGF mechanism rewards projects based on their demonstrated contributions to the community. The guiding principle is that "impact should be rewarded," and therefore projects creating ecosystem value should be financially supported. This principle parallels utilitarian and proportional notions in social choice theory. For instance, in Round 4, large allocations were awarded to projects like L2Beat and Gitcoin, reflecting their visible impact on infrastructure and community support.

These application requirements form the basis for our analysis of voting rules. In particular, we focus on how well various mechanisms perform with respect to efficiency, strategic resistance, and fairness under realistic voter models. While a symmetric preference scenario may lead to agreement on allocations, we argue that the presence of individual biases, reputational considerations, and information asymmetries necessitates a more nuanced modeling of badgeholder behavior.

3 Related Work

Research at the intersection of public good funding, computational social choice, and blockchain governance has developed significantly over the past decade. Early models such as participatory budgeting [7] and quadratic funding [8] have been adapted to decentralized contexts, raising new challenges in designing fair, efficient, and strategy-resistant allocation mechanisms. More recently, retroactive funding systems have emerged as a novel paradigm, where reward is based on verified impact rather than anticipated outcomes. This shift demands mechanisms that can robustly aggregate diverse preferences and uncover ground truth contributions—a setting where social choice theory, particularly in its algorithmic and strategic dimensions, becomes highly relevan [9].

Public Good Funding Public good funding distributes resources to benefit communities, with decentralized models such as quadratic funding [10–12] amplifying smaller contributions to ensure fairness. Participatory budgeting [7, 13] allows voters to decide on resource allocation prior to implementation. RetroPGF, as used in Optimism, instead rewards projects based on their *proven* impact, representing a shift from ex-ante to ex-post evaluation.

RetroPGF and Portioning Optimism's RetroPGF evaluates completed projects to reward those with the most community value [14]. This approach parallels the setting of *portioning* [15], where resources are divided after evaluating outcomes. In both settings, the role of the voter is evaluative rather than predictive, and the aggregation mechanism must navigate heterogeneous signals of impact.

Optimism's RetroPGF Operating within a DAO framework, Optimism's RetroPGF integrates blockchain transparency and social choice theory [16], leveraging majoritarian decision-making to align token distribution with perceived community value. The design space intersects with work on blockchain governance [17] and computational social choice in digital settings [18], raising questions about fairness, robustness, and decentralization in large-scale decision-making.

Uncovering the Ground Truth A central challenge in RetroPGF is to accurately aggregate badgeholder votes to reveal the true impact of projects. Prior work in elicitation and aggregation under uncertainty, such as Bayesian Truth Serum [19, 20] and noisy preference models [21], offer tools for designing mechanisms that align collective outcomes with objective contribution measures. These methods are particularly relevant for blockchain-based voting systems, where preference aggregation must also resist manipulation while remaining transparent.

4 Formal Model

We formalize the token-based Retroactive Project Funding process as a voting-based budget allocation mechanism. Let $N = \{1, \ldots, n\}$ be the set of voters and $P = \{1, \ldots, m\}$ the set of projects. The total available budget is B, which we normalize to 1, ensuring that all allocations are expressed as fractions of the total budget. Each voter is allocated c tokens, with the constraint that the total number of tokens does not exceed the budget, i.e., $c \cdot n \leq B$.

A feasible allocation is a vector $\mathbf{a} = (a_1, \ldots, a_m)$ where:

$$a_p \geq 0, \quad \forall p \in P, \quad \text{and} \quad \sum_{p \in P} a_p \leq B.$$

Each voter i submits a cumulative ballot $X_i = (x_{i,1}, \ldots, x_{i,m})$, where $x_{i,p} \geq 0$ represents the fraction of their tokens allocated to project p, subject to:

$$\sum_{p \in P} x_{i,p} \leq c.$$

Since voters benefit from fully utilizing their allocated tokens, we assume:

$$\sum_{p \in P} x_{i,p} = c, \quad \forall i \in N.$$

The final allocation $\mathbf{a}$ is determined by a voting rule, formally defined as a function:

$$f : (X_1, \ldots, X_n) \to \mathbf{a} = (a_1, \ldots, a_m),$$

which satisfies the budget constraint:

$$\sum_{p \in P} a_p \leq B.$$

Preference Structure. Although the RetroPGF process aims to reward projects according to their objective impact, we assume that badgeholders may exhibit heterogeneous preferences, modeled via different cumulative ballots. This heterogeneity reflects several practical considerations:

- *Epistemic diversity:* Voters possess varying knowledge about the ecosystem and specific projects, leading to different interpretations of what constitutes impact.
- *Domain affinity:* Some voters may prioritize projects aligned with their expertise or values (e.g., governance vs. infrastructure).
- *Reputational strategy:* Badgeholders might consider not only what is best for the ecosystem, but also how their votes will be perceived within the community.

As a theoretical benchmark, we consider the *symmetric preference case*, in which all badgeholders submit the same ballot, i.e., $X_1 = \cdots = X_n$. This case serves as a useful baseline for evaluating how different rules behave under full alignment. However, since empirical data from past rounds (e.g., Round 4) shows clear variation in allocations, we argue that modeling badgeholder preferences as heterogeneous provides a more realistic and informative foundation for mechanism evaluation.

5 Voting Rules

This section reviews the voting rules used in Optimism's RetroPGF rounds and introduces improved mechanisms.

Quadratic Voting (Round 1). Quadratic Voting (QV) [22] allows voters to allocate $x_{i,p}$ tokens to project p, with the effective vote weight given by:

$$a_p = \frac{\sum_{i \in N} \sqrt{x_{i,p}}}{\sum_{i \in N} \sum_{p' \in P} \sqrt{x_{i,p'}}}.$$

Mean Rule (Round 2). Allocations are proportional to the total tokens received:

$$a_p = \frac{\sum_{i \in N} x_{i,p}}{\sum_{i \in N} \sum_{p' \in P} x_{i,p'}}.$$

Quorum Median Rule (Round 3). Allocations are based on the median vote with quorum constraints q_1 (minimum tokens) and q_2 (minimum voters):

$$b_p = \frac{\text{median}\{x_{i,p} \mid x_{i,p} > 0\}}{\sum_{p' \in P} \text{median}\{x_{i,p'} \mid x_{i,p'} > 0\}}.$$

If $b_p \geq q_1$ and at least q_2 voters contribute, then $d_p = b_p$; otherwise, $d_p = 0$. The final allocation is:

$$a_p = \frac{d_p}{\sum_{p' \in P} d_{p'}}.$$

Capped Median Rule (Round 4). A variant of the Quorum Median Rule, with an upper bound K_1 and redistribution of excess funds:

$$c_p = \frac{\text{median}\{x_{i,p}\}}{\sum_{p' \in P} \text{median}\{x_{i,p'}\}} \cdot B, \quad d_p = \min(c_p, K_1) + \frac{\sum_j \max(0, c_j - K_1) \cdot c_p}{\sum_j c_j}.$$

Projects below K_2 are eliminated, and their allocations redistributed:

$$b_p = \begin{cases} 0, & d_p < K_2, \\ d_p + \frac{\sum_{p'} d_{p'} < K_2}{\sum_{p'} d_{p'} \geq K_2} \cdot d_p, & \text{otherwise}. \end{cases}$$

Final normalization ensures:

$$a_p = \frac{b_p}{\sum_{p'} b_{p'}}.$$

Midpoint Rule. The allocation minimizes the ℓ_1 distance from all voter allocations [23]:

$$\mathbf{x} = X_{i^*}, \quad i^* = \arg\min_{i \in N} \sum_{j=1}^{n} \|X_i - X_j\|_1.$$

Moving Phantoms. The Moving Phantoms mechanism [1] addresses budget inconsistencies in median-based voting by introducing phantom voters whose influence dynamically adjusts allocations while preserving strategyproofness. The final allocation is determined using a median-based adjustment:

$$\mathcal{A}^F(a_p) = \text{med}(f_0(t^*), \ldots, f_n(t^*), x_{1,p}, \ldots, x_{n,p}),$$

where t^* is chosen such that:

$$f_0(t^*) + \sum_{i=1}^{n} f_i(t^*) + \sum_{i=1}^{n} \sum_{p=1}^{m} x_{i,p} = 1.$$

This constraint ensures that the total allocation remains within budget. The optimal value of t^* can be computed efficiently using binary search.

Two variants of the Moving Phantoms mechanism are considered:

Independent Markets Algorithm. In this variant, phantom influence follows a linear distribution:

$$f_k(t) = \min\{t(n-k), 1\}.$$

Majoritarian Phantoms Algorithm. This variant prioritizes majority preferences by defining:

$$f_k(t) = \begin{cases} 0, & 0 \leq t \leq \frac{k}{n+1}, \\ t(n+1) - k, & \frac{k}{n+1} < t \leq \frac{k+1}{n+1}, \\ 1, & \frac{k+1}{n+1} \leq t \leq 1. \end{cases}$$

.

6 Properties and Metrics

To evaluate voting rules in the Retroactive Project Funding framework, we consider key theoretical properties and performance metrics. These criteria incorporate classical social choice principles [24] and RetroPGF-specific requirements. To define these metrics and properties, we first establish the agent utility function based on the

ℓ_1 distance, as prior work commonly assumes that agents assess budget distributions by their ℓ_1 distance from their ideal allocation [1, 25].

Resistance to Manipulation. A voting rule should be robust against strategic behavior, including bribery and control. The *cost of bribery* is the minimum expenditure required to increase project p's allocation by X tokens:

$$b = \sum_{i=1}^{n} \sum_{q \in P} |x_{i,q} - x'_{i,q}|,$$

where $V = \{X_1, \ldots, X_n\}$ and $V' = \{X'_1, \ldots, X'_n\}$ are the original and modified vote profiles, and $\mathbf{x}$ is the outcome. The *cost of control* measures the minimal number of voters that must be added or removed to increase p's allocation by r. A rule is *robust* if the expected deviation in outcomes due to small vote perturbations remains bounded:

$$\mathbb{E}[d(\mathbf{x}, \mathbf{x}')],$$

where d is a distance metric such as ℓ_1 or ℓ_2. The *Voter Extractable Value (VEV)* quantifies the maximum allocation shift a single voter can induce:

$$\text{VEV} = \max_{i \in [n], k \in [m]} d(\mathbf{x}, \mathbf{x}^{(i,k)}),$$

where $\mathbf{x}^{(i,k)}$ is the outcome after voter i reallocates $r\%$ of their vote to project k.

Incentive Compatibility. A voting rule is *strategyproof* if truthful reporting is a weakly dominant strategy for all voters. Formally, for every $i \in N$, let $u_i(X_i, X_{-i})$ be their utility when reporting truthfully and $u_i(X'_i, X_{-i})$ their utility when submitting a strategic misreport X'_i. The rule is strategyproof if:

$$u_i(X_i, X_{-i}) \geq u_i(X'_i, X_{-i}) \quad \forall i \in N, \quad \forall X'_i \neq X_i, \quad \forall X_{-i}.$$

Outcome Quality. A voting rule satisfies *Pareto efficiency* if there exists no alternative allocation $\mathbf{x}'$ that strictly improves the utility of at least one voter without making any other voter worse off. Formally, an allocation $\mathbf{x} = (a_1, \ldots, a_m)$ is Pareto efficient if:

$$\forall \mathbf{x}' \in \mathbb{R}^m_{\geq 0}, \quad \exists i \in N \text{ such that } U_i(\mathbf{x}') > U_i(\mathbf{x}) \Rightarrow \exists j \in N \text{ such that } U_j(\mathbf{x}') < U_j(\mathbf{x}).$$

This ensures that no allocation $\mathbf{x}'$ is strictly better for all voters simultaneously.

A voting rule satisfies *monotonicity* if increasing support for a project cannot decrease its allocation. That is, for any two voter profiles V and V', where V' is obtained by increasing the support for project p for all voters:

$$f(V', p) \geq f(V, p) \quad \text{for } V' \text{ where } x'_{i,p} \geq x_{i,p} \text{ for all } i.$$

The rule satisfies *reinforcement* if combining two disjoint voter groups that yield the same outcome separately does not change the result:

$$f(V_1 \cup V_2) = f(V_1) = f(V_2).$$

Fairness and Representation. A rule should balance majority rule with minority protection.

Utilitarian social welfare measures how well the outcome reflects voter preferences:

$$W = \frac{1}{n} \sum_{i=1}^{n} \|\mathbf{x} - X_i\|_1.$$

Proportionality ensures that any subset $S \subseteq N$ with $|S| \geq n/k$ that exclusively supports a single project p guarantees p at least B/k of the total budget:

$$\forall S \subseteq N, \quad |S| \geq \frac{n}{k}, \quad \forall i \in S, \quad x_{i,p} = c, \quad x_{i,p'} = 0 \text{ for } p' \neq p \Rightarrow a_p \geq \frac{B}{k}.$$

Allocation inequality is quantified using the *Gini index*, which measures the disparity in allocated resources:

$$G = \frac{\sum_{i=1}^{m} \sum_{j=1}^{m} |a_i - a_j|}{2m \sum_{i=1}^{m} a_i}.$$

Participation and Ground-Truth Alignment. A rule satisfies *participation* if no voter is worse off by voting, meaning that submitting a ballot cannot result in a lower utility than abstaining. Formally, for every voter i, let $\mathbf{x} = (a_1, \ldots, a_m)$ denote the allocation when i does not participate, and let $\mathbf{x}' = (a'_1, \ldots, a'_m)$ be the allocation when i submits a ballot X_i. The rule satisfies participation if:

$$u_i(\mathbf{x}') \geq u_i(\mathbf{x}) \quad \forall i \in N.$$

This ensures that participation is always beneficial or neutral.

Alignment with ground truth measures the deviation from an objective allocation $\mathbf{x}^* = (a_1^*, \ldots, a_m^*)$, which represents the theoretically correct funding distribution assuming perfect voter expertise and full knowledge of project impact. The alignment metric is given by:

$$d_{\text{GT}} = \sum_{i=1}^{m} |a_i^* - a_i|.$$

This ensures that the allocation reflects the true contribution of funded projects [21, 26].

7 Theoretical Results

We provide Table 1 that summarizes the theoretical results. For space considerations proofs are in the appendix. Note that we have added the Normalized median rule that is a generalization of R3 and R4 voting rules (since it does not include using of capping or quorum).

8 Experimental Design

Experiments were conducted using artificial voter data and a simplified version of Optimism's Round 4 dataset, the only fully available real-world Optimism voting dataset, in which 108 badge-holders collectively allocated 8 million tokens across 229 projects. The analysis compares the voting rules employed in Optimism Rounds 1-4 with the Majoritarian Phantoms mechanism, selected for its capacity to maximize ℓ_1-based social welfare while ensuring strategyproofness–two fundamental properties aligned with the application's requirements.

Vote Generation. Cumulative ballot instances were generated using Mallows' model [27, 28], ensuring structured yet diverse voter preferences. The process is as follows:

1. A base vote X_{base} is sampled from a Dirichlet distribution with parameters $\alpha^m = 1^m$, ensuring it sums to 1:

$$\sum_{p \in P} X_{\text{base},p} = 1.$$

2. An independent vote $X_{\text{independent}}$ is sampled from the same Dirichlet distribution ($k = 1$).
3. Each voter's ballot is computed as a weighted combination:

$$X_i = 0.5 \cdot X_{\text{base}} + 0.5 \cdot X_{\text{independent}}.$$

Experimental Setup. To evaluate different voting rules, we conduct simulations across multiple scenarios, each designed to assess specific properties of the mechanisms. The experimental conditions are as follows:

- Bribery, Control, Robustness, and Voter Extractable Value (VEV) Experiments: These experiments use a setup with 40 voters distributing 8 million OP tokens across 145 projects.
- Social Welfare, Gini Index, and Alignment Experiments: To analyze broader allocation trends, these experiments use an expanded setting with 145 voters, 600 projects, and 30 million OP tokens.

Table 1 Properties of voting rules

Voting Rule	Reinforcement	Pareto- Efficiency	Monotonicity	Participation	Proportionality	Max Social Welfare	Strategyproofness
R1 Quadratic	✓	×	✓	×	×	×	×
R2 Mean Rule	✓	✓	✓	✓	✓	×	×
R3 Quorum Median	×	×	×	×	×	×	×
R4 Capped Median Rule	×	×	✓	×	×	×	×
Normalized Median Rule	✓	✓	✓	✓	×	×	×
Midpoint Rule	✓	✓	✓	✓	×	×	×
Independent Market [16]	✓	× for ($m \geq n^2$)	✓	✓	✓	×	✓ (for $m > 2$)
Majoritarian Phantom [16]	✓	✓	✓	✓	×	✓	✓ (for $m > 2$)

– Trial Averaging: Each experimental condition is repeated for 100 independent trials to ensure statistical reliability and minimize variance.

Resistance to Manipulation. To examine the vulnerability of each voting rule to strategic behavior, we conduct two experiments:

1. Control Experiment: This experiment assesses how resistant a voting rule is to the addition or removal of voters. We measure the minimum number of strategically placed voters required to increase the funding of a specific target project by a predetermined percentage. The experiment systematically varies the target funding increase from 1% to 30% and runs 10 independent trials per setting.
2. Bribery Experiment: This experiment quantifies the cost of influencing the outcome by reallocating tokens. Assuming a unit cost per token reallocated, we measure the minimum expenditure required to shift funding in favor of a given project. Similar to the control experiment, we vary the targeted funding increase from 1% to 30% and conduct 10 trials per condition.

Robustness and Voter Influence. These experiments assess the stability of allocations under small perturbations and the extent of influence exerted by individual voters:

1. Robustness Experiment: We introduce controlled random variations to individual voter preferences and measure the impact on the final allocations. The robustness of a voting rule is quantified by computing the ℓ_1 distance between the original allocation and the perturbed allocation. This process is repeated over 100 trials to evaluate stability across different scenarios.
2. Voter Extractable Value (VEV) Experiment: This experiment measures the maximum impact a single voter can exert on the allocation. A voter is allowed to concentrate between 90% and 99% of their total tokens on a single project, and we observe the resulting change in the project's final funding allocation. The goal is to quantify how susceptible each rule is to concentrated voting power.

Alignment with Ground Truth. To assess how well each voting rule reflects the true distribution of voter preferences, we compute the ℓ_1 distance between the final allocation produced by a voting rule and a benchmark reference distribution. We set the benchmark to be the base vote used in the generation of all ballots.

9 Experimental Results

We present Figure 1, which summarizes the key findings from our simulations on bribery costs, control, robustness, and VEV using Round 4 data (108 voters, 229 projects, 8M tokens).

Majoritarian Phantom outperforms other rules across strategic robustness metrics, including higher bribery and control costs, stronger stability under noise, and reduced voter extractable value. However, as shown in the other figures in the appendix, the advantage is less pronounced for metrics like Gini index and alignment with

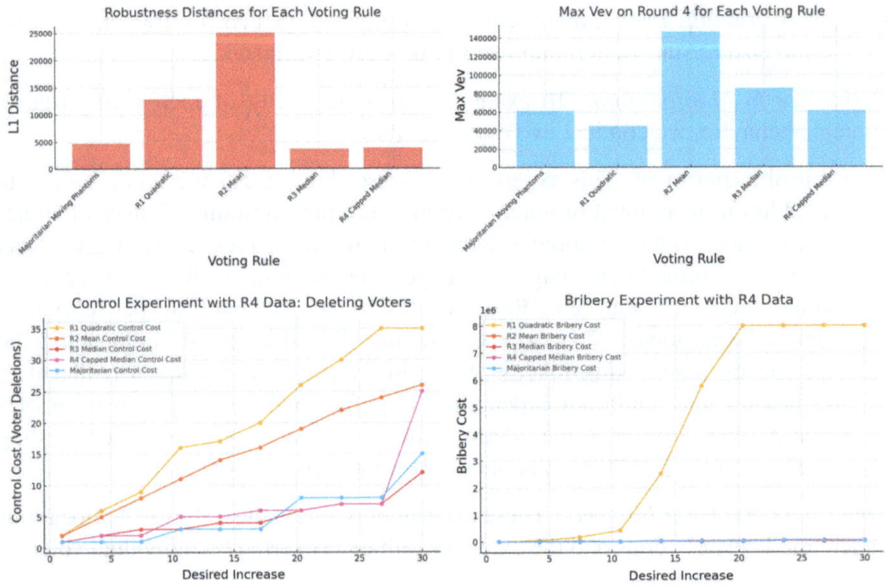

Fig. 1 Bribery costs, cost of control by deleting voters, robustness, and Max VEV for each voting rule using Round 4 data

ground truth. In those cases, differences between Majoritarian Phantom and the R3/ R4 median-based rules are often small and not statistically significant, indicating that the practical gains, while consistent, may be incremental rather than large.

10 Discussion and Outlook

Our theoretical and simulation results indicate that the Majoritarian Phantom rule is the most effective mechanism for RetroPGF among those tested, based on the application requirements set in Sect. 2. It maximizes ℓ_1 social welfare, satisfies key axioms such as Pareto and Participation, maintains a high Gini index (favoring impactful projects over equal distribution), and exhibits strong resistance to manipulation. It also aligns well with the ground truth–although it ranks third in this metric after Quadratic and Mean rules. However, as shown in our simulations, the empirical advantage of Majoritarian Phantom over median-based rules (R3 and R4) is often modest. In fairness and alignment metrics, the differences are typically small and not statistically significant. This suggests that while the rule offers strong theoretical benefits, its practical improvements may be incremental.

Our analysis focuses on the voting stage of the allocation process, assuming fixed distributions of voting tokens. We do not model pre-voting dynamics, such as trading or influence between badgeholders. In settings where more biased voters accumulate voting power through such exchanges, the choice of voting rule may interact with deeper strategic incentives. While Majoritarian Phantom remains strategy-resistant in the voting stage, its resilience under pre-voting manipulation is an open question warranting further study.

In addition, our current framework does not account for dynamic reputation costs. In practice, badgeholders face reputational consequences for misaligned or self-serving behavior, which could deter manipulation even without formal enforcement. Modeling such costs explicitly could improve the realism of strategic analyses and explain observed behavior in real-world rounds.

We formalized RetroPGF as a majority-based, token-weighted allocation process and analyzed its voting mechanisms through the lens of computational social choice. Our results contribute a structured framework for evaluating decentralized funding mechanisms, identifying tradeoffs between fairness, efficiency, and strategic robustness. We conclude with several directions for future work.

Comparison with Other Retroactive Project Funding Models. Other ecosystems such as Filecoin's RetroPGF[4] use similar mechanisms. A comparative analysis could reveal institutional design insights across DAOs.

Metric-Based, Indirect Voting. Optimism is experimenting with metric-based voting,[5] where badgeholders vote on evaluation criteria rather than projects. This may reduce cognitive load and limit manipulation. Evaluating this model is a promising research direction.

Mechanism Design Refinements. Future refinements include reputation-weighted voting [29, 30], mitigation of pseudonymity risks [31], moving phantoms [25], and adaptations of VCG-like or Continuous Thiele rules [32, 33]. Bayesian truth serum methods [19, 20] may further help validate whether a rule meaningfully uncovers ground truth.

Missing Proofs

Reinforcement

Theorem 1 The Mean, Normalized Median, and Midpoint Rules satisfy reinforcement.

Proof For two profiles V_1 and V_2, let:

$$a_p^1 = \frac{\sum_{i \in N_1} x_{i,p}}{\sum_{i \in N_1} \sum_{p' \in P} x_{i,p'}}, \quad a_p^2 = \frac{\sum_{i \in N_2} x_{i,p}}{\sum_{i \in N_2} \sum_{p' \in P} x_{i,p'}}.$$

[4] https://filecoin.io/blog/posts/unveiling-fil-retropgf-1-retroactively-funding-filecoin-public-goods/.

[5] https://gov.optimism.io/t/experimentation-impact-metric-based-voting/7727.

Since allocation summation is linear (Mean Rule) or preserves order statistics (Median Rule), the combined profile maintains relative rankings:

$$a_p^3 = \frac{\sum_{i \in N_1 \cup N_2} x_{i,p}}{\sum_{i \in N_1 \cup N_2} \sum_{p' \in P} x_{i,p'}}.$$

For the Midpoint Rule, the voter minimizing ℓ_1 remains unchanged under profile union, ensuring reinforcement.

Corollary 1 The Quadratic Rule satisfies reinforcement as it follows the Mean Rule after square-root transformation.

Example 1 The R3 Quorum Median and R4 Capped Median Rules violate reinforcement due to quorum effects. Consider two projects p_1, p_2 with quorum 0.2. - V_1: v_1 votes $[0.9, 0.1] \rightarrow$ Winner: $[1, 0]$. - V_2: v_2 votes $[0.9, 0.1] \rightarrow$ Winner: $[1, 0]$. - $V_1 \cup V_2$: Quorum applies, shifting the result to $[0.8, 0.2]$.

Pareto Efficiency

Theorem 2 The Mean Rule satisfies Pareto efficiency.

Proof The Mean Rule distributes the budget proportionally among projects. Any reallocation that benefits one voter must reduce another project's allocation due to the budget constraint, making at least one voter worse off. Thus, no Pareto improvement is possible, proving Pareto efficiency.

Theorem 3 The Normalized Median Rule satisfies Pareto efficiency.

Proof The median allocation minimizes absolute deviations from voter preferences. Increasing a project's allocation necessarily reduces another's, harming at least one voter. Thus, no Pareto improvement exists, proving Pareto efficiency.

Theorem 4 The Midpoint Rule satisfies Pareto efficiency.

Proof The selected allocation corresponds to a voter's input. Any alternative would increase some voters' distance from their preferred allocation, making them worse off, ensuring Pareto efficiency.

Example 2 The Quadratic Rule does not satisfy Pareto efficiency.

A voter allocating $[0.7, 0.3]$ receives an outcome based on square roots, deviating from their preference and allowing a Pareto improvement.

Example 3 The R3 Quorum Median Rule does not satisfy Pareto efficiency.

A voter allocating $[0.7, 0.3]$ with a quorum of 0.4 results in $[1, 0]$, which is strictly worse for the voter.

Corollary 2 The R4 Capped Median Rule does not satisfy Pareto efficiency due to the quorum constraint K_2.

Monotonicity

Theorem 5 The Mean Rule satisfies monotonicity.

Proof Increasing a voter's allocation to project p increases the numerator in:

$$a_p = \frac{\sum_{i \in N} x_{i,p}}{\sum_{i \in N} \sum_{p' \in P} x_{i,p'}}$$

while the denominator grows less significantly, ensuring a_p does not decrease.

Theorem 6 The Normalized Median Rule satisfies monotonicity.

Proof Increasing $x_{i,p}$ either shifts the median upward or leaves it unchanged. Thus, a_p does not decrease.

Theorem 7 The Midpoint Rule satisfies monotonicity.

Proof If a voter increases their allocation to p, it reduces their ℓ_1-distance to the Midpoint outcome, preventing a worse allocation.

Corollary 3 The Quadratic Rule satisfies monotonicity.

Theorem 8 The R3 Quorum Median Rule does not satisfy monotonicity.

Example 4 Voters v_1, v_2, v_3 cast $[0.5, 0.5]$, $[0, 1]$, $[1, 0]$, yielding $[0.5, 0.5]$. If v_2 changes to $[0.1, 0.4]$, the new allocation is $[0.4, 0.6]$, violating monotonicity.

Theorem 9 The R4 Capped Median Rule satisfies monotonicity.

Proof If a project's allocation is below the cap K_1, additional votes increase a_p. If at or above K_1, it remains unchanged. If below quorum K_2, additional votes push a_p above quorum. If a project falls below quorum, fewer competing projects benefit from redistribution. Thus, monotonicity holds.

Participation

Theorem 10 The Mean Rule satisfies participation.

Proof If voter i abstains, their influence on allocations is removed, generally resulting in a worse outcome for them, as their preferred projects may receive less funding. Thus, abstaining never increases utility.

Theorem 11 The Normalized Median Rule satisfies participation.

Proof Abstaining shifts the median in a way that can only worsen or maintain the voter's preferred outcome. If $x_{i,p}$ is below the median, abstaining does not improve it; if above, abstaining reduces the median allocation.

Theorem 12 The Midpoint Rule satisfies participation.

Proof If the voter's ballot is selected as the midpoint, participation directly benefits them. Otherwise, it follows from the Mean Rule proof, as their participation reduces total ℓ_1-distance.

Example 5 The Quadratic Rule does not satisfy participation.

A voter with [0.8, 0.2] in a setting where the initial allocation is also [0.8, 0.2] may, by participating, shift the outcome away due to the square root transformation.

Example 6 The R3 Quorum Median Rule does not satisfy participation.

A project p_2 is close to funding but does not meet quorum. If voter v adds a small vote $[1 - \epsilon, \epsilon]$, p_2 suddenly receives significant funding, potentially harming v.

Corollary 4 The R4 Capped Median Rule does not satisfy participation as it includes a quorum K_2.

Proportionality

Theorem 13 The Mean Rule satisfies proportionality.

Proof The Mean Rule aggregates votes by summing across all voters, ensuring each project receives funding proportional to its total allocation. Since the final allocation mirrors the proportion of tokens assigned, the rule satisfies proportionality.

Example 7 The Normalized Median Rule does not satisfy proportionality.

Consider three voters with allocations [1, 0], [1, 0], and [0, 1]. The median allocation is [1, 0], while proportionality requires [2/3, 1/3], meaning the rule fails proportionality.

Example 8 The Midpoint Rule does not satisfy proportionality.

With the same three voters as above, the rule selects [1, 0], minimizing the ℓ_1 distance rather than providing [2/3, 1/3], violating proportionality.

Example 9 The Quadratic Rule does not satisfy proportionality.

For three voters voting [9, 1], [5, 5], and [4, 6], the rule outputs [5.6, 4.4] instead of the proportional outcome [6, 4], failing proportionality.

Example 10 The R3 Quorum Median Rule does not satisfy proportionality.

With voters [1, 0], [1, 0], and [0, 1], and a quorum of 2 voters with 1.1 tokens, the rule yields [1, 0] instead of [2/3, 1/3], violating proportionality.

Corollary 5 The R4 Capped Median Rule does not satisfy proportionality as it includes a quorum $K3$ and is median based.

Strategyproofness

Theorem 14 The Mean Rule is not strategyproof.

Example 11 Consider two voters with votes [0.75, 0.25] and [0, 1]. The Mean Rule outputs [0.375, 0.625], giving voter 1 an ℓ_1 distance of 0.75. If voter 1 misreports [1, 0], the new allocation [0.5, 0.5] reduces their ℓ_1 distance to 0.5, demonstrating manipulability.

Theorem 15 The Normalized Median Rule is not strategyproof.

Example 12 Three voters vote [0.57, 0.24, 0.19], [0.39, 0.48, 0.13], and [0.44, 0.09, 0.48]. The Normalized Median Rule outputs [0.506, 0.276, 0.218], giving voter 1 an ℓ_1 distance of 0.1285. If they misreport [0.6, 0.2, 0.2], the new outcome [0.524, 0.238, 0.238] lowers their ℓ_1 distance to 0.0962.

Theorem 16 The Midpoint Rule is not strategyproof.

Example 13 Three voters vote [0.9, 0.1], [0.4, 0.6], and [0.2, 0.8]. The Midpoint Rule outputs [0.4, 0.6], with voter 1's ℓ_1 distance at 1. By misreporting [0.5, 0.5], they reduce their distance to 0.8.

Theorem 17 The Independent Markets Rule is strategyproof.

Proof Follows from [16] [Theorem 4.8] for $m > 2$.

Theorem 18 The Majoritarian Phantom Rule is strategyproof.

Proof Follows from [16] [Theorem 4.8] for $m > 2$.

Theorem 19 The Quadratic Rule is not SP.

Example 14 Three voters vote [0.7, 0.3], [0.4, 0.6], and [0.3, 0.7]. The Quadratic Rule outputs [0.483, 0.517], with voter 1's ℓ_1 distance at 0.434. Misreporting [0.8, 0.2] changes the outcome to [0.502, 0.498], lowering their distance to 0.396.

Theorem 20 The R3 Quorum Median Rule is not strategyproof.

Example 15 Three voters vote [0.2, 0.8], [0.1, 0.9], and [0.5, 0.5] with a quorum of 0.3 tokens and 2 voters per project. The R3 Quorum Median Rule outputs [0, 1], giving voter 1 an ℓ_1 distance of 0.4. If they misreport [0, 1], the new allocation [0.25, 0.75] reduces their distance to 0.1.

Corollary 6 The R4 Capped Median Rule is not strategyproof since it includes a quorum $K3$ and is median based.

Maximal Social Welfare (Minimal L1)

An allocation satisfies maximal social welfare (SWF) if no alternative allocation results in a smaller total ℓ_1 distance between the final allocation and voter ballots.

Theorem 21 The Mean Rule does not satisfy maximal SWF.

Example 16 Three voters vote $(1, 0)$, $(1, 0)$, and $(0.2, 0.8)$. The Mean Rule outputs $(0.733, 0.267)$ with a total ℓ_1 distance of 2.133. An alternative allocation $(1, 0)$ reduces the total ℓ_1 distance to 1.6, proving that the Mean Rule is suboptimal.

Remark 1 The Mean Rule satisfies maximal SWF if measured by minimizing ℓ_2 distance [5].

Theorem 22 The Normalized Median Rule does not satisfy maximal SWF.

Example 17 Three voters vote $(0.1, 0.9)$, $(0.4, 0.2)$, and $(0.6, 0.1)$. The Normalized Median Rule outputs $(0.667, 0.333)$ with a total ℓ_1 distance of 1.834. The alternative allocation $(0.5, 0.5)$ reduces the distance to 1.7, showing suboptimality.

Remark 2 The Median Rule satisfies maximal SWF if it directly minimizes ℓ_1 distance without normalization [5].

Theorem 23 The Midpoint Rule does not satisfy maximal SWF.

Example 18 Four voters vote for four projects: $(0.8, 0.1, 0.05, 0.05)$, $(0.1, 0.8, 0.05, 0.05)$, $(0.05, 0.05, 0.8, 0.1)$, $(0.05, 0.05, 0.1, 0.8)$. The Midpoint Rule selects any voter's ballot, leading to a total ℓ_1 distance of 4.6. An alternative allocation $(0.25, 0.25, 0.25, 0.25)$ reduces it to 4.4, proving suboptimality.

Theorem 24 The Independent Markets algorithm does not satisfy maximal SWF, following [16] [Theorem 6.1].

Theorem 25 The Majoritarian Phantoms algorithm satisfies maximal SWF, following [16] [Theorem 6.1].

Theorem 26 The Quadratic Voting Rule does not satisfy maximal SWF.

Example 19 Three voters vote $(0.01, 0.99)$, $(0.01, 0.99)$, and $(0.99, 0.01)$. Quadratic Voting outputs $(0.364, 0.636)$ with a total ℓ_1 distance of 2.668. The alternative allocation $(0.2, 0.8)$ reduces the distance to 2.34, proving suboptimality.

Corollary 7 The R3 Quorum Median Rule does not satisfy maximal SWF, as Median-based rules require normalization.

Corollary 8 The R4 Capped Median Rule does not satisfy maximal SWF, as it relies on Median-based normalization.

Missing Figures

See Figs. 2, 3, 4, 5, 6, 7, 8, 9.

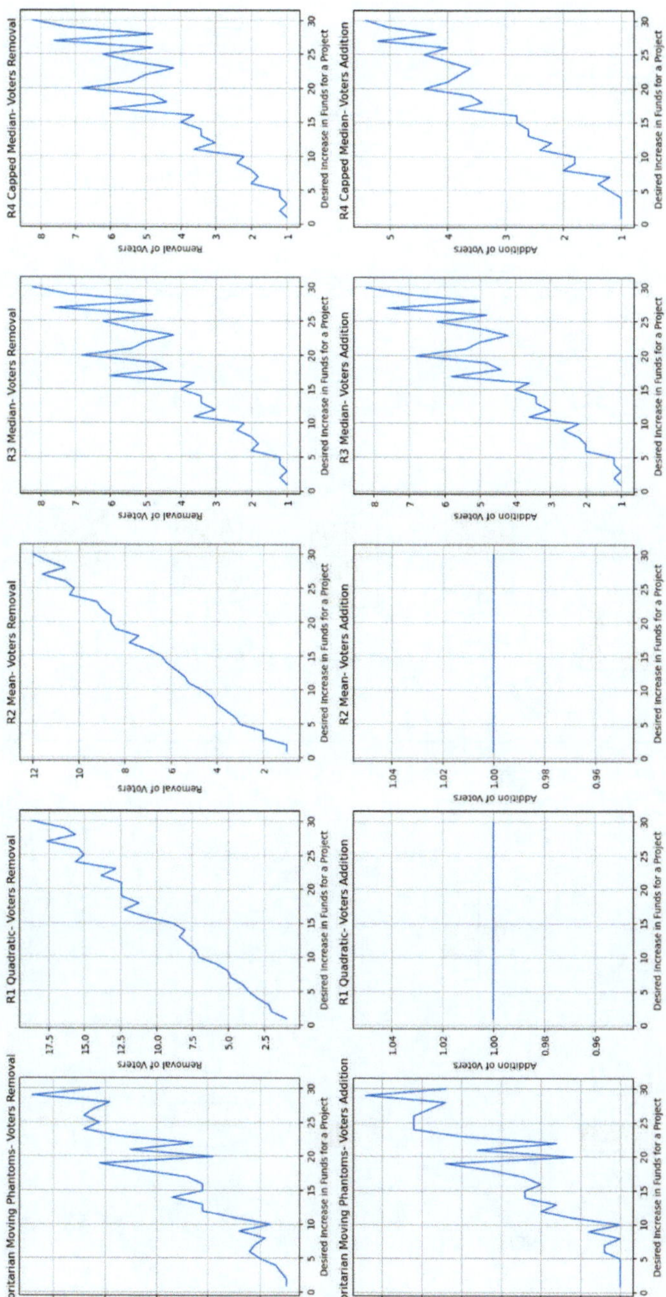

Fig. 2 Cost of Adding and deleting voters as a function of the desired funding increase

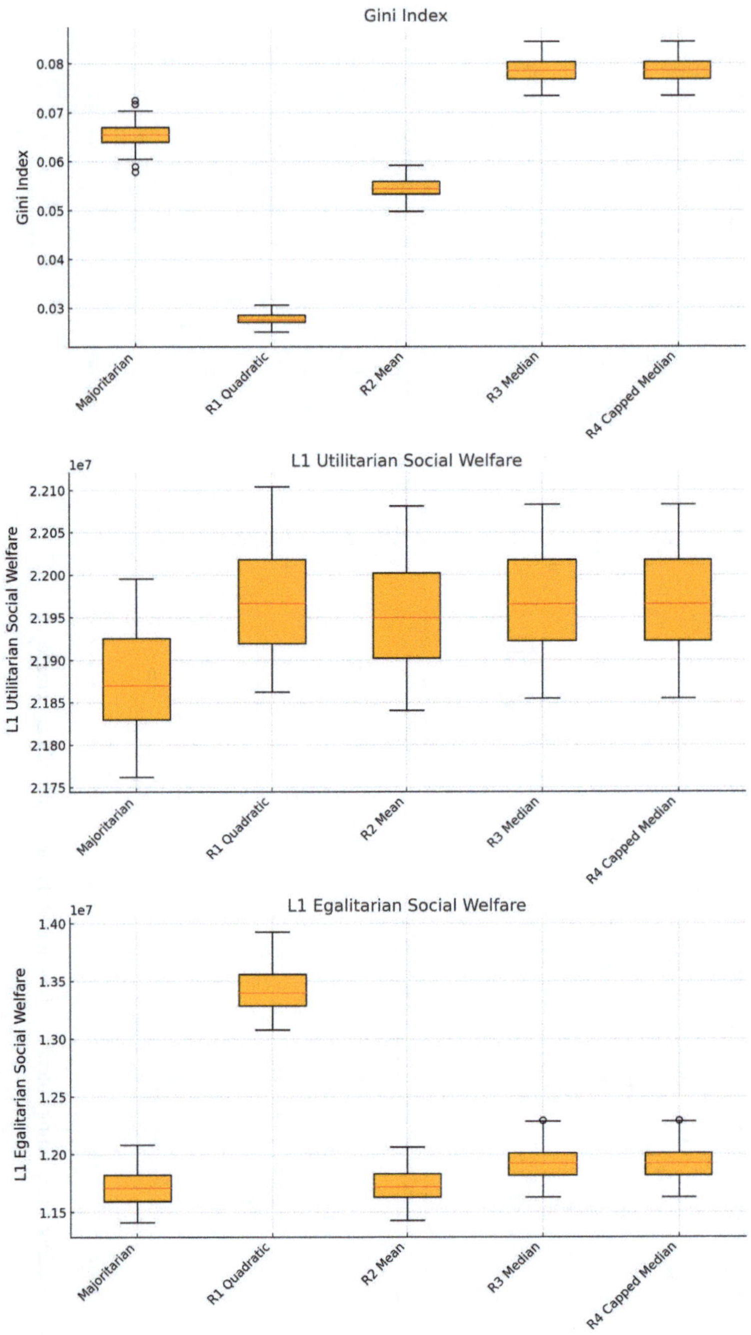

Fig. 3 Comparison of Gini Index, L1 Utilitarian Social Welfare, and L1 Egalitarian Social Welfare across voting rules

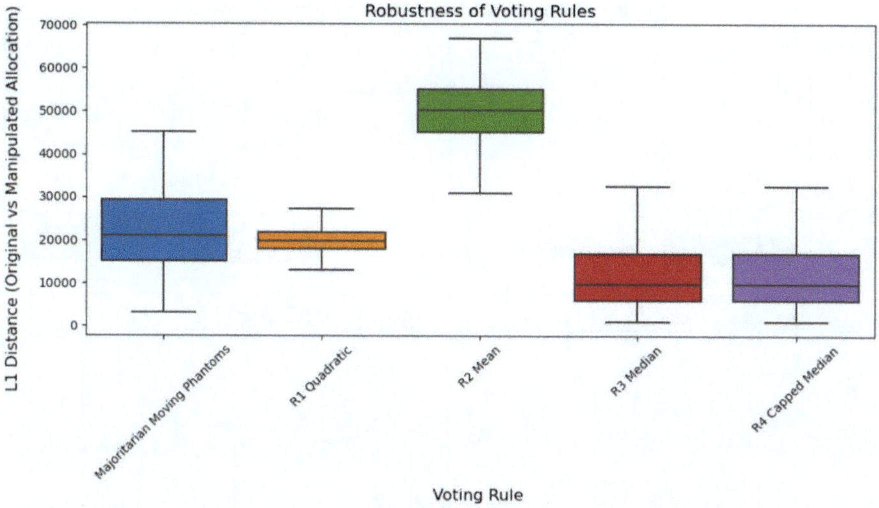

Fig. 4 Robustness of voting rules under manipulation, represented by L1 distance between original and manipulated allocations

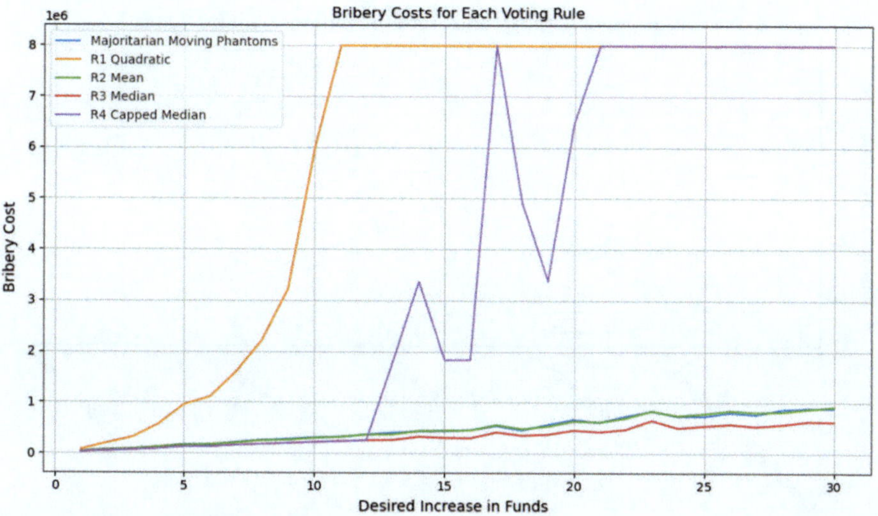

Fig. 5 Bribery costs for different voting rules as a function of desired increase in funds for a project

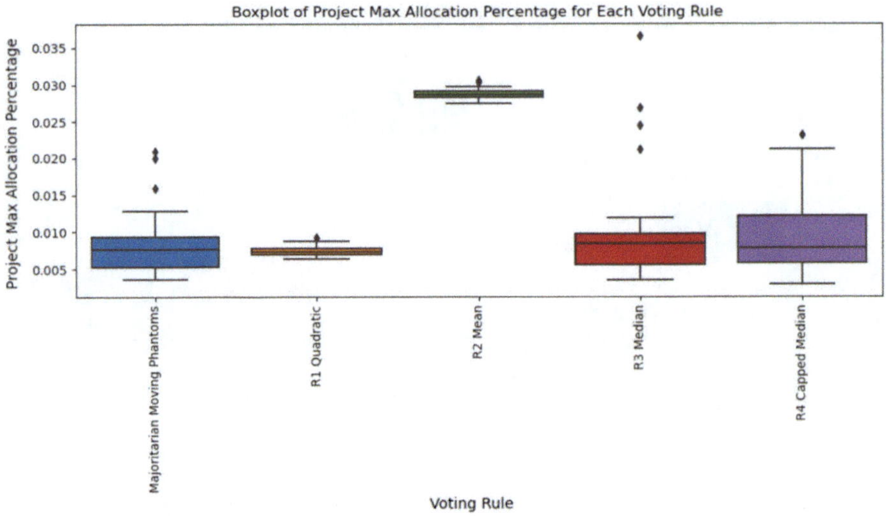

Fig. 6 The maximal new project allocation caused by one voter skewing the outcome divided by the total number of tokens to be funded for each voting rule

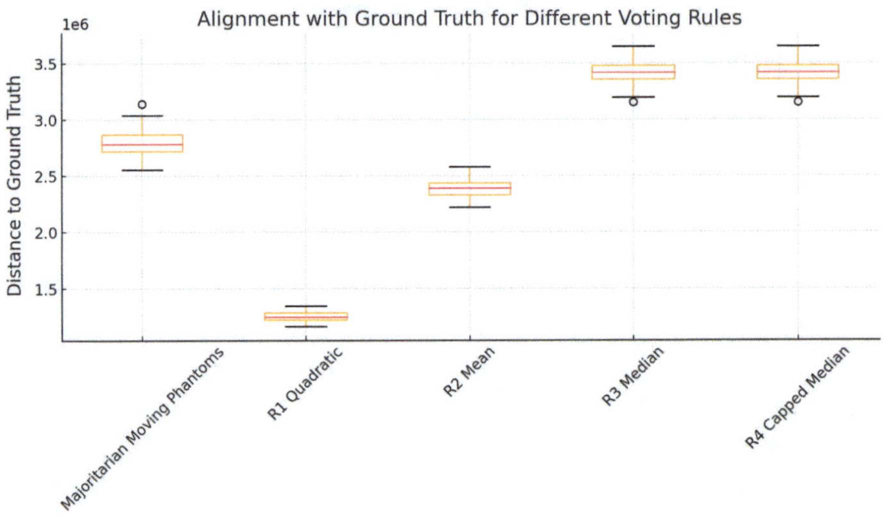

Fig. 7 Alignment with ground truth for different voting rules, measured by distance to ground truth

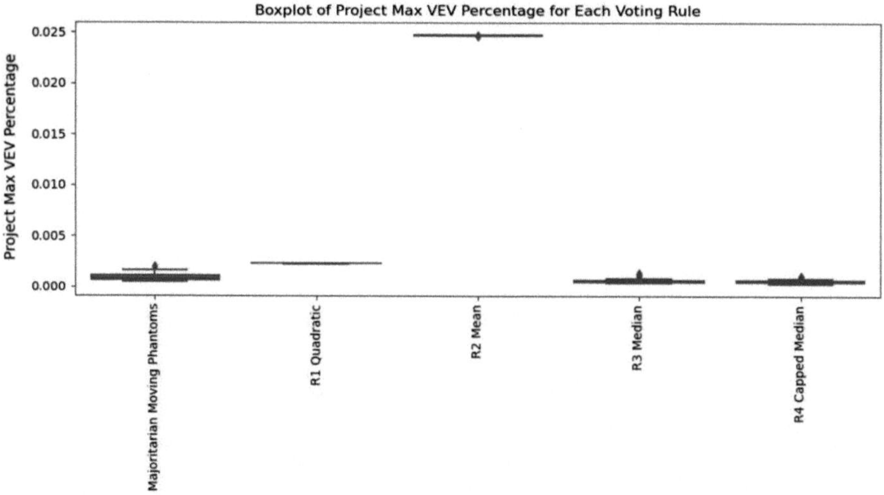

Fig. 8 The maximal difference in token allocation caused by one voter skewing the outcome, divided by the total number of tokens to be funded for each voting rule

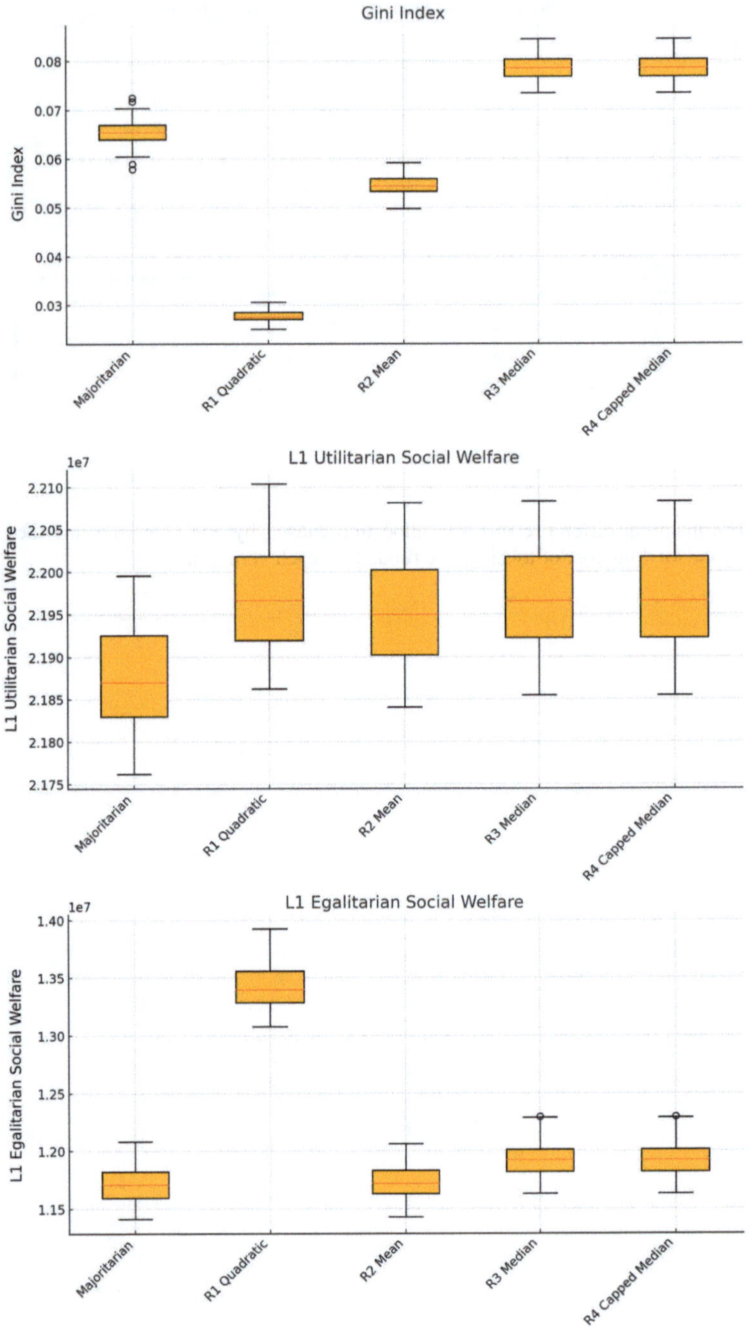

Fig. 9 Gini Index, Utilitarian Social Welfare (ℓ_1 distance), and Egalitarian Social Welfare (maximum ℓ_1 distance) for each voting rule on round 4 data

References

1. Freeman, R., Pennock, D.M., Peters, D., Vaughan, J.W.: Truthful aggregation of budget proposals. In Proceedings of the 2019 ACM Conference on Economics and Computation, pp. 751–752 (2019)
2. Optimism: The retropgf experiment (2021). Accessed 10 July 2024
3. Optimism Collective. Retropgf round 2 (2022)
4. Optimism Collective Governance. Retropgf 3 round design (2023)
5. Optimism Collective. Retropgf round 4 (2023)
6. Optimism Collective Governance. Retro funding 5: Op stack round details (2024). Accessed 10 July 2024
7. Aziz, H., Shah, N.: Participatory budgeting: models and approaches. In Pathways Between Social Science and Computational Social Science: Theories, Methods, and Interpretations, pp. 215–236. Springer (2021)
8. Pasquini, R.A.: Quadratic funding and matching funds requirements. arXiv preprint arXiv: 2010.01193 (2020)
9. Cohen, J.: An epistemic conception of democracy. Ethics **97**(1), 26–38 (1986)
10. Buterin, V., Hitzig, Z., Weyl, E.G.: A flexible design for funding public goods. Manage. Sci. **65**(11), 5171–5187 (20190
11. Georgescu, L., Fox, J., Gautier, A., Wooldridge, M.: Fixed-budget and multiple-issue quadratic voting. arXiv preprint arXiv:2409.06614 (2024)
12. Dimitri, N.: Quadratic voting in blockchain governance. Inf. **13**(6), 305 (2022)
13. Fairstein, R., Benadè, G., Gal, K.: Participatory budgeting designs for the real world. In Proceedings of the AAAI Conference on Artificial Intelligence, vol. 37, pp. 5633–5640, Palo Alto, CA, USA (2023)
14. Zichichi, M., Contu, M., Ferretti, S., D'Angelo, G.: Likestarter: a smart-contract based social dao for crowdfunding. In IEEE INFOCOM 2019-IEEE Conference on Computer Communications Workshops (INFOCOM WKSHPS), pp. 313–318. Piscataway, NJ, USA. IEEE (2019)
15. Airiau, S., Aziz, H., Caragiannis, I., Kruger, J., Lang, J., Peters, D.: Portioning using ordinal preferences: Fairness and efficiency. Artificial Intell. **314**, 103809 (2023)
16. Talmon, N.: Social choice around decentralized autonomous organizations: on the computational social choice of digital communities. In: Proceedings of the 2023 International Conference on Autonomous Agents and Multiagent Systems, pp. 1768–1773, New York, NY, USA, ACM (2023)
17. Jones, K.: Blockchain in or as governance? evolutions in experimentation, social impacts, and prefigurative practice in the blockchain and dao space. Inf. Polity **24**(4), 469–486 (2019)
18. Grossi, D.: Social choice around the block: on the computational social choice of blockchain. arXiv preprint arXiv:2203.07777 (2022)
19. Prelec, D.: A bayesian truth serum for subjective data. Sci. **306**(5695), 462–466 (2004)
20. Prelec, D.H., Seung, S., McCoy, J.: A solution to the single-question crowd wisdom problem. Nature **541**(7638), 532–535 (2017)
21. Caragiannis, I., Procaccia, A.D., Shah, N.: When do noisy votes reveal the truth? ACM Trans. Econo. Comput. **4**(3), 1–30 (2016)
22. Lalley, S.P., Weyl, E.G.: Quadratic voting: how mechanism design can radicalize democracy. In AEA Papers and Proceedings, vol. 108, pp. 33–37, Nashville, TN, USA, American Economic Association (2018)
23. Nehring, K., Puppe, C., Linder, T.: Allocating public goods via the midpoint rule. Preprint (2008)
24. Brandt, F., Conitzer, V., Endriss, U., Lang, J., Procaccia, A.D.: Handbook of Computational Social Choice. Cambridge University Press, Cambridge, UK (2016)
25. de Berg, M., Freeman, R., Schmidt-Kraepelin, U., Utke, M.: Truthful budget aggregation: beyond moving-phantom mechanisms. arXiv preprint arXiv:2405.20303 (2024)

26. Cohensius, G., Meir, R.: Proxy voting for revealing ground truth. In Proceedings of the 4th Workshop on Exploring Beyond the Worst Case in Computational Social Choice (EXPLORE) (2017)
27. Boehmer, N., Bredereck, R., Faliszewski, P., Niedermeier, R., Szufa, S.: Putting a compass on the map of elections. arXiv preprint arXiv:2105.07815 (2021)
28. Szufa, S., Faliszewski, P., Skowron, P., Slinko, A., Talmon, N.: Drawing a map of elections in the space of statistical cultures. In Proceedings of the 19th International Conference on Autonomous Agents and Multiagent Systems, pp. 1341–1349, New York, NY, USA, ACM (2020)
29. Leonardos, S., Reijsbergen, D., Piliouras, G.: Weighted voting on the blockchain: improving consensus in proof of stake protocols. Int. J. Netw. Manage. **30**(5), e2093 (2020)
30. de Oliveira, M.T., Reis, L.H., Medeiros, D.S., Carrano, R.C., Olabarriaga, S.D., Mattos, D.M.: Blockchain reputation-based consensus: a scalable and resilient mechanism for distributed mistrusting applications. Comput. Netw. **179**, 107367 (2020)
31. Perez, A.J., Ceesay, E.N.: Improving end-to-end verifiable voting systems with blockchain technologies. In 2018 IEEE International Conference on Internet of Things (iThings) and IEEE Green Computing and Communications (GreenCom) and IEEE Cyber, Physical and Social Computing (CPSCom) and IEEE Smart Data (SmartData), pp. 1108–1115, Piscataway, NJ, USA, IEEE (2018)
32. Wagner, J., Meir, R.: Strategy-proof budgeting via a vcg-like mechanism. In International Symposium on Algorithmic Game Theory, pp. 401–418, Springer (2023)
33. Wagner, J., Meir, R.: Distribution aggregation via continuous thiele's rules. arXiv preprint arXiv:2408.01054 (2024)
34. Bulteau, L., Shahaf, G., Shapiro, E., Talmon, N.: Aggregation over metric spaces: proposing and voting in elections, budgeting, and legislation. J. Artifi. Intell. Res. **70**, 1413–1439 (2021)

Bridging Social Capital and Financial Incentives: Navigating Liability and Regulatory Challenges in DAO Governance

Lukas Weidener, Benjamin Heurich, and Bence Lukács

Abstract Decentralized Autonomous Organizations (DAOs) promise to transform governance through blockchain-enabled transparency and communal decision-making. However, unresolved legal responsibilities and speculative governance token dynamics complicate their ability to maintain trust, encourage participation, and secure legitimacy. Drawing primarily on Social Capital Theory (SCT), this study shows how bonding, bridging, and linking social capital intersect with liability ambiguities and token concentration to undermine institutional confidence and grassroots engagement. Public Goods Theory (PGT) clarifies how free-rider tendencies can deter infrastructural support, while Principal-Agent Theory (PAT) highlights incentive misalignments when whales prioritize short-term gains over collective welfare. Through a theoretical lens, this study illuminates how token-based power asymmetries, a lack of regulatory clarity, and conflicting motivations strain the viability of DAOs in fulfilling the promise of decentralized governance. In synthesizing these frameworks, this study advocates tailored governance strategies, ranging from reputation-based voting models to legally compliant organizational wrappers, to mitigate power imbalances, foster inclusive decision-making, and ultimately strengthen DAOs' resilience in an evolving blockchain ecosystem. By bridging the sociological, economic, and legal perspectives, this study illustrates the interplay of trust, accountability, and incentives that shape DAO sustainability.

Keywords Decentralized Autonomous Organizations (DAOs) · Governance · Social capital theory

L. Weidener (✉)
Eduard-Wallnöfer-Zentrum, UMIT Tirol—Private Universität für Gesundheitswissenschaften und -technologie, Hall in Tirol, Austria
e-mail: lukas@weidener.eu

B. Heurich · B. Lukács
Institute for Applied Blockchain (IABC), Berlin, Germany

M. Lustenberger et al. (eds.), *Decentralized Autonomous Organizations—Governance, Technology, and Legal Perspectives*, Springer Proceedings in Business and Economics,
https://doi.org/10.1007/978-3-032-03273-7_6

1 Introduction

Decentralized Autonomous Organizations (DAOs) have emerged as a transformative governance model capable of restructuring decision-making and exercising authority. By intertwining blockchain technology with community-driven oversight, DAOs promise a recalibration of the traditional organizational hierarchy, turning it from a top-down system into a network of stakeholders who, in principle, coordinate transparent and collective decision-making processes [1]. Indeed, these organizations typically rely on cryptographic tokens and smart contracts to govern day-to-day operations, allocate resources, and confer voting rights to members worldwide [2, 3]. Within such an environment, the virtues of decentralization, openness, accessibility, and resistance to centralized censorship often come into tension with the practical issues of regulatory compliance, liability assignment, and the underlying social dynamics that shape human cooperation [4]. The recent legal ruling involving Lido DAO, in which the U.S. District Court for the Northern District of California ruled that a DAO could be liable under general partnership laws and signals the novel legal environment that decentralized entities must navigate [5, 6]. This case underscores that DAOs, while technologically innovative, are not immune to the traditional legal principles that hinge on concepts of accountability, fiduciary duty, and personal liability. If token holders, developers, or core contributors can be treated as partners in a general partnership, they may find themselves confronting significant legal obligations. From a policy standpoint, the decision raises profound questions about how DAOs reconcile ambitions for open, trustless governance with the real-world demands of regulation and dispute resolution [7, 8]. From a scholarly perspective, this development invites an urgent rethinking of how theoretical frameworks, particularly those drawn from the social sciences, can illuminate the interplay between human behavior, economic incentives, and technological enforcement within these emerging ecosystems [9]. Although initial enthusiasm for DAOs centered on the efficiency and transparency afforded by blockchain and smart contracts, it has become increasingly clear that the success or failure of a DAO does not hinge solely on the reliability of its code [10]. Rather, social architecture is equally influential if not more so. DAOs are not machines that autonomously govern themselves, despite the word "autonomous" in their name. They are human-technology hybrids, wherein code-based rules structure certain forms of interaction, however, human relationships, negotiations, and trust-building remain pivotal for ensuring long-term viability [11]. Governance tokens exemplify this duality: they grant holders financial stakes in the organization's performance, yet they also endow them with decision-making power that may shape the DAO's trajectory [12]. This coalescence of economic and participatory dimensions engenders a unique set of sociological concerns, from how token-induced incentives might skew communal ethos to how large token holders, often called "whales," can control governance to advance their private interests over collective welfare [13].

Social Capital Theory (SCT) provides a foundation for dissecting interconnected social and economic processes [14]. Rooted in the seminal works of Bourdieu,

Coleman, and Putnam, SCT contends that social networks, norms, and trust relationships have tangible value [15–17]. In Bourdieu's formulation, social capital is more than a neutral resource, it is a form of symbolic power that can be mobilized to reinforce hierarchies or facilitate collective aims, depending on who wields it and under what circumstances [15]. Coleman's approach complements this by emphasizing the functional qualities of social capital: trust, shared norms, and reciprocity decrease transaction costs and expand possibilities for coordinated action [16]. Putnam's influential distinction between bonding and bridging social capital captures a tension particularly relevant to DAOs: strong internal ties can catalyze swift decision-making and unity of purpose, but they may hinder broader outreach and innovation if the group closes itself off from external perspectives [17]. Putnam's further notion of linking social capital and the vertical ties that connect communities to formal institutions resonates with the contemporary scenario in which DAOs seeking legitimacy, stability, or major funding must establish rapport with regulators, courts, and institutional investors [17]. Nonetheless, an overreliance on relational conceptions of trust and reciprocity can inadvertently downplay the essential role of economic and legal structures in shaping behavior. DAOs embed a financial layer through utility and governance tokens, which, while not inherently structured as financial instruments, acquire market valuations and liquidity in secondary exchanges [18]. This economic dimension can exert a distortive influence, potentially subordinating altruistic and communal imperatives to market-driven incentives [19].

Power asymmetries can arise when those with more tokens (and, by extension, more financial influence) dominate the voting outcomes [13]. Moreover, legal ambiguities complicate relational trust, if participants sense that the organization lacks clear accountability mechanisms, they may disengage or participate in a superficial manner [8]. Here, Public Goods Theory (PGT) and Principal-Agent Theory (PAT) supplement SCT [18, 19]. PGT highlights how decentralized communities might underfund essential infrastructural tasks, such as code audits or user education, owing to free-rider tendencies [19]. If there is no formal structure to ensure that all beneficiaries of a public good contribute proportionally, then short-term, profit-driven incentives might overshadow collective interest [12]. Meanwhile, PAT focuses on incentive misalignments between principals (those who hold decision-making power or capital) and agents (those who carry out tasks but may not be fully aligned with the principals' goals) [18]. In traditional corporations, legal frameworks emphasize trust-based obligations. However, in DAOs where accountability is diffused among token holders of varying anonymity, these lines of responsibility remain unclear [4]. Consequently, DAOs must contend with legal accountability in a domain that is not designed to handle decentralized or pseudonymous actors. The Lido DAO case is emblematic: it illustrates how courts might interpret seemingly "leaderless" organizations as general partnerships, exposing each participating individual to potential liabilities [6]. For the average token holder, institutional investor, or prospective contributor, this specter of unbounded liability could deter substantive engagement, thereby depriving the DAO of the crucial bridging capital that fosters external partnerships and draws in diverse skill sets [1]. Thus, the tension between decentralization and accountability is a pivotal challenge. DAOs that adhere too strongly to ideals of maximal decentralization may forgo vital legal protections, whereas those that adopt extensive legal wrappers or hierarchical elements risk alienating crypto-native participants who treasure the open, egalitarian ethos that attracted them in the first place [20]. Concurrent with legal uncertainties, governance tokens introduce a precarious balance between financial and participation motivations. While tokens can align individual interests with the DAOs' overall well-being, they can also breed speculative mindsets in which participants push for policies that inflate token prices, even if such policies undermine longer-term initiatives such as building robust infrastructure, engaging with regulators, or promoting equitable resource distribution [11]. The short-term horizon of many retail token holders can exacerbate free-rider dynamics, participants might wait for philanthropic whales or dedicated core teams to supply essential services, effectively shirking their own responsibility to sustain the community's health [9]. This cyclical dynamic threatens both bonding capital, which depends on mutual trust, and bridging capital, which comes from an active, diverse membership base [14]. This cyclical dynamic threatens both bonding and bridging social capital [14]. Accordingly, the interplay between technological rules and human incentives must be examined through a multi-faceted theoretical lens. This cyclical dynamic threatens both bonding and bridging social capital [14]. Accordingly, the interplay between technological rules and human incentives must be examined through a multi-faceted theoretical lens. Although many practical governance solutions exist, a deeper theoretical groundwork is crucial for understanding the complexities of DAOs. In what follows, this research draws on empirical examples (such as MakerDAO, Uniswap, and Curve) and conceptual insights to demonstrate how these interwoven theories can frame the core governance dilemmas faced by DAOs [10].

The overarching objective is to move beyond celebratory or purely technical narratives of decentralized governance and instead offer a nuanced understanding that includes the complexities of symbolic authority, moral legitimacy, and the changing regulatory landscapes [12]. This study aims not only to provide theoretical clarity but also to point toward practical recommendations, including governance token design, liability structuring, and ways of fortifying trust among disparate participants [13]. By doing so, the analysis contributes to the broader discourse on how DAOs can realize their transformative potential, potentially addressing the pitfalls of legal unpredictability [6], power imbalances [11], and free-rider vulnerabilities [19]. As DAOs progress from niche experiments to mainstream phenomena, these issues will become increasingly urgent [8]. Regulatory bodies worldwide are already struggling with how to classify and oversee decentralized finance platforms [21], whereas institutional investors are exploring how best to incorporate crypto assets and DAO governance tokens into their broader portfolios [1]. The decisions made in these early phases of the DAO evolution will likely shape how deeply the model penetrates traditional sectors, from finance to supply chain management to creative industries [4]. For DAOs to mature, they must demonstrate not only robust technological foundations but also governance processes perceived as fair, inclusive, and accountable [10]. SCT, along with PGT and PAT, illuminates the path forward by exposing the intricate and often fragile web of relationships and incentives upon which DAOs depend [13].

2 Objective

The objective of this study is to critically analyze the impact of unresolved legal accountability and the financialization of governance tokens on the participation, engagement, and attractiveness of DAOs using SCT as the primary analytical framework. In pursuit of this goal, this study employs a conceptual approach that integrates the authors' direct experience in DAOs with a structured review of existing research and illustrative case references, thereby systematically highlighting how relational trust dynamics inform decentralized governance outcomes.

2.1 Research Questions

1. How does the unresolved legal accountability for investments and contributions to DAOs influence their ability to attract institutional and individual investors?
2. If the ownership of governance tokens acts as de facto financial stakes, how does it influence participation and engagement in DAOs?

2.1. How does the concentration of governance tokens among holders' impact power asymmetries and their influence on participation in DAOs?

3 Methodology

The authors' continued engagement as contributors to multiple DAOs, including active participation in governance discussions, proposal evaluations, and token-based voting, informed their selection of SCT as the primary analytical framework for this study. This dual (practical experience and academic expertise, e.g., in social sciences) perspective enabled a grounded evaluation of relevant theoretical models. A literature review identified several candidate theories, each contributing valuable insights but failing to comprehensively address the unique dynamics of DAOs.

Oliver E. Williamson's Transaction Cost Economics, which explains how organizations minimize costs and reduce uncertainty, provides an important foundation for understanding organizational efficiency [22]. However, its focus on traditional organizational hierarchies overlooks the relational trust dynamics, decentralized decision-making, and liability ambiguities inherent to DAO ecosystems [4, 8]. Similarly, New Institutionalism in Organizational Analysis by Walter W. Powell and Paul J. DiMaggio articulates how norms influence organizational legitimacy [23]. While relevant for understanding how governance legitimacy evolves in DAOs, it does not address the fluid participation and token-based power asymmetries that define these decentralized organizations [1, 13]. Paul Cilliers' Complexity and Postmodernism: Understanding Complex Systems offers a valuable lens for analyzing emergent behavior within distributed networks [24]. However, its applicability is limited when confronting accountability gaps and incentive misalignments that arise in financialized, decentralized systems [18, 19]. Bruno Latour's Reassembling the Social: An Introduction to Actor-Network-Theory highlights the interplay between human and non-human actors, such as smart contracts, in socio-technical systems [25]. However, it lacks a robust framework for addressing governance procedures, legal liability, and practical decision-making in DAOs [6, 9].

These theoretical limitations underscore the need for a framework that can address the intricate interplay of trust, accountability, and participation in DAOs. SCT, with its emphasis on bonding, bridging, and linking forms of social capital, has emerged as the most suitable lens for examining decentralized, community-driven governance [15–17]. Supplementing SCT with Public Goods Theory (PGT) and Principal-Agent Theory (PAT) further enhances its capacity to analyze how relational networks, incentive structures, and governance processes converge within DAO ecosystems [18, 19, 26].

4 Theoretical Analysis

This chapter applies SCT as its primary framework, integrated with PGT and PAT to offer a multi-layered understanding of DAOs' governance challenges. SCT highlights how trust, reciprocity, and social networks underpin collaboration and collective actions. However, the inherent financial dimensions of DAOs, such as token-based voting and resource allocation, also invoke issues of free-rider behavior (PGT) and incentive misalignment (PAT). By integrating these perspectives, the ways in which liability ambiguities, token concentration, and economic stakes converge to shape the DAO participation, legitimacy, and sustainability will be emphasized.

4.1 Research Question 1—How Does the Unresolved Legal Accountability for Investments and Contributions to DAOs Influence Their Ability to Attract Institutional and Individual Investors?

DAOs present a novel model of organizational governance, one in which power is supposedly decentralized and critical decisions are made through on-chain voting [3]. Within SCT, persistent ambiguities regarding liability and cross-jurisdictional regulatory compliance erode trust upon which new forms of collective organization, such as DAOs, rely [15, 16, 27]. Bonding, bridging, and linking social capital suffer when the question of who bears responsibility for wrongdoing or regulatory infraction remains unanswered [27]. Linking social capital, which connects decentralized communities to traditional institutions (e.g., regulators, venture capital firms, courts), is particularly compromised in this environment [23]. Institutional investors, such as venture capital funds and private equity firms, typically require enforceable governance structures, defined fiduciary duties, and clear liability frameworks before making investments ([28]; Wong 2023). However, in DAOs, the absence of direct contractual obligations and concerns over joint liability among token holders has made institutional players hesitant to allocate significant capital [29]. When the possibility arises that token holders might be treated as general partners or that developers could be retroactively held accountable for collective decisions, the perceived reliability of DAOs in the eyes of seasoned investors may decline sharply [6]. Consequently, bridging the gap between decentralized governance and mainstream financial standards demands heightened legal clarity, an essential precondition for forging the robust linking of social capital that large-scale institutional investment typically requires [29]. From a PAT perspective, opacity regarding who is legally responsible for contract breaches or securities violations compounds agency problems [18]. In contrast, in many DAOs, these lines of accountability are blurred, large token holders may steer decisions, but without a formal position that can be sanctioned under law [12]. This structural fluidity undermines the straightforward contracting processes that PAT assumes. While institutional investors emphasize accountability, retail participants ranging from small-scale crypto enthusiasts to individual community developers experience liability ambiguities differently [13]. Many retail actors are motivated by the ideals of decentralization and community ownership [9]. Smaller contributors or "casual" investors face a disproportionate risk of personal liability in jurisdictions that interpret token ownership as a form of general partnership, potentially exposing them to legal claims [29, 30]. Rather than actively engaging in governance or voting, many prefer passive token-holding to minimize legal exposure, exacerbating the concentration of decision-making power among a few dominant actors (e.g., "whales") [13]. This dynamic undermines bridging social capital by discouraging broad-based participation and governance diversity, further deterring institutional and grassroots involvement [31]. Consequently, this stunting effect undercuts one of the advantages of DAOs: their ability to attract a global open community of problem solvers and innovators [1]. PGT clarifies the scope of this problem: under conditions of legal risk, participants may underprovide essential resources, such as proposal drafting, knowledge sharing, and code audits, if they foresee potential liabilities overshadowing collective gains [31]. In short, the communal well-being of the DAO is jeopardized by a climate of legal uncertainty that, ironically, was never intended to plague an organization formed to dismantle traditional gatekeeping [20].

Despite these challenges, many DAOs attempt to maintain internal cohesion, bonding social capital, through trust, shared purposes, and consistent community norms [16, 17]. Developers or core contributors, who face an increased risk of being singled out in lawsuits or enforcement actions, may disengage or insist on operating pseudonymously [6]. While pseudonymity offers some shield, it also complicates direct accountability and the forging of strong personal ties that underlie bonding capital [15]. In response, some DAOs adopt legal wrappers (e.g., LLCs, Swiss Associations, or Foundations) to delineate liability, at least partially [27]. Although such structures can reduce the risk to token holders, they can also introduce hierarchical elements that might appear to undermine the ideal of fluid and decentralized decision-making [25]. From a PAT perspective, formalizing certain roles might reduce overall ambiguity, however, it also reintroduces a managerial layer, potentially re-creating classic agency problems [18]. Meanwhile, from an SCT lens, having a recognized legal entity can fortify linking social capital with regulators and established financial institutions, but it might also alienate purist segments of the community who perceive any regulatory compliance as antithetical to true decentralization [23]. Institutional investors tend to engage in thorough risk assessments, demanding legal wrappers (LLCs, Foundations), compliance assurances, and structured governance roles such as reserved seats on DAO governance councils before committing capital ([28]; Wong 2023). Conversely, retail investors often prioritize speculative opportunities, viewing DAOs primarily as short-term profit vehicles rather than sustainable governance models [13, 29]. This dynamic exacerbates token price volatility, leading to governance instability and making it even harder for DAOs to establish long-term financial credibility [31]. The absence of cohesive bridging capital between these cohorts can cause confusion about strategic priorities such as short-term price appreciation or long-term protocol sustainability [14]. Overall, unresolved legal accountability remains a formidable barrier to DAOs' capacity to attract and sustain diverse investor bases [6, 8]. In SCT terms, it corrodes the trust essential to forging strong linking social capital, reduces bridging opportunities with broader communities, and strains bonding ties between core contributors [17]. PGT and PAT add to this picture by showing how risk aversion and uncertain recourse mechanisms drive inefficiencies and undermine alignment among stakeholders [18, 19]. Consequently, efforts to develop standardized legal frameworks, or at least widely accepted "safe harbor" provisions, are vital, not as a means of capitulating on centralized authority but as a pragmatic strategy for mitigating existential threats to DAOs' growth [27]. Through such clarity, DAOs may realize their full potential as novel engines of collaborative innovation, unencumbered by a perpetual climate of doubt around legal responsibility [20].

4.2 Research Question 2—If the Ownership of Governance Tokens Acts as De Facto Financial Stakes, How It Influences Participation and Engagement in DAOs?

Governance tokens function as hybrid financial instruments, granting voting rights while exposing holders to protocol revenue, treasury management, and market speculation [3, 32]. Their liquidity and price volatility fundamentally shape DAO participation dynamics, often creating tensions between community-driven governance and profit-seeking behavior (Wong 2023). This duality intensifies the interplay between the economic incentives and collaborative governance. SCT illuminates how trust and reciprocity might shift when governance becomes inseparable from market-driven tokens [15–17], PGT underscores the vulnerabilities in shared-resource funding [19], and PAT reveals why large token holders may act primarily to maximize short-term gains [18]. When governance tokens are tradable and liquid, economic self-interest ca35.n overshadow community-driven motivations [13]. Financialization shifts social capital dynamics in DAOs, while initial members may be ideologically driven, later participants often treat their governance role as an investment opportunity rather than a community responsibility [33, 34]. The conversation shifts from "How do we best fulfill the DAOs' vision?" to "How do we maximize token value?" While such a shift can galvanize engagement, particularly if rising token prices signal successful governance, it can also diminish altruistic interest that originally animated many decentralized projects [9]. Bridging social capital, which fosters broad-based participation, weakens financialized DAO environments, as token-weighted voting disproportionately amplifies whale influence, discouraging small and medium stakeholders from engaging in governance [34, 35]. Smaller or newer participants tend to calibrate their involvement based on the perceived financial upside [4]. If whales hold disproportionate voting power, smaller holders may conclude that their marginal influence is negligible, leading them to free ride on others' governance efforts [19]. PGT explains that free-rider tendencies intensify when financial incentives skew governance priorities, leading participants to vote for token price maximization over community-building efforts, such as security audits or infrastructure upgrades [34]. This dynamic disincentivizes long-term contributions, further exacerbating DAO governance asymmetries. Indeed, the intangible nature of "community well-being" is seldom priced in the token [15]. The capacity of DAOs to connect with hierarchies in the financial or regulatory spheres acquires new contours under financialization [23]. On the one hand, the existence of a robust token economy can draw on hedge funds, crypto-specific venture capitalists, and other deep-pocketed investors [22]. On the other hand, these external stakeholders may prioritize quarterly returns over communal ethos or experimental democratic processes that define DAOs [6]. This tension risks fracturing the internal trust upon which bonding capital depends, as founding members may sense a drift toward a purely profit-driven structure [17].

Recent analyses of DAOs such as Compound, Uniswap, and Curve reveal that governance is frequently dominated by a small number of large token holders, leading to lower participation rates among smaller stakeholders [34]. This dynamic, consistent with PAT, indicates that bigger holders, acting as "principals," can shape the DAO in ways that secure immediate returns (e.g., token buybacks or liquidity mining programs) rather than investing in less glamorous but vital initiatives like user support, developer training, or security audits [18]. Over time, short-termism can degrade a DAOs' resilience and brand reputation, especially when critical upgrades or expansions are perpetually deferred [12]. From a PGT lens, even well-meaning participants may avoid volunteering time or expertise if they fear that large token holders will capture most of the financial benefits [19]. This "governance capture" by whales can suppress creativity and hamper the entrepreneurial energy that often fuels decentralized innovation [9]. In an ecosystem designed to harness crowd wisdom, the overshadowing influence of a few people can corrode bridging social capital by signaling to newcomers that their voices, however informed, hold limited weight [16, 17]. Bourdieu's concept of symbolic capital highlights that governance tokens confer social status, reinforcing informal hierarchies in which whales accumulate both economic and reputational power [15, 27]. This dynamic concentrates on decision-making influence, subtly shaping DAO narratives and governance norms [32]. Whales accumulate financial stakes and gain social prestige, which translates into an informal leadership role [27]. Some whales may become figureheads, whether they intend to or not, their decisions tend to anchor community discourse and shape acceptable standards for proposals [23]. Smaller participants may acquire tokens anticipating that aligning with whale-endorsed proposals could indirectly elevate token prices or yield intangible social rewards such as invitations to exclusive channels or the promise of future collaboration [15]. Simultaneously, behavioral economics reminds us that many participants, especially retail investors, exhibit short time horizons [13]. They are prone to vote in ways that immediately inflate token prices, ignoring intangible or long-term infrastructure investments [19]. This bias can reinforce the free-rider syndrome, as these voters wait for someone else, perhaps the core development team or a philanthropic whale, to assume the burden of building the essential layers of the ecosystem [20]. In summary, the financialization of DAO governance can overshadow altruistic or community-driven impulses, weakening broad participation.

4.3 Research Question 2.1: How Does the Concentration of Governance Tokens Among Holder Affect Power Asymmetries and Their Influence on Participation in DAOs?

A central critique of DAO governance is the concentration of voting power among a small elite of token holders, which undermines decentralization and participatory legitimacy [13, 36]. Studies reveal that as few as 1–5% of token holders control governance in leading DAOs, reinforcing financial stratification rather than democratic decision-making [36]. This concentration not only distorts the egalitarian ideals commonly associated with DAOs but also potentially threatens their long-term viability [17, 27]. By using SCT in tandem with PGT and PAT, we see how such concentration erodes trust, fosters a perception of unfairness, and drives talented contributors away [14, 16]. Governance capture arises when whales leverage their disproportionate voting power to steer DAOs toward self-enriching policies, often at the expense of collective welfare [12, 36]. Empirical studies show that large token holders frequently dominate high-stakes proposals, effectively pre-determining governance outcomes before community votes occur [35]. Bonding social capital erodes in governance-captured DAOs, as smaller token holders recognize that their votes hold minimal weight, leading to lower voter turnout and disengagement [17, 34]. Research shows that DAOs with extreme token-weighted voting disparities experience sub-20% participation rates, exacerbating governance inequalities [34]. Over time, these stakeholders may disengage from working groups or critical discussions, disillusioned by the reality that "major" votes are effectively sealed before they can rally support [4]. The fracturing of bonding social capital further manifests in developers' frustration, particularly if whales allocate resources to short-term token price manipulation or self-serving yield strategies rather than crucial tasks, such as contract auditing, community outreach, or user interface improvements [19]. In line with Coleman's view of social structures, a breakdown in reciprocity can be devastating to informal norms that sustain trust in a shared mission [16]. Even if the code remains open-source, the intangible glue that makes collaborative innovation feasible starts to dissolve [15]. Similarly, bridging social capital suffers when newcomers detect an entrenched hierarchy [17]. Many are initially drawn to DAOs by the promise of merit-based governance, where well-argued proposals stand on their own independent of capital holdings [9]. However, if large token holders can systematically overrule community sentiment, the pool of prospective contributors diminishes [20]. From a PGT perspective, token concentration skews incentives away from collective investment, leading to the chronic underfunding of essential DAO infrastructure [19]. Research highlights that DAOs with higher governance token concentration levels allocate over 70% of treasury funds to yield-based incentives, neglecting developer grants, security audits, and contributor incentives.

Linking social capital, which connects DAOs to institutional spheres, presents parallel challenges [23]. Regulatory bodies and institutional investors wary of "pseudo-decentralization" may question the integrity of a system that claims to be community-driven yet is, in practice, controlled by a handful of influential addresses [6]. Off-chain institutional investors frequently acquire DAO tokens not for governance participation but for fee extraction and treasury redirection, prioritizing short-term arbitrage over long-term ecosystem sustainability [4, 29]. This pattern mirrors traditional financial rent seeking, where large capital holders dictate terms without engaging in meaningful governance [29]. This dynamic can discourage more public-minded institutions or philanthropic donors, who might otherwise appreciate the decentralized model's community-led orientation [8]. The symbolic capital associated with large token holdings often translates into de facto governance authority, as whales position themselves as "visionary leaders" or "founding architects" of the DAO's success, reinforcing an informal power hierarchy [15, 32]. Empirical studies show that DAOs frequently defer whale-endorsed proposals, even when alternative governance models are proposed [32]. Community members may then defer, sometimes uncritically, to whale decisions, conflating high-token balances with visionary leadership [23]. This conflation can stymie critical debate and lead to a uniform opinion that leaves blind spots in the DAOs' strategic planning [13]. Over time, the very structure that DAOs were designed to circumvent hierarchical control, emerges in a new form, framed as "market efficiency" or "liquidity provision" [27]. The lines of accountability become further blurred: whales can set the agenda and disburse funds yet hold no formal fiduciary duty to smaller token holders or the DAOs' user base [12]. Consequently, the agents (i.e., developers, smaller contributors) experience constraints on budget or policy decisions that might reflect the entire community's preferences under a more balanced governance model [18]. Hence, the overall concentration of governance tokens can bring about a quasi-hierarchical power dynamic, diminishing the decentralized ethos that DAOs aim to uphold.

5 Discussion

The findings of this study underscore the potent yet partial explanatory power of SCT in highlighting key tensions and dynamics within DAO governance [14, 17]. SCT demonstrates how bonding, bridging, and linking social capital can sustain communal trust in decentralized ecosystems [15, 16]. Specifically, bonding social capital strengthens internal cohesion among core contributors [17], bridging capital fosters collaboration across diverse stakeholder groups [14], and linking capital helps integrate DAOs with institutional actors and regulatory frameworks [23]. Empirical illustrations ranging from Compound to Uniswap and Curve reveal that when relational capital is weak or absent, DAOs struggle to attract consistent engagement and maintain investor confidence [12, 13]. However, recent studies have demonstrated that the financialization of governance tokens and liability ambiguities endemic to decentralized environments exposes SCT limits [8, 35]. The increasing dominance of large token holders ("whales") fosters participation asymmetries, whereby smaller stakeholders feel disenfranchised, further fracturing social cohesion [36]. This suggests that while SCT provides an important framework for understanding community engagement, it must be supplemented with theories that account for the economic and legal constraints shaping DAO governance. Token-based power imbalances, which incentivize short-term profit-taking and free-rider behavior, highlight the necessity of integrating PGT and PAT [18, 19]. PGT captures how shared resources (such as a DAO's treasury) can be underfunded or misallocated if individual stakeholders prioritize immediate gains over communal resilience [20].

Empirical analyses of DAOs indicate that treasury fund allocations overwhelmingly favor yield incentives, with over 72% of the total spending directed toward liquidity incentives, staking rewards, and speculative yield strategies, less than 22% is invested in infrastructure development, governance research, or protocol security upgrades [1, 3]. This allocation dynamic exacerbates free-rider problems and governance capture, as large token holders prioritize short-term financial gains over long-term ecosystem sustainability [13]. PAT further exposes how principal-agent misalignments shape governance inefficiencies [18]. Large token holders (principals) can unilaterally shape governance proposals to secure immediate financial returns, leaving smaller participants (agents) without effective recourse mechanisms [35, 36]. This not only exacerbates power asymmetries but also undermines merit-based governance, as token-weighted voting reinforces entrenched hierarchies rather than promotes participatory engagement [32]. Governance capture by institutional investors, who may acquire DAO tokens purely for rent-seeking purposes rather than contributing to ecosystem development, further complicates the principal-agent problem [29]. The tensions among these theoretical perspectives manifest in practical design solutions that attempt to correct power asymmetries through technical and economic interventions [22]. PAT-inspired safeguards, such as capping voting power or imposing multi-signature requirements, can prevent governance capture, but simultaneously risk alienating participants who see such constraints as antithetical to decentralization [4]. Similarly, PGT-driven approaches, such as token-burning mechanisms or tiered staking rewards, may mitigate free-rider problems, but inadvertently concentrate power among capital-intensive actors [19]. Quadratic voting has been proposed as a countermeasure to mitigate whale influence, however, it remains susceptible to Sybil attacks and identity verification challenges, limiting its scalability as a governance model [11, 36]. Further complicating DAO governance is an external regulatory requirement that increasingly collides with internal governance structures [6]. DAOs navigating securities laws or seeking to limit liability exposure often introduce centralized governance elements, which paradoxically undermine the decentralization ethos that originally attracted participants [8]. Examples such as Lido DAO, facing classification under general partnership laws, demonstrate how regulatory uncertainty erodes bridging social capital by deterring smaller stakeholders from governance participation out of fear of legal liability [6, 29]. Moreover, as DAOs seek to professionalize and attract institutional funding, their reliance on centralized funding structures may further entrench governance disparities. Large venture capital funds and hedge funds that acquire governance tokens often demand governance privileges such as board representation or treasury veto power, replicating traditional corporate governance hierarchies [29]. In this sense, the practical evolution of DAOs reflects a gradual transition from decentralized experimentation to hybrid governance models that blend decentralized decision-making with institutional oversight [32]. Thus, the dual imperative for DAOs is to strike a workable balance between the economic and legal rigor advocated by PGT and PAT and the communal trust emphasized by SCT [17]. Future empirical research should systematically examine how DAOs experiment with hybrid governance solutions, such as partial off-chain deliberation, on-chain automated enforcement, and adaptive token-weighted voting models, to balance decentralization with governance efficiency [9, 20]. In addition, emerging governance mechanisms, including reputation-weighted voting and dynamic identity verification systems, warrant further investigation. Reputation-based governance models, which weigh voting power based on long-term contributions rather than financial stakes, have been proposed to rebalance power dynamics. However, empirical research is needed to assess real-world effectiveness and resistance to collusion [16, 27]. Other mechanisms, such as vesting schedules or time-locked tokens, could potentially realign incentives by discouraging speculative behavior while promoting long-term ecosystem stability [18]. The interplay between SCT, PGT, and PAT underscores the complexity of decentralized governance, in which social capital must be nurtured along with economic and legal safeguards [14]. Although SCT remains a foundational framework for understanding trust formation and community engagement, it must be complemented by economic and legal theories that account for the material constraints that shape DAO decision-making [15, 16]. Interventions designed to solve governance inefficiencies, such as quadratic voting, treasury allocation reforms, and regulatory compliance strategies, must be critically assessed to ensure that they do not unintentionally undermine the collective ethos that distinguish DAOs from traditional corporate hierarchies [17, 36]. Achieving this balance is vital for the long-term legitimacy and resilience of decentralized ecosystems, ensuring that DAOs fulfill their promise as dynamic, transparent, and participatory governance structures rather than replicating the systemic inequalities of traditional institutions [27].

5.1 Limitations

While SCT highlights the crucial role of trust, reciprocity, and social networks in sustaining DAO governance, its explanatory scope remains incomplete when confronted with persistent governance asymmetries, regulatory unpredictability, and the dominance of economic self-interest over community-driven decision-making. SCT, which originates in the context of comparatively stable social structures, does not fully address the implications of the pseudonymity, vote delegation, and liquidity-driven governance structures that define many DAOs. Moreover, unclear regulations regarding liability or token classification can attenuate linking social capital, since participants often hesitate to engage with a system they perceive as legally precarious. The Lido DAO case and broader concerns over token classification as securities have underscored how regulatory anxieties deter participation, especially among risk-averse investors and nontechnical contributors. Many DAOs claim to be decentralized, but in practice, function under de facto oligarchies because of token concentration, a factor that SCT does not fully theorize. These factors suggest that purely relational theories are insufficient to understand DAOs. For instance, PGT highlights how DAOs systematically underfund shared infrastructure, whereas PAT reveals how governance incentives tend to favor large stakeholders at the expense of broader community interests. They also cannot, on their own, diagnose or measure latent power asymmetries when decision-making shifts from public, on-chain discussions to private negotiations among influential token holders. Future research, especially qualitative in nature, should investigate how trust, responsibility, and accountability are negotiated informally through discourse, reputation, and consensus norms across the manifold spaces in which DAO governance unfolds. Nevertheless, the empirical measurement of these informal dynamics remains challenging. On-chain metrics provide visibility into governance participation, proposal outcomes, and token distributions, yet they fail to capture strategic abstentions, backchannel negotiations, or the role of dominant narratives in shaping decision-making.

6 Conclusion

This study highlights how SCT explains how trust, reciprocity, and social ties shape DAO governance; it alone cannot address the financialization, regulatory challenges, and power asymmetries inherent in these ecosystems. The integration of PGT and PAT reveals why free-rider problems persist, why treasury allocations often prioritize short-term incentives over long-term resilience, and how large token holders distort participatory decision-making. The findings emphasize that purely relational trust is insufficient when token holdings dictate governance influence and algorithmic mechanisms replace human discretion. Without well-designed incentives and regulatory clarity, DAOs risk entrenching power imbalances rather than enabling decentralized, community-driven governance. To preserve their participatory ethos, DAOs must rethink governance models, rebalance incentive structures, and adopt hybrid mechanisms that balance decentralization with accountability. Future research should empirically assess governance innovations, such as reputation-based voting, hybrid deliberation models, and liability-sensitive legal structures. As DAOs evolve, understanding how trust, power, and incentives interact across different governance models is crucial for their long-term legitimacy and resilience.

References

1. Bellavitis, C., Fisch, C., Momtaz, P.: The rise of decentralized autonomous organizations (DAOs): a first empirical glimpse. Ventur. Cap. **25**, 187–203 (2022). https://doi.org/10.1080/13691066.2022.2116797
2. Alexopoulos, C., Ferro, E., Lampoltshammer, T.J.: Editorial: blockchain and tokenomics for sustainable development. Front. Blockchain **8**, 1567925 (2025). https://doi.org/10.3389/fbloc.2025.1567925
3. Sharma, T., Kwon, Y., Pongmala, K., Wang, H., Miller, A., Song, D., Wang, Y.: Unpacking how decentralized autonomous organizations (DAOs) work in practice. 2024 IEEE International Conference on Blockchain and Cryptocurrency, 416–424. https://doi.org/10.1109/ICBC59979.2024.10634404 (2023)
4. Axelsen, H., Jensen, J.R., Ross, O.: When is a DAO decentralized? Complex Syst. Inf. Model. Q. **31**, 51–75 (2022). https://doi.org/10.7250/csimq.2022-31.04
5. Lustenberger, M., Spychiger, F., Küng, L., Bassi, E., Wollenschläger, S.: DAO research trends: reflections and learnings from the first European DAO workshop (DAWO). SSRN. https://ssrn.com/abstract=4944742 or https://doi.org/10.2139/ssrn.4944742 (2024)
6. United States District Court, Northern District of California. Andrew Samuels v. Lido DAO et al. Case No. 23-cv-06492-VC (2024)
7. Black, K.H.: Investing in Cryptocurrencies and Digital Assets: A Guide to Understanding Technologies, Business Models, Due Diligence, and Valuation. Wiley, Hoboken (2024)
8. Han, J., Lee, J., Li, T.: DAO governance. SSRN https://ssrn.com/abstract=4346581(2023)
9. Nabben, K.: Governance by algorithms, governance of algorithms: human-machine politics in decentralized autonomous organisations (DAOs). pIJ **8**(1) (2023)
10. Kitzler, S., Balietti, S., Saggese, P., Haslhofer, B., Strohmaier, M.: The governance of decentralized autonomous organizations: a study of contributors' influence, networks, and shifts in voting power. arXiv:2309.14232v2 (2023)
11. Ding, Q., Xu, W., Wang, Z., Lee Kuo Chuen, D.: Voting schemes in DAO governance. SSRN https://ssrn.com/abstract=4442470 (2023)
12. Jungnickel, M., Sönmez, F.Ö., Mulligan, C., Knottenbelt, W.J.: DAO governance: Voting power, participation, and controversy—a review and an empirical analysis. SSRN https://ssrn.com/abstract=5008958 (2024)
13. Fritsch, R., Müller, M., Wattenhofer, R.: Analyzing voting power in decentralized governance: who controls DAOs? Block. Res. Appl. **5**, 100208. https://doi.org/10.1016/j.bcra.2024.100208 (2024)
14. Adler, P., Kwon, S.: Social capital: Prospects for a new concept. Acad. Manage. Rev. **27**, 17–40 (2002). https://doi.org/10.5465/AMR.2002.5922314

15. Bourdieu, P.: Outline of a Theory of Practice. The New Social Theory Reader. Routledge, Abingdon (2020)
16. Coleman, J.S.: Social capital in the creation of human capital. Am. J. Sociol. **94**, S95–S120 (1988)
17. Putnam, R.D.: Bowling Alone: The Collapse and Revival of American Community. Simon & Schuster, New York (2000)
18. Ross, S.: The economic theory of agency: the principal's problem. The American Econ. Rev. **63**, 134–139 (1973)
19. Samuelson, P.A.: The pure theory of public expenditure. In: Public Goods and Market Failures, pp. 29–33. Routledge, London (2024)
20. Chohan, U.: Decentralized autonomous organizations (DAOs): their present & future. SSRN https://ssrn.com/abstract=3082055(2024)
21. Perestrelo de Oliveira, M., Rolo, A.G.: Decentralized autonomous organisation (DAO) regulation: Principles and perspectives for the future. OAPEN Library (2024)
22. Williamson, O.E.: Transaction cost economics. Handbook Ind. Organ. **1**, 135–182 (1989)
23. Powell, W.W., DiMaggio, P.J.: The New Institutionalism in Organizational Analysis. University of Chicago Press, Chicago (2012)
24. Cilliers, P.: Complexity and Postmodernism: Understanding Complex Systems. Routledge, London (2002)
25. Latour, B.: Reassembling the Social: An Introduction to Actor-Network-Theory. Oxford University Press, Oxford (2007)
26. Zatti, F.: The DAO between the nation state and the network state. SSRN. https://ssrn.com/abstract=4933647 or https://doi.org/10.2139/ssrn.4933647 (2024)
27. Rikken, O., Janssen, M., Kwee, Z.: Governance challenges of blockchain and decentralized autonomous organizations. Inf. Polity **24**(4), 357–373 (2019)
28. Schneider, B., Ballesteros, R., Moriggl, P., Asprion, P.: Decentralized autonomous organizations—Evolution, challenges, and opportunities. In Bork, D., Barat, S., Asprion, P., Marcelletti, A., Morichetta, A., Schneider, B., Kulkarni, V., Breu, R., Zech, P. (eds.), *Proceedings of the PoEM 2022 Workshops and Models at Work*. https://doi.org/10.26041/fhnw-7346 (2022)
29. Shenk, M., Weinberger, J.: Legal uncertainty and DAOs in the digital economy. In: Decentralized Autonomous Organizations, pp. 123–138. Routledge, London (2024)
30. Bodellini, M., Dalvinder, S.: Decentralized autonomous organizations: looking for a suitable regulatory treatment. Open Review of Management, Banking & Finance. https://openreviewmbf.org/2021/04/05/decentralised-autonomous-organizations-looking-for-a-suitable-regulatory-treatment/ (2021)
31. Blaszczyk, M.: Decentralized autonomous organizations and regulatory competition: a race without a cause. 99 N.D. L. Rev. 107. Available at SSRN: https://ssrn.com/abstract=4509636(2024)
32. Monaco, V.L., Momtaz, P., Vismara, S.: Distributed governance and value creation in decentralized autonomous organizations: evidence from a regression discontinuity design. Econ. Lett. 112233 (2025)
33. Guo, D., Kwon, H.E., Huang, N., Hong, Y.: How does shielded (vs. open) voting shape collective actions? evidence from decentralized autonomous organizations. SSRN https://ssrn.com/abstract=4982940 or https://doi.org/10.2139/ssrn.4982940 (2024)
34. Peña-Calvin, A., Arroyo, J., Schwartz, A.: Concentration of power and participation in online governance: The ecosystem of decentralized autonomous organizations. ACM. https://doi.org/10.1145/3589335.3651481 (2024)
35. Han, J., Lee, J., Li, T.: A review of DAO governance: recent literature and emerging trends. In European Corporate Governance Institute—Finance Working, 1044/2025, Available at SSRN: https://ssrn.com/abstract=5074046 or http://doi.org/10.2139/ssrn.5074046 (3, November 2024)

36. Spychiger, F., Lustenberger, M., Küng, L.: Decision-making in decentralized autonomous organizations (DAOs). In Handbook of blockchain technology, pp. 142–163. Edward Elgar Publishing (2025)

Regulation of Financial Protocol DAOs: Addressing the Problems of Decentralization and AI Governance

Salvatore Luciano Furnari and Chiara Villani

Abstract This article examines the legal challenges of regulating Decentralized Autonomous Organizations (DAOs) within financial markets, particularly those offering decentralized financial (DeFi) services. After classifying DAO in Social DAO, Investment DAO and Protocol DAO, it discusses the ambiguous legal status of DAOs, their decentralized and autonomous governance structure, and the obstacles these pose to traditional regulatory frameworks. DAOs are typically governed by smart contracts and operate on blockchain, complicating regulatory enforcement due to their decentralized, non-hierarchical structure. Additionally, the integration of artificial intelligence (AI) in DAOs introduces further complexities regarding accountability and liability, as AI lacks legal personhood. The paper reports innovative regulatory approaches, including "embedded supervision", which integrates monitoring mechanisms within DAO operations, and "polycentric co-regulation", which involves collaborative regulatory input from industry stakeholders. Ultimately, it suggests that Protocol DAOs might be more suitably considered as "infrastructural assets" rather than traditional business entities, encouraging voluntary compliance and adapting standards to their unique, decentralized nature.

Keywords Financial protocol DAO · Decentralization · Artificial intelligence

---

S. L. Furnari (✉) · C. Villani
Università Degli Studi Di Roma "Tor Vergata", Rome, Italy
e-mail: salvatore.furnari@leplex.it

C. Villani
e-mail: chiara.villani.tv@alumni.uniroma2.eu

M. Lustenberger et al. (eds.), *Decentralized Autonomous Organizations—Governance, Technology, and Legal Perspectives*, Springer Proceedings in Business and Economics,
https://doi.org/10.1007/978-3-032-03273-7_7

1 DAOs and Their "Unclear" Legal Status[1]

According to Wikipedia "[a] *decentralized autonomous organization (DAO), sometimes called a decentralized autonomous corporation (DAC), is an organization managed in whole or in part by decentralized computer program, with voting and finances handled through a blockchain. In general terms, DAOs are member-owned communities without centralized leadership. The precise legal status of this type of business organization is unclear*" [1].

The most significant aspect of this citation is not the attempts to provide a definition but rather the final statement, which notes that "*The precise legal status of this type of business organization is unclear*" [2]. An analysis of the revision history of this Wikipedia page reveals that, while the page was created in 2014, this statement was added in 2016. This means that, from 2016, the ambiguous legal status of this phenomenon has been highlighted on the internet's most popular encyclopedia—and it remains unchanged to this day.

In order to contribute to the mission of providing a legal status for DAO, this article in paragraph 2 offers definition and classification of DAO, examines the absence of a clear legal status, emphasizing the regulatory difficulties arising from their decentralized management and blockchain-based operations. It also highlights DAO role in financial markets through "financial" protocols (decentralized exchanges, lending protocol and yield aggregator) that operate without being traditional intermediaries. In paragraph 3, the article analyzes how the decentralized and global nature of DAOs complicates regulatory oversight and enforcement. Additionally, it explores how the integration of AI within DAOs, lacking legal accountability, challenges regulatory frameworks traditionally reliant on human oversight. Paragraph 4 discusses innovative regulatory approaches tailored to the unique characteristics of DAOs, considering their decentralized structure and the role of AI components. Paragraph 5 concludes by advocating for a shift in perspective: considering (correctly) DAOs as infrastructure rather than enterprises could be a solution to find a way to regulate these entities (*rectius* "*res*"), adopting a model based on voluntary compliance.

2 Financial Markets DAOs

2.1 Breaking the Term to Get a Definition

Beginning with definitions, a useful approach to defining a DAO is to break down the acronym into its components, focusing on the concepts of "*Decentralized Organization*" (DO) and "*Autonomous*" (A) [3].

[1] While the article reflects a joint collaboration, authorship of Par. 2, 3.1 and 5 is attributed to Salvatore Luciano Furnari, Par. 1 and 3.2 to Chiara Villani and Par. 4 to both Authors.

The middle term of DAO, "*Autonomous*" comes from "*Autonomous Agent*" [4], which in the IT sector refers to "entities" whose existence depends on humans only in their creation. Indeed, once created, their operation is indifferent to the action or will of their programmers.

A common example of autonomous agents are computer viruses, which can replicate on its own, from computer to another without any form of intervention by its creator. Like viruses, the simplest autonomous agent is bound to limited purposes; once achieved, emphatically, they die (or, rather, stop working).

Creating fully autonomous agents requires highly complex artificial intelligence systems, capable of surviving any changes in their computing environment.[2] This is far from being something to be seen in a distant future. As AI complexity advanced in recent years, it has been seen a transition from machine learning, which relies on binary code and statistical processing, to deep learning, where reprocessing capabilities and response complexity both increases. This progression leads to self-learning and self-modifying processes, driving those autonomous agents toward greater autonomy. These characteristics mark the most advanced AI systems, known as "strong" [5] systems, which can operate independently of initial inputs from creators, programmers, or users [6]. These systems make autonomous decisions, often labeled "*black box*" because the processes behind these decisions are not transparent [7]. In contrast, primordial AI systems, so-called "weak" systems, are limited to problem solving on the basis of human instructions, realizing an intelligence that is simulated but not capable of autonomous thinking. The core characteristic of autonomous agents, as relevant here, is their autonomy in performing tasks without human interference.[3]

The outer terms of DAO refer to "*Decentralized Organization*", that can be defined as a non-hierarchical organization, for the lack of a "central body" that direct its operations. To compensate for the lack of hierarchical control, "actions" within these organizations are governed by *ex ante* established rules shared by participants or incentivized through reward mechanisms. With modern technology, these rules and rewards can be entrusted to computer systems (also "*smart contracts*") that impartially guide members toward shared objectives.

The concept of a decentralized organization, or the decentralization of traditional organizations, poses theoretical challenges since hierarchy and centralization are

[2] Consider, for example, an Autonomous Agent programmed to run on the Ethereum blockchain. At the extreme, to be considered completely independent, the Autonomous Agent would have to have the ability to migrate to a different blockchain should the Ethereum network "shut down" for any reason.

[3] For greater understanding, it is useful to quote an example from Buterin [4]. According to the author, an Autonomous Agent performing an entrepreneurial activity could be a data storage Web service, which is programmed not only to store information received from users, but also to employ the revenues from the sale of its storage services to acquire new space on which to store more and more data, doing so as the demand for the service offered increases. In this example, the Autonomous Agent is not a mere executor of orders to achieve a specific and defined purpose (e.g., storing a precise number of data), but adapts the goal it has been given (providing the data storage service) based on the demand and availability of its surrounding environment in order to continue to perform its function in complete autonomy and for as long as possible.

deeply embedded in human organizations [8]. Typically, modern organizations function in pyramid structures, where contributions from lower-level members support those of higher levels, ultimately benefiting those at the top who, accumulating the "utility" provided by the other, then redistribute wealth downward. In contrast, decentralized organizations allow each participant to selfishly achieve the "ultimate utility" rather than contributing to a central hierarchy.[4] Benkler [9] through reward mechanisms, members achieve personal utility, and in striving to attain it, they may incidentally create a utility for another subject within the organization who pursue different, non-competitive objectives.[5]

Decisions affecting the organization are made on a widespread basis, with implementation usually requiring majority approval among voters. The ability to initiate a vote generally belongs to all token holders.

A DAO can be simply defined as a decentralized organization managed by an autonomous agent.[6] In other words, it is an organization composed of people and assets, structured without a central authority and managed autonomously (i.e., by a software that operates independently of both participants and programmers) from the individuals who participate in it[7] [10].

[4] DAOs find their roots in the concept of commons-based peer production, a model initially developed by Benkler [9]. Benkler's [9] model describes a system in which individuals work collectively on projects without traditional hierarchy or centralized control. This form of collaborative production enables self-organizing individuals to participate in various projects, as seen in examples like open-source software (e.g., Linux) and community-led platforms (e.g., Wikipedia). In these settings, control is decentralized, and resources are shared among participants without ownership by a central authority, emphasizing community governance and shared contributions. DAOs expand upon Benkler's [9] model by integrating blockchain technology and smart contracts, which provide an additional layer of automation and transparency to decision-making processes. Through blockchain, DAOs enable members to vote and govern collectively, and smart contracts automate key functions, eliminating the need for a central authority altogether.

[5] An example of this is the operation of Bitcoin's blockchain. Considering, for simplicity, two types of participants—the miner and the trader—the former supports the organization by earning bitcoin through mining, while the latter benefits from this activity by trading bitcoin with others. This system is governed by strict protocols within the Bitcoin network, which denies expected utility (e.g., bitcoin rewards or transaction validation) to participants who fail to adhere to the behavioral rules necessary for the organization's proper functioning. According to Buterin [4], Bitcoin's could even be considered on a par with a DAO and not just as a simple decentralized organization.

[6] This is from the words of Buterin [4], according to whom a DAO is "an entity that lives on the internet and exists autonomously, but also heavily relies on hiring individuals to perform certain tasks that the automaton itself cannot do".

[7] The concept of DAOs is not, as one would guess, exclusive to the business world. DAOs, while assuming (as an "organization") the possibility of owning or managing assets, does not have among its "ideological" assumptions the production or distribution of profits. For the purpose of distinguishing DAOs with a properly entrepreneurial vocation from others, the different acronym DAC or "Decentralized Autonomous Corporation" has also been coined.

2.2 Types of DAOs

Although DAO concept dates to 2013 [11], efforts to classify this phenomenon have emerged only recently.

The most important classification is the one based on their function. DAOs can be, indeed, classified into at least three categories: (i) Grant or Social DAO; (ii) Protocol DAO; (iii) Investment DAO [12].

Grant or Social DAOs focus essentially on philanthropic purposes and their goal is to distribute the monies raised when the DAO is established to projects selected by the DAO participants. Examples of grant or social DAOs include MolochDAO, [13] GitCoin DAO [14], Big Green DAO [15]; these projects collect and distribute resources to worthy projects, usually selected by the entire community of token holders.

Protocol DAOs are DAOs that primarily aim to "manage" a decentralized protocol. Examples include projects like Uniswap [16], MakerDAO [17], ICP [18] o Yearn [19] projects.

Uniswap, for instance, in its original version, is one the best example to understand protocol DAOs. Uniswap operates as a so-called "*decentralized exchanges*" (DEX) using a so-called "*automated market maker*" (AMM) model, where users deposit crypto-asset pairs of equal value into so-called "*pools*" managed by smart contracts. These "*liquidity pair*" enable exchanges between assets in each pair without needing to identify, directly, a specific counterparty. In fact, when an exchange order is sent, the smart contract holds the originator's crypto-asset and returns an equivalent value of the crypto-asset requested and present in the liquidity pair. The exchange is based on a mathematical formula embedded in the algorithm implemented in the smart contract; the most popular AMMs employ a formula that ensures that the product of the values in each liquidity pair remains constant before and after each transaction[8] [20]. Users who deposit crypto assets into "*liquidity pools*" participate in the distribution of "*fees*" generated by each exchange in proportion to what they deposit.[9]

The Investment DAO category includes DAOs whose purpose is to raise funds to invest in entrepreneurial projects with the aim of dividing the profits for the benefit of the participants in the DAO itself. Within the latter category falls the first project to have claimed to "take on" the form of a DAO: it dates back to 2016 and is known as the DAO.[10] The DAO is one of the most cited projects in the blockchain community,[11]

---

[8] For this reason they are also referred to as "Constant Product Market Maker". Variations to this formula involve, for example, the sum of value being constant; others involve "hybrid" or "dynamic" formulas. The reference is to the systems known as Constant Mean Market Maker (CMMM), Constant Sum Market Maker (CSMM), Hybrid Function Market Maker (HFMM) and Dynamic Automate Market Maker (DAMM).

[9] This trading fee is usually between 0.30% and 0.10% of the value of the exchange.

[10] The notoriety of this project may have been caused by the 2017 report of the Security Exchange Commission that, for the first time, sanctioned the applicability to Initial Coin Offerings of the regulations on public offerings of financial instruments.

[11] The project saw the light of day in 2016 with the publication on the GitHub site (a development platform frequently employed by computer programmers to make their creations public and receive

often regarded as a landmark crowdfunding experiment due to the significant funds raised in a short period. However, the project was abandoned, both because of a hacker attack,[12] and in relation to a report by the Security Exchange Commission, which acknowledged the nature of "*security*" to the DAO tokens offered to the public.[13]

2.3 DAO Applications in Financial Markets

DAOs have established a transformative role in the financial sector, particularly *Protocols DAO*, enabling and governing decentralized finance (DeFi) [21] protocols, but also in the still slightly less common form of *Investment DAO*. In their first form, DAOs are commonly deployed to manage and operate protocols that offers services that (in a non-juridical way) can be defined as financial services [21].[14] The most common example are decentralized exchanges (DEXs) such as the above-mentioned Uniswap, which facilitates peer-to-peer trading of digital assets without the need for

---

feedback from the community) of the source code of the smart contracts underlying its operation. On April 30, 2016, these smart contracts were executed on the Ethereum blockchain, and within 15 days the project managed to raise nearly $100 million. Within a month of its publication, some users had identified the existence of some computer errors in the source code on which the operation of the DAO was based. A few days later, before the token holders had time to "vote" on correcting the mentioned errors, a hacker attack, exploiting them, managed to steal about a third of the collected resources. the DAO's protocol, however, stipulated that in order for sums to be withdrawn from the project, it would be necessary to wait 28 days. In order to avoid the subtraction of at least a third of the entire amount collected, the entire Ethereum community was asked to vote on one of the first "forks" of a DLT network in the history of these technologies. Since a DLT network is unchangeable, the only way to avoid sum subtraction was to have all the network's supporters (the so-called "nodes") resume storing information from the version of the registry prior to the subtraction of resources. Some of the nodes that supported the Ethereum blockchain did not agree to "rewind the tape", continuing to record new transactions as if nothing had happened. Most of the miners that supported the blockchain voted to resume recording information from the transaction that preceded the hacker attack. This made it possible to "return" resources to their rightful owners and prevent their theft. From this diversity of behavior, the fork was generated that led to the birth of the Ethereum Classic blockchain (alongside the Ethereum blockchain), which continues to be supported by nodes opposed to the fork.

[12] The attack would appear to have been facilitated by the need to call a vote among all Ethereum token holders to correct a computer error found within a smart contract of the DAO. The execution of a smart contract, in fact, implies that it is no longer modifiable without the consent of a majority of the computing power supporting the underlying DLT network. Thus, the programmers of the the DAO project were forced to call an actual vote even to correct a blatant programming error. This procedure, needing time to be concluded, has meanwhile allowed malicious parties to exploit the same computer errors that should have been corrected, resulting in the near-subtraction of part of the monies collected.

[13] The DAO project aimed to raise capital to be conveyed within entrepreneurial projects based on DLT technology. Specifically, token holders had the power to choose which project the sums raised should be invested in and would receive profits commensurate with the success of the entrepreneurial project in which they invested.

[14] Here the term "financial" is used in its economic meaning and not in its legal one. The reason is that from a legal purpose it is very difficult to classify a protocol as a financial intermediary.

centralized intermediaries. Through DEXs, users can trade tokens directly via smart contracts that execute trades automatically, with liquidity pools managed and funded by individual participants instead of traditional market makers.

Additional example of "financial" protocols are the *lending protocols*, such as Aave [22] or Venus [23], which offer services that are very similar to the one offered by banks, or *yield aggregator protocols* such as Yearn [19], which offer services similar to investment companies, considering their ability to distribute (and so invest) the crypto-asset provided within the protocols offering better returns, giving back crypto-assets to the users with an increase in their amount.

Financial Protocol DAOs export the role of decentralized governance in financial markets. Unlike traditional financial institutions, where corporate boards or regulatory bodies dictate policy, these particular kinds of DAO allow protocol stakeholders—typically token holders—to vote on key decisions [24]. This community-based governance model enables participants to influence aspects like protocol upgrades and fee structures, thus decentralizing control and empowering users [25]. Additionally, DAOs serve as a mechanism for transparency and accountability [2]; by voting on proposed changes and maintaining an open record of decisions, DAOs promote a level of trust and reliability rarely seen in traditional financial institutions.

But one of the most important characteristics of the use of Protocol DAOs in financial markets is their distributed way of functioning that do not just rely in the absence of a central body under which (as it has been said) a fake scheme is created just to avoid regulation [26].[15] DeFi innovation reside in their impossibility to function without a collaborative participation transcending a sort of "mutualistic symbiosis" relation.[16] In DEXs, for instance, liquidity providers earn rewards proportionate to the volume of transactions in their respective pools, creating an incentive for users to supply liquidity and support the protocol's stability. This decentralized, automated approach to liquidity provision would be impractical in traditional finance, where market-making relies on centralized entities and where liquidity supply functions could not be directly offered by investors. By distributing financial markets "tasks" to all possible stakeholders of a financial markets (together with financial incentives that are no more "absorbed" by few big financial intermediaries) among a broad participant base, Financial Protocol DAOs not only enable a scalable and resilient financial ecosystem that adapts organically to market needs [2], but also favor the distribution of wealth within all the stakeholder of a financial markets.

---

[15] This has been argued by [27] and [28], where the authors argue that the notion of decentralization, often portrayed as a core feature of DeFi protocols, is largely illusory. They observe that, while many DeFi projects are marketed as decentralized, significant control over these protocols frequently resides with certain key actors, particularly the developers who design and manage the code. These individuals not only retain the power to modify the protocol but, in some cases, can even disable its functionality. As such, the authors suggest that "decentralization" is more of a strategic tool to avoid regulatory costs than a fundamental aspect of the technology.

[16] In this sense, the function of DeFi protocols can be likened to the framework of mutualistic symbiosis—a form of biological interaction between two organisms of different species, where both parties gain benefits from the relationship. Unlike parasitism, in mutualism, both symbionts contribute positively to each other's welfare, creating a partnership that supports the survival and reproduction of both parties. For the cited notions of biology, please refer to Rózsa and Garay [29].

3 Regulation Obstacles

3.1 A Decentralized Structure...

While DAOs empower participants and reduce entry barriers to "financial" services,[17] they also necessitate a re-evaluation of regulatory frameworks to accommodate their decentralized and autonomous structures within the financial sector.

From a "macro" perspective, governments are limited to exerting only weak controls over DAOs. The intrinsic design of DAOs, which are built and operate on blockchain networks, restricts traditional regulatory powers. Unlike centralized entities that rely on a physical or digital presence easily targeted by enforcement actions, DAOs exist in a decentralized environment where the *locus* of control is dispersed across anonymous, global participants. Since DAOs are hosted on public blockchains, their code and data are not bound to a single geographic location or entity, making enforcement challenging. Authorities cannot simply "shut down" a DAO in the conventional sense, as there is no centralized server or organizational headquarters to target.

The most immediate recourse for governments is to restrict access to the DAO's web interface, often through blocking its associated website domain. However, this measure remains superficial and largely ineffective due to technological workarounds; users can circumvent such restrictions with a simple VPN, masking their location and accessing the DAO interface regardless of imposed bans. Additionally, since DAOs can interact directly with users via blockchain addresses and digital wallets, blocking a website domain has a limited impact on core functionalities. Furthermore, DAOs often have open-source front-ends that can be replicated or "mirrored" across multiple domains, making it nearly impossible to prevent access entirely.

The limited jurisdictional reach of any single government over DAOs highlights an unprecedented regulatory challenge. Traditional enforcement mechanisms fail to account for the unique resilience and fluidity of blockchain-based entities, which can adapt or migrate in response to enforcement actions. This leads to questions of whether alternative regulatory frameworks are needed. In sum, the decentralized architecture of DAOs raises significant barriers to conventional regulatory efforts, calling for innovative regulatory approaches to address these digital and boundaryless entities.

[17] In truth, Atzori [30] critically scrutinizes this profile and posits that Blockchain-based governance is frequently praised for its egalitarian potential, but it often concentrates power among a few key actors—such as developers, miners, and tech entrepreneurs—who influence decision-making within platforms like Bitcoin and Ethereum. This concentration of power raises concerns about transparency and democratic legitimacy, as decision-making tends to fall into the hands of a small elite, challenging the ideal of decentralized, egalitarian control.

3.2 … and an AI Governance

Artificial intelligence (AI) systems, while often integrated into DAO operations for automation and decision-making support, lack the legal capacity to act as agents in the formal and legal sense, meaning they cannot enter into contracts or be held accountable in the way human managers or corporate officers can. Legally, an AI cannot assume the role of a "director", "manager", or "entrepreneur" of a DAO, as these positions require an entity capable of bearing rights and obligations [31, 32]

The most famous active DAOs, such as the Bitcoin protocol infrastructure (considered by some [33] one of the first DAOs to be implemented) and other decentralized finance DAOs like Uniswap or MakerDAO, don't always rely on formal structures. The famous the DAO project itself lacked a formal structure for external representation, operating instead as a mere "IT entity"; its interaction with the external world occurred through DAO.LINK, an entity under Swiss law [34], and a series of agents called "*contractors*", [35] who helped channel funds to selected projects.[18]

At present, no legal system recognizes the personhood of algorithms, nor does this path appear likely to be pursued in the future.

A related issue specific to DAOs is identifying the entity to be sued in the event of damages caused by such decentralized entities: the lack of a centralized legal entity complicates the identification of a responsible party.

In jurisdictions requiring identifiable and accountable leadership for corporate entities, the responsibility gap presents a challenge. Unlike human directors or managers, who can be scrutinized, sanctioned, or held liable, an AI remains outside the reach of traditional corporate governance laws. Without a legal person to hold accountable, regulators face challenges in enforcing compliance standards or penalizing misconduct within DAOs, raising questions about how existing corporate governance frameworks must evolve to address the unique nature of AI governance within DAOs.

The "problem" is so serious that the idea of giving legal personality to artificial agents to establish a center of responsibility for their acts had been considered at the European Level.[19]

However, this stance was soon abandoned by both the legal scholarship and the EU institutions themselves, recognizing numerous obstacles to framing AI in terms

[18] The creation of an entity that merely "assists" the DAO, enabling it to enter into legally binding contracts with the outside world (as opposed to the IT world in which the DAO finds itself), without properly representing its organizational structure, is quite common. Further example can be found in the Aragon DAO [36], a project aimed at developing tools to create other DAOs running on the Ethereum network, which uses the Aragon Association as its "manager" ("*stewardship*").

[19] The European Parliament's Resolution of 16 February 2017, containing Recommendations to the Commission on civil law rules on robotics (2015/2103(INL)), proposed, in paragraph 59(f) to «*creat(e) a specific legal status for robots in the long run, so that at least the most sophisticated autonomous robots could be established as having the status of electronic persons responsible for making good any damage they may cause, and possibly applying electronic personality to cases where robots make autonomous decisions or otherwise interact with third parties independently.*»

of legal personhood.[20] In particular, if a criminal penalty is imposed, there remains the issue that artificial agents cannot fulfill the rehabilitative, general-preventive, or special-preventive functions of a sanction [37].

Similarly, the High-Level Expert Group on Artificial Intelligence (AI HLEG), established by the European Commission in June 2018, in its Report on Liability for Artificial Intelligence and other emerging digital technologies, after determining that «*there is currently no need to give a legal personality to emerging digital technologies*», stated that: «*[h]arm caused by even fully autonomous technologies is generally reducible to risks attributable to natural persons or existing categories of legal persons, and where this is not the case, new laws directed at individuals are a better response than creating a new category of legal person*» [38]. This issue becomes doubly problematic in the context of DAOs, as there is both a general difficulty in determining to which title responsibility for the actions committed by the AI should be attributed and the challenge of identifying any entity upon whom such responsibility might rest: in DAOs, indeed, there is typically no designated, legally accountable individual, and participants are often anonymous or dispersed across multiple global jurisdictions. Therefore, in the context of DAOs, the frequently advocated approach of enhancing human involvement in AI decision-making processes—known as "*human-in-the-loop*"—is impractical.

In particular, this concept belongs to the EU's human-centric AI paradigm, which aims to align AI functionality with human objectives[21]: it centers on the notion of trustworthiness, defined by the requirement that intelligent systems must adhere to certain standards to ensure respect for fundamental rights, as well as human freedom and autonomy in interactions with these systems [39]. Human-centric AI has been operationalized through the human-in-the-loop framework, which assigns specific roles and consequent responsibilities to humans in AI-driven processes to address issues related to accountability attribution.

---

[20] At present, not even U.S. laws recognize legal personhood for artificial intelligence. Some recent proposals and discussions have begun to explore the legal responsibilities of advanced AI and algorithms without conferring them the same legal status as natural or legal persons. Reference is made to Algorithmic Accountability Act of 2022, H.R. 6580, 117th Cong. (2022): it aims to hold companies accountable for the societal impacts of their algorithms, focusing on organizational and developer responsibility rather than AI as an independent entity; and Federal Trade Commission, Aiming for Truth, Fairness, and Equity in Your Company's Use of AI (April 2021): those are guidelines emphasizing the ethical and responsible use of AI, highlighting corporate and individual accountability in AI development. This framework reinforces human and organizational responsibility, implicitly dismissing AI's independent legal status.

[21] Recall Art. 3 of the 2021 Proposal for a Regulation of the European Parliament and of the Council laying down harmonized rules on artificial intelligence, which defined the intelligent system as: "*software that is developed with one or more of the techniques and approaches listed in Annex I and can, for a given set of human-defined objectives, generate outputs such as content, predictions, recommendations, or decisions influencing the environments they interact with*" The definition was taken verbatim from the 2019 OECD Recommendation on AI and, earlier, from the 2018 Commission Communication Artificial Intelligence for Europe. It is noteworthy that this nuance has been lost in the final version of the AI act (Regulation (EU) 2024/1689 of the European Parliament and of the Council of June 13, 2024 laying down harmonized rules on artificial intelligence).

This perspective is not only unsuitable for the aforementioned practical reasons but is also conceptually incompatible with DAOs. The fundamental rationale underpinning DAOs is their design to minimize human intervention, thereby enhancing decentralized governance and autonomy within the system. Imposing a human-in-the-loop framework on DAOs would counteract their core purpose, as DAOs are specifically structured to operate independently of continuous human oversight, relying instead on automated decision-making mechanisms. Consequently, requiring human oversight within DAOs would fundamentally conflict with their intended autonomous operational model and could undermine their functionality and efficiency.

Even regressing back to the time of creation of the DAO in which the AI system is embedded, the imputation of liability to producers or programmers is also problematic: the autonomy of strong AI systems complicates the identification of a causal link between the human subject's inputs and the output produced by the algorithm, due to the opacity of the AI's decision-making process.[22] This increases the risk of creating a sphere of irresponsibility, a phenomenon known as the "*responsibility gap*" [41].

Not even the provisions of the 2022 Artificial Intelligence Liability Directive (AILD)[23] Consulich et al. [42] succeed in resolving some of the most critical issues related to civil liability for damages caused by artificial intelligence systems, particularly due to the ever-growing degree of autonomy and independence of such systems from human users, which gives rise to the well-known *black box* problem.

In fact, although it provides for a relative presumption of causation in cases of fault between the failure to comply with a duty of care and the production or non-production of an output from the AI system that caused the damage,[24] it is still

[22] Actually, someone constructed a liability model based on abstract foreseeability, aligning with the assumption of risk by producers and programmers who have deliberately activated an artificial agent with unpredictable behavior. In this sense Magro [40] asserted the necessity of attributing liability to human actors in any case, maintaining that the lack of predictability and scientific explainability of robotic actions does not absolve the designer from criminal liability for negligence, as, according to the concept of negligence in existing law, abstract foreseeability does not require a detailed or specific prediction of potential harmful outcomes This reconstruction, however, evidently collides with the principle of personal imputation of criminal responsibility: indeed, unlike civil law, which also adopts imputation models of liability on an objective basis, criminal law does not provide similar criteria for objective imputation.

[23] The Artificial Intelligence Liability Directive (AILD) is a European Commission proposal submitted in October 2022 and not yet adopted as binding legislation. This proposal is part of a broader regulatory framework that aims to regulate the safe and responsible use of artificial intelligence technologies within the European Union. In addition to the AILD, this framework also includes the Artificial Intelligence Regulation (AI Act), which entered into force On August 1, 2024. If the AI Regulation focuses on preventing potential harm caused by AI systems, the AI Directive, by contrast, is aimed at harmonizing the liability regime applicable when such systems do cause harm.

[24] Specifically, Article 4(1) of the AI Directive, in light of the difficulty for claimants to demonstrate the causal link between non-compliance with a duty of care and the generation or failure to generate an output from the AI system that caused the damage, provides for a rebuttable presumption of causation in cases of fault; this presumption applies only where the national court deems it excessively difficult for the claimant to fulfill the burden of proof, and the following conditions are met:

incumbent on the injured party to prove the fault of the defendant and the causal link between the damage suffered and the operation of the AI system. This requirement continues to place a significant evidentiary burden on the claimant. Although fault can be established through a breach of duty of care as defined by AI legislation or other EU regulations, the effectiveness of such proof is limited in practice. The specific content of these "duties of care" must ultimately be interpreted by national courts; this carries the risk of interpretive divergence and regulatory fragmentation across the EU, potentially leading to a variety of national approaches that paradoxically undermine the Directive's core objective of harmonization. The same concern applies to the definition of "fault": the Directive does not interfere with national rules in this regard, thus allowing for differing interpretations among Member States. This situation creates additional uncertainty and potential fragmentation, as each state may maintain distinct criteria for determining fault in relation to damages caused by AI systems [43].

Considering all of this, it becomes evident that the primary issue identified with AI is its opacity: as the autonomy of the system increases, there is a growing disconnect between the inputs introduced by the designer, developer, or user, and the outputs produced. Particularly in the case of advanced AI systems, there exists the black box phenomenon, where the logical decision-making path leading to the final output is not traceable and it is complicated the attribution of responsibility.

This concern is echoed in the ESMA 2023 report, which identifies AI as a factor that negatively impacts transparency [44]. In light of this, one proposed solution is to make the decision-making process of AI systems more explainable and less opaque. The ESMA 2023 report provides a definition of the "explainability of artificial intelligence" which, in its narrow sense, refers to a technical and objective understanding of an algorithm's behavior that enables identification of the specific variables and their impact in producing a particular output. In a broad sense, explainability also refers to the comprehensibility of a given AI model for human users. However, ESMA itself acknowledges that this definition is somewhat shallow and lacks broad consensus, leading to uncertainty about the precise meaning of explainability.

Generally, an output is considered explainable if its decision-making process can be linearly traced backward. In contrast, deep neural networks are typically

(a) the claimant has demonstrated, or the court has presumed, the fault of the defendant; (b) it is reasonably probable that the defendant's negligent behavior influenced the generation or failure to generate the AI system's output; (c) the claimant has demonstrated that the damage was caused by the output generated or not generated by the AI system. Additionally, exceptions are provided for systems classified as high risk by the AI Act: the application of the causation presumption is limited under paragraph 2 to cases of non-compliance with certain obligations set out by the AI Regulation, and it does not apply under paragraph 4 if the defendant demonstrates that the claimant had sufficient evidence and expertise available to establish causation. A further exception is provided under paragraph 6 for cases where the AI system was used in the course of a non-professional personal activity: in such cases, the causation presumption applies only if the defendant materially interfered with the conditions of the AI system's operation or if the defendant was under an obligation and was able to determine the conditions of the AI system's operation and failed to do so.

considered to have low explainability due to their highly nested logic, where inputs are combined and transformed at each level, producing outputs that represent entirely new and unpredictable representations. In practice, however, this definition can create ambiguities [44].

4 The Need for a Different Regulatory Approach to Overcome AI and Decentralization Issues

The integration of AI within DAOs introduces an additional layer of complexity to an already intricate set of challenges. This raises a fundamental question: can regulation—or, more broadly, human intervention—effectively address the unique issues arising from the intersection of AI and decentralization?

Starting from the opacity issue, this specific problem could fade out into the specific domain of DAOs, as it operates within a framework characterized by transparency, owing to the features of blockchain technology. Indeed, blockchain provides an immutable record of actions, which is essential for ensuring transparency in DAO operations. In this context, AI can also help improve transparency and regulatory compliance within DAOs by analyzing data recorded on the blockchain and suggesting interventions to maintain adherence to evolving regulations.

This could actually have influence also with reference to the liability problem. In this context, one proposed solution has been to integrate preventive measures within the algorithm's structure, specifically by incorporating a "*deterrence formula*" within the AI system itself [43, 45].[25] This would enforce the certification that the algorithms include mechanisms to inhibit their operation in the event, for instance, of market manipulation risks. This preventive measure, originally proposed by legal scholars in relation to MiFID II[26] and algorithmic trading, in line with its risk-based approach, seems extendable to DAOs. Given the increasing learning capabilities of autonomous algorithms, it is believed that they could soon predict the impact of a specific output, self-restricting their actions in negative circumstances. Such negative conditions could be programmed directly *into-the-code* from the outset or emerge from subsequent learning processes.

[25] Azzutti [45] finds two possible shortcomings encountered in this approach: the first concerns possible technical or legal barriers; the second, assuming there are no technical or legal barriers, concerns the difficulty an autonomous and self-apprehending artificial intelligence would have in adapting to changes in regulations and market dynamics in such a way as to achieve effective deterrence. He believes that this difficulty could only be overcome by moving to more machine-intelligible regulation in terms of objectivity and quantifiability, yet the current European framework is extremely vague and leaves too much room for legal interpretation to be machine learnable. These criticisms have been rejected by other parts of the doctrine: see Annunziata [43], which believes that as far as possible technical or legal barriers are concerned, these have not yet been identified. Instead, for the second objection, it is noted that the European legislation is well specified, with the consequence of being learnable by algorithms.

[26] Directive 2014/65/EU.

This is connected to the idea of using AI to implement automated supervision embedded within DAOs: a concept called "*embedded supervision*" [46]. In this context, AI can monitor actions and transactions within a DAO in real time, reporting suspicious or noncompliant activities directly on the blockchain. This allows for continuous and transparent monitoring of algorithmic intermediaries through the ability to create automated and auditable compliance rules and enables authorities to exercise more effective and timely control than traditional supervisory systems.

Among the examples of the potential application of "*embedded supervision*" [47, 48], one that makes this principle clearer is the one that describes the possibility of verifying compliance with a financial intermediary's capital requirements by monitoring its crypto-wallets in real time [46].

The innovative approach suggested certainly has the advantage of reducing the management and compliance costs of individual intermediaries, while at the same time ensuring better supervision. Activity that, thanks to algorithms, also becomes simpler and more effective for the authorities, who, at the same time, will be able to receive real-time and qualitatively superior information.

However, it is possible to point out that it may be of no use to apply traditional regulation through the concepts of *embedded supervision* to "fully" algorithmic intermediaries. With regard to these, it is already the imposition of "classical" capital requirements that, upstream, loses its meaning. In these cases, the stability of the individual algorithmic intermediary cannot be guaranteed by its capital structure, which is essentially non-existent, but rather by the "stability"[27] of the code it employs. It might, therefore, be useful to espouse the approach of "embedded supervision", but on condition that it focuses on verifying requirements more suited to the management of algorithmic intermediaries' criticalities. These will necessarily be ad hoc requirements (i.e., absence of *bugs* in the computer code used, monitoring aimed at the prevention of attacks by hackers) as they are significantly different from those envisaged by the regulation of "traditional" intermediaries.

The search for new possibilities to innovate the way "decentralized" financial markets are regulated has already seen the emergence of new hypotheses to structure a different regulatory approach for this sector.

Another innovative regulatory approach can be found in what is known as "*polycentric co-regulation*", according to which regulation must be the result of a collaborative approach between authorities, industry players, and other stakeholders. [49] This approach is considered particularly suitable for the regulation of the decentralized finance sector because, given the difficulty of regulating a highly decentralized sector such as this "from above", if regulation also found its source in a decentralized structure, it could gain greater consensus (and thus *compliance*) on the part of the regulated parties [48].

The concept of *co-regulation* has seen an evolution into the different principle known as "participatory regulation" [48] in which market participants collaborate with the regulator from the development stages of the technology, which thus seems to lose its "traditional" characteristic of neutrality [50].

---

[27] Stability in this context must be understood as resistance to cyber-attacks.

In general, therefore, there are several hypotheses on how to renew and innovate today's regulatory approach to decentralized finance. Hypotheses and approaches all share the idea that the rules that should be enacted for algorithmic intermediaries should be significantly different from those currently in place for traditional intermediaries. On the contrary, the approach used today by the European legislator within the regulations already in force does not differ significantly from the ways in which traditional intermediaries are already regulated. The reference is to Regulation (EU) 2023/1114 (so-called MiCAR), which regulates crypto-asset service *providers* (so-called *crypto-asset service providers* or CASPs) by almost completely transposing the regulations envisaged for traditional financial intermediaries [21].

Despite these considerations, two legal issues arising from the absence of legal personality for AI systems within DAOs remain unresolved: the establishment of a responsibility regime and the capacity to enter into contracts.

Specifically, all the above-mentioned approaches do not address the issue of responsibility: assuming the inclusion of a deterrence formula (embed within the code and being the result of a co-regulation process) should it fail, an AI cannot be held legally responsible for its actions, which in a DAO context typically involve autonomous decision-making and operational tasks. This creates a concerning regulatory gap, as there is no legally accountable entity[28] to which claims for damages or violations can be directed. The gravity of the situation is heightened by the fact that DAOs themselves lack a formal structure for external representation: due to this lack, there is no clear, legally responsible entity that can interface with the outside world; when the management is handled by AI, which also lacks legal personality, it doubles the accountability vacuum: there's no legal person to answer for, or represent, the organization in case of disputes or breaches.[29]

[28] In the context of DAOs, it has been suggested that any token holder could be held liable, similar to the structure of a general partnership. However, this is not a general approach for several key reasons: (1) not all DAOs are organized or operate like traditional businesses. Many DAOs lack of the formal structure or activities of a traditional enterprise. In these cases, the application of such liability frameworks is complicated; (2) in many DAOs token holders and participants remain anonymous or operate under pseudonymous identities. In these cases, applying liability rules that assume identifiable individuals, such as those used in general partnerships, becomes practically and legally problematic. (3) DAOs are typically decentralized across multiple jurisdictions. Legal enforcement becomes a significant issue when participants are based in multiple regions with differing laws on liability and corporate governance. If token holders are located in jurisdictions with less stringent regulations on DAOs, or where DAOs are not explicitly recognized by law, holding them liable could be ineffective [8].

[29] As an attempt to regulate the phenomenon, mention should be made of the State of Vermont (USA), which sought to bridge the legal gap between traditional entities and decentralized organizations such as DAOs through an amendment to its LLC (Limited Liability Company) legislation. With this 2020 amendment, the creation of blockchain-based LLCs was permitted, allowing for the use of technology in governance. In this context, LLCs can be programmed to operate through smart contracts, with a voting and management system utilizing blockchain technology, while still maintaining the limited liability protection typical of an LLC. Nonetheless, given that DAOs are global entities, it would be beneficial to develop an international regulatory framework that enables greater interoperability between different jurisdictions and establishes common principles regarding the liability, governance, and transparency of DAOs [51].

Secondly, without legal personality, an AI cannot own assets, enter into contracts, or exercise property rights—essential functions for the operation of DAOs. As a result, DAOs managed by AI must rely on legal workarounds, such as delegating activities to developers or DAO members, which contrasts with the principle of decentralization and increases the risk of manipulation or conflicts of interest, undermining the DAO's core objective of operating without centralized authority.

All the above being true, a solution could be to stop trying to regulate DAOs in a "traditional" manner, namely, by insisting on identifying a "classical" responsible party. Indeed, even if a "scapegoat" were identified through legal means, the outcome would likely remain unsatisfactory.

For instance, if this should be identified with the programmers of the algorithm providing the service, the risk would be that of extending to them a potentially indefinite liability considering the impossibility of guaranteeing that an algorithm is free from computer programming errors and that it will remain so, given its many possible uses, its diverse and unpredictable interactions, and the possible subsequent innovations of the underlying technology. Not to mention the fact that *software* is considered by the sector's legislation as creative works of the intellect and that their "programming" liability could even collide with freedom of expression.

It would be different, however, to reverse the "liability" (and so the related risk) regime on users. Several years of *overprotective* regulation of the investor have had no effect on his growth and preparation.[30] Indeed, there is no legal obstacle to holding accountable a user that deliberately exploits an undiscovered computer error for personal gain at the expense of others. Such actions, driven by intent and resulting harm, fall within the scope of existing liability frameworks, ensuring that malicious exploitation does not evade legal repercussions. This principle underscores the importance of distinguishing between accidental interactions with flawed systems and intentional misuse aimed at deriving unfair advantages. In this context, blockchain technology is particularly well-suited for tracking, with significant advancements being made through the development of increasingly sophisticated blockchain forensic tools.

These considerations could lead to the possibility of giving a different "legal status" to DAO and, in particular, to Protocol DAOs. Indeed, considering DAOs as enterprises, with corresponding governance and accountability implications, it something that suits most Investment DAOs. Such organizations often resemble traditional enterprises, as they involve a collective entrepreneurial effort aimed at generating and distributing revenues. This process is typically preceded by a contribution, often used to acquire tokens that confer both administrative rights and a stake in the organization.

On the other hand, Protocol DAOs are more akin to infrastructures. For example, a protocol like a DEX can be compared to a public "iron bridge". It functions as a neutral platform facilitating interactions among diverse stakeholders and it shall be distinguished from the private entity (usually an enterprise) holding a concession to operate the bridge and that use it as its principal business asset. The DEX itself is

---

[30] Suffice it to say that Italy is still among the countries with the lowest levels of financial literacy [52].

an asset—an infrastructural tool—and should be assessed and qualified from a legal perspective as such.

From this standpoint, attempting to assign legal personality to (certain) DAOs is an unproductive exercise, analogous to trying to attribute legal personality to an inanimate object, like a rock.

In other words, if the combination of AI and blockchain technology results in the creation of mere assets or infrastructures—entities capable of interacting with humans but that are not, themselves, human—the regulatory framework designed for these new *res* will need to adapt accordingly. Specifically, it may require the removal of certain regulatory obligations that are inherently inapplicable to autonomous infrastructures as such.

Another conceivable (and less anarchic) solution would be to subject only the code that makes up the algorithms used by the protocols to prior authorization, in the specific same way as it is done by the rules that provide how to build the above-mentioned iron bridge.

Although it does not resolve them completely, this approach may provide more opportunities for the regulatory "management" of these entities. Focusing the audits on the code of these entities rather than on the "human" part of the organization already seems to be more in line with the essence of these IT entities.

Notwithstanding the fact that their international nature could not prevent the creation of Protocol DAO in countries that will not adopt such rules, the impossibility of showing the public the obtaining of the authorization (for instance with a *label*[31] confirming the consistency of the algorithms employed with the regulatory standards) would certainly favor spontaneous *compliance* due to the greater trust that obtaining the *label* would convey to investors.

In this case, a potential investor deciding to interact with a Protocol DAO that has not received the authorization *label* will bear full risk and responsibility of his acts (as it happens to investors deciding to interact with financial intermediaries having their seat in off-shore countries).

With reference to investors that will interact with authorized Protocol DAO, a sort of insurance system could be created and imposed by the regulator for obtaining the authorization, considering the possibility of this being financed by part of the fee collected by the Protocol itself [53].[32]

---

[31] For example, in France, the "digital asset service providers" who wish to offer services related to the custody of crypto assets, exchange with other crypto assets or with fiat currency, the management of an exchange or other services related to crypto assets, can optionally obtain a license issued by the Autorité des marchés financiers (AMF). This license merely allows them to display the "label" proving their possession to the public.

[32] However, it should be noted that while an insurance system may help mitigating potential risks, it also raises concerns regarding "*moral hazard*": this concept pertains to the risk that subjects covered by insurance may engage in reckless behavior. In the context of DAOs and AI, users might feel less accountable for associated risks, thereby incentivizing riskier actions. Consequently, insurance could inadvertently diminish the incentive for DAO developers and users to implement adequate precautions. Furthermore, traditional insurance models are poorly equipped to deal with the complexities of risks posed by DAOs, unique and often dynamic, while simultaneously offering coverage at a reasonable cost.

At the end of the day, given the decentralized nature of these entities and the inherent difficulty in "imposing" rules on them, the preferred regulatory approach would likely focus on demonstrating the benefits of compliance. This strategy aims to encourage voluntary adherence by highlighting its practical value to such organizations.

5 Considering DAO as Infrastructure to Solve Regulatory Uncertainty

This paper tries to contribute to the definition of DAO legal status by analyzing the regulatory issues that characterize this phenomenon.

Indeed, the attempt to regulate DAOs as if they were conventional financial market entities reveals a fundamental flaw deeply connected with their legal status: it assumes that DAOs operate as (and *are*) traditional "businesses". In reality, the concept of a DAO encompasses a broader range of organizational forms, many of which do not align with traditional business structures. As shown in various classifications, only Investment DAOs resemble enterprises, while most active DAOs (Protocol DAOs) today function more like infrastructures.

This shift in perspective calls for an innovative regulatory approach tailored to these new phenomena. Rather than imposing rigid "top-down" solutions, regulatory frameworks should embrace flexibility and incentivize DAOs toward voluntary compliance. Considering a DAO's inherent ability to evade conventional regulatory control, a more effective approach could involve incentive-based regulations that encourage DAOs to adopt standards for secure code development, maintain "cyber insurance", and adhere to best practices for risk management.

Moreover, the classification of DAOs as infrastructure aligns with their inherent challenges, such as the lack of legal personhood, which complicates accountability and regulatory compliance. A forward-thinking regulatory model could leverage these unique qualities, aiming to foster voluntary adherence to standards rather than enforce rigid oversight.

References

1. Wikipedia: Decentralized autonomous organization. https://en.wikipedia.org/wiki/Decentralized_autonomous_organization, last accessed 2025/04/14
2. Wang, S., Ding, W., Li, J., Yuan, Y., Ouyang, L., Wang, F.: Decentralized autonomous organizations: concept, model, and applications. IEEE Trans. Comput. Soc. Syst. **6**(5), 876 (2019)
3. Borgogno, O., Martino, E.: Decentralised autonomous organizations: targeting the potential beyond the hype. European Banking Institute Working Paper Series No. 161 (2024)

4. Buterin, V.: DAOs, DACs, DAs and more: an incomplete terminology guide. https://blog.ethereum.org/2014/05/06/daos-dacs-das-and-more-an-incomplete-terminology-guide/, last accessed 2025/04/14
5. Proietti, G.: Definire l'indefinibile? I sistemi di intelligenza artificiale alla ricerca di un inquadramento sistematico. Contratto e impresa **3**, 832–925 (2024)
6. Searle, J.R.: Minds, brains, and programs. Behav. Brain Sci. **3**(3), 417–457 (1980)
7. Russell, S., Norvig, P.: Artificial Intelligence: A Modern Approach, 4th edn. Pearson, Boston (2021)
8. De Filippi, P., Wright, A.: Blockchain and the Law. Harvard University Press, Cambridge (2018)
9. Benkler, Y.: The Wealth of Networks: How Social Production Transforms Markets and Freedom. Yale University Press, New Haven (2006)
10. Kaal, W.A.: Decentralized autonomous organizations—internal governance and external legal design. Ann. Corp. Governance, Univ. of St. Thomas Legal Studies Research Paper No. 20–14, 6–7 (2021)
11. Ortolani, P.: Decentralized autonomous organizations: inquadramento giuridico de jure condito e prospettive de jure condendo. In: Battaglini, R., Giordano, M.T. (eds.) Blockchain e Smart Contract, pp. 404–420. Giuffrè Francis Lefebvre, Milano (2019)
12. Moduoran, C.: The complete guide to crypto DAO. https://milkroad.com/dao/, last accessed 2025/04/14
13. MolochDAO official website. https://molochdao.com/, last accessed 2025/04/14
14. Gitcoin official website. https://www.gitcoin.co/, last accessed 2025/04/14
15. Big Green DAO official website. https://dao.biggreen.org/home, last accessed 2025/04/14
16. Uniswap official website. https://uniswap.org/, last accessed 2025/04/14
17. MakerDAO official website. https://makerdao.com/, last accessed 2025/04/14
18. Internet Computer official website. https://internetcomputer.org/, last accessed 2025/04/14
19. Yearn Finance official website. https://yearn.fi/, last accessed 2025/04/14
20. Mohan, V.: Automated market makers and decentralized exchanges: a DeFi Primer. Financ. Innov. **8**, 20 (2022)
21. Furnari, S.L.: La Finanza Decentralizzata. Cripto-attività, protocolli, questioni giuridiche aperte. Editrice Minerva Bancaria, Roma (2023)
22. Aave official website. https://aave.com/, last accessed 2025/04/14
23. Venus Protocol official website. https://venus.io/, last accessed 2025/04/14
24. Dupont, Q.: Cryptocurrencies and blockchains. Wiley, Cambridge (2019)
25. Powell, W.W.: Neither market nor hierarchy: network forms of organization. Res. Organ. Behav. **12**, 295–336 (1990)
26. Bank for International Settlements: The crypto ecosystem: key elements and risks, p. 9 (2023)
27. Anker-Sørensen, L., Zetzsche, D.: From centralized to decentralized finance: the issue of "Fake-DeFi". Working Paper (2021)
28. Aramonte, S., Huang, W., Schrimpf, A.: DeFi risks and the decentralisation illusion. BIS Q. Rev., December (2021)
29. Rózsa, L., Garay, J.: Definitions of parasitism, considering its potentially opposing effects at different levels of hierarchical organization. Parasitol. **150**(9), 761–768 (2023)
30. Atzori, M.: Blockchain technology and decentralized governance: is the state still necessary? J. Govern. Regul. **6**(1), 45–62 (2017)
31. Tullio, P.: Diritto societario degli algoritmi. E se I robot diventassero imprenditori commerciali? Anal. giur. econ. **1**, 225–246 (2019)
32. Mosco, G.D.: Roboboard. L'intelligenza artificiale nei consigli di amministrazione. Anal. giur. econ. **1**, 247–258 (2019)
33. Voshmigir, S.: DAOs & Purpose-Driven Tokens. Elvas (2024)
34. DAO Link—Blockchain and real-world business. https://blog.slock.it/announcing-dao-link-the-bridge-between-blockchain-and-brick-and-mortar-companies-9510ba04d236#.z0z9xwbpa, last accessed 2025/04/14

35. On Contractors and Curators. https://blog.slock.it/on-contractors-and-curators-2fb9238b2553, last accessed 2025/04/14
36. Aragon Association official website. https://aragon.org/association, last accessed 2025/04/14
37. Cappellini, A.: Machina delinquere non potest? Brevi appunti su intelligenza artificiale e responsabilità penale. disCrimen (2019)
38. Expert Group on Liability and New Technologies: Report on Liability for Artificial Intelligence and other emerging digital technologies. European Commission (2019)
39. High-Level Expert Group on AI: Ethics Guidelines for Trustworthy AI. European Commission (2019)
40. Magro, M.B.: Decisione umana e decisione robotica. Legislazione penale, 10 May (2020)
41. Consulich, F., Maugeri, M., Milia, M., Poli, T.N., Trovatore, G.: AI e abusi di mercato: le leggi della robotica si applicano alle operazioni finanziarie? Quad. Giuridici, CONSOB 29 (2023)
42. Proietti, G.: Responsabilità civile, inadempimento e sistemi di intelligenza artificiale. Giust. Civile.com, 07.02.2023
43. Annunziata, F.: Artificial Intelligence and Market Abuse Legislation. Edward Elgar, Cheltenham (2023)
44. ESMA: Artificial intelligence in EU securities markets. ESMA TRV, 1 February 2023, ESMA50-164-6247
45. Azzutti, A.: AI-driven Market Manipulation and Limits of the EU law enforcement regime to credible deterrence. ILE Working Paper Series No. 54, Univ. of Hamburg (2022)
46. Auer, R.: Embedded supervision: how to build regulation into blockchain finance. BIS Working Paper No. 811 (2019)
47. Lessig, L.: Code and Other Laws of Cyberspace. Basic Books, New York (1999)
48. Ostercamp, P.: From 'Code is Law' to 'Code and Law': Polycentric Co-Regulation in Decentralized Finance (DeFi), SSRN working paper (2022)
49. Flick, M.: Digital Regulation: Designing a Supranational Legal Framework for the Platform Economy. LSE Law, Society and Economy Working Papers 15/2017, 23–28 (2017)
50. Bassan, F.: Digital Platforms and Blockchains: The Age of Participatory Regulation. Eur. Bus. Law Rev. (2023)
51. Wright, A.: The rise of decentralized autonomous organizations: opportunities and challenges. Stanford J. Blockchain Law Policy (2021)
52. Eurobarometer: https://europa.eu/eurobarometer/surveys/detail/2953, last accessed 2025/04/14
53. Faure, M., Li, S.: Artificial Intelligence and (Compulsory) Insurance. J. Eur. Tort Law **13**(1), 1–24 (2022)

Decentralized Autonomous Organizations: Is a New Liability Regime Possible? Current Landscape of German and Turkish Company Law and a New Liability Regime Recommendation

Barış C. Cantürk

Abstract The socio-economic developments and the volume of Decentralized Autonomous Organizations ("DAO") are increasing day by day. However, debates in the field of law regarding the DAOs are still vigorous. One of the most crucial issues pertaining to DAOs is liability, which is related to their legal nature. Hence, this work first briefly reveals the current liability regime of DAOs within the context of the current landscape of German and Turkish Company Law. Particularly ordinary partnerships, joint-stock companies and limited companies will be examined. Then, the new liability regime for DAOs will be proposed, as a part of the recommendation of a "New Code". Finally, this work will be concluded with the outcomes and recommendations.

Keywords DAO · Liability · Legal nature

This paper is reproduced from the dissertation successfully defended at the Faculty of Law, Leipzig University, entitled 'The Future of Company Law: Decentralized Autonomous Organization (DAO)—The Existing Legal Wrappers and A New Form Recommendation: A Comparative Perspective from Civil Law and Common Law.' It aims to introduce the New Liability Regime Recommendation proposed in the said dissertation. The dissertation was subsequently published by Nomos. The full text of the dissertation can be accessed through the bibliographic reference provided in footnote 20.

The original version of the chapter has been revised. A correction to this chapter can be found at https://doi.org/10.1007/978-3-032-03273-7_10

B. C. Cantürk (✉)
Department of IT Law, Faculty of Law, Marmara University, Istanbul, Türkiye
e-mail: b.canturk@marmara.edu.tr

Future Finance Law Hub, Munich, Germany

M. Lustenberger et al. (eds.), *Decentralized Autonomous Organizations—Governance, Technology, and Legal Perspectives*, Springer Proceedings in Business and Economics,
https://doi.org/10.1007/978-3-032-03273-7_8

1 Introduction

The socio-economic developments and the volume of Decentralized Autonomous Organizations ("DAO") are increasing day by day.[1] However, debates in the field of law regarding the DAOs are still vigorous. One of the most crucial issues pertaining to DAOs is liability, which is related to their legal nature. Because of the fact that, the main reason behind the preference for a new or existing legal wrapper in DAOs, especially after the SEC's legal explanations on "the DAO" [2–8] and "the bZx DAO case" [9], is the desire to limit the liability of DAO token holders and creators [10].

Therefore, this work first briefly reveals the current liability regime of DAOs within the context of the current landscape of German and Turkish Company Law. Particularly ordinary partnerships, joint-stock companies and limited companies will be revealed briefly. Then, the new liability regime for DAOs will be proposed, as a part of the recommendation of a "New Code". Finally, this work will be concluded with the outcomes and recommendations.

2 Current Landscape of German and Turkish Company Law

2.1 General

After the token holders of a DAO were deemed liable under the premise of a general partnership in the United States [9], concerns about the liability regime for DAOs and their legal nature have risen. Therefore, the current liability regime for DAOs under Civil Law jurisdictions also becomes a crucial issue to be examined. Recognizing said liability regime requires checking the compatibility of the legal wrappers of the said jurisdictions. For that purpose, the most common legal wrappers of German and Turkish Company Law are preferred to be examined.[2] This examination will be generally conducted through these two jurisdictions' common features. Due to the page limitations, direct results will be presented instead of detailed examinations. For the same reason, only the most common legal wrappers, particularly ordinary partnerships, joint-stock companies and limited companies will be evaluated.

[1] As of 3rd of the March 2025 there were a total of 50,845 aggregated governances, encompassing all DAOs and sub-DAOs, with a total asset value of USD 21.8 billion, 11.8 million token holders and 3.3 million active voters and proposal makers [1].

[2] Undoubtedly, Civil Law comprises many significant jurisdictions such as French and Swiss Law, in addition Turkish and German Law. However, Turkish and German Company Law selected deliberately based on the following reasons: Analysing French, Swiss, or other Civil Law jurisdictions would exceed the length limitations of this study. Moreover, the author does not claim expertise in those jurisdictions. In contrast, the author has studied and is familiar with Turkish and German Law. Additionally, the similarities between these two legal systems are well established, making a comparative analysis not only feasible but also conducive to drawing joint conclusions.

2.2 *Ordinary Partnerships*

Ordinary partnership ("OP") could be basically defined as an agreement where more than one natural or legal person pools their assets (i.e. tangible, intangible or efforts) for a common purpose [11–18]. As a default form, OPs are regulated under Art. 620 et. seq. of Turkish Code of Obligations ("TCO") and Art. 705 German Civil Code ("BGB") aF/nF. According to said regulations, if an entity does not fall into any forms of specific entities regulated by law, OP regulations shall be applied [Art. 620/2 TCO, § 705 BGB, 12, 13, 16–19].

Both in German and Turkish Law, OP does not have a legal personality [20], thus partners are jointly, severally, and personally liable [11, 12, 14, 15, 18]. Even after the Act on the Modernization of Partnerships ("MoPeG"), which came into force as of January 1, 2024, registered OP (*eingetragenen GbR*, "eGbR") [21–25] does only have legal capacity ("*Rechtsfähigkeit*") but not have a legal personality which prevents liability limitation [23, 25].

Owing to its comprehensive nature, OP emerges as a frequently encountered structure possessing various facets that may be deemed suitable for DAO. Indeed, either DAO may opt for the OP structure or fall into that wrapper. Although prima facie and roughly classifying DAO as an OP may seem plausible *de lege lata*, the existence of numerous challenges becomes evident in the application of relevant provisions.

Firstly, it would be beneficial to reiterate the reservation regarding the ontological incongruity between DAO and centrally governed corporate forms. Secondly, it is noteworthy that in both Turkish and German Law, OP lacks legal personality, thereby rendering partners jointly, severally, and personally liable [11, 12, 14, 15, 18]. Besides the ongoing liability of partners [§ 708 BGB aF; § 721BGB nF, 17], the attribution of the status of a merchant to partners in the current state of Turkish Law and the potential disputes over the attribution of the merchant status in the evaluation of BGB nF, especially in the context of eGbR, pose a significant issue for DAO. This is due to the negative consequences, particularly for members, arising from the implications attributed to being a merchant [26, 27]. Furthermore, other vulnerabilities for DAO include, for instance, the liability of a new partner for pre-existing debts under Art. 721b BGB. Moreover, eGbR stipulates several obligations in various scenarios concerning the newly introduced register through the MoPeG [21–25]. Additionally, the necessary consent process for the admission of new partners, as well as the termination and liquidation process, will pose considerable challenges.

2.3 *Joint-Stock Companies*

Joint-stock company ("JSC"), which assumes a pivotal type of company in Turkish and German Law, is generally defined as a legal entity with a specified capital divided into shares, solely responsible for its debts with its own assets, possessing separate legal personality and thus limited liability regime [Art. 329 TCC, Art. 125 TCC, § 1 AktG, 28, 11, 19, 29, 30].

Especially owing to attributes such as legal personality, limited liability, the current structure of shareholders, shares, and the decision-making process, the JSC has been acknowledged as a construct well-aligned with the operational principles of DAO.

Conversely, even procedural aspects like notarization and formal registration pose impediments to categorizing DAO as a JSC [*q.v.* 7, 19]. Furthermore, significant attention has been directed towards mandatory provisions regime [§ 23/5 AktG, 28, 30–35]. Within this framework, considering that numerous facets are explicitly "dictated" by law, JSCs find themselves constrained in adapting regulations to meet their specific requirements. This inherent constraint proves disadvantageous for innovative structures like DAOs, each of which boasts a distinctive organizational framework.

Moreover, formation audit is regulated under the German Stock Corporation Act ("AktG") [§ 33 AktG, 31] in addition to several other official procedures and approval requirements for certain sectors both in Turkish [Art. 339 et seq. TCC, 28, 11, 35] and German Law stands as important obstacles. Furthermore, it is opined that under both Turkish [36–38] and German Law [19, 39–42], the fulfilment of capital debt via tokens remains highly controversial within the existing regulations, in addition to several other incompatibilities.

Finally, despite recognizing the potential for opportunity within this constraint, it remains assertable, within the existing legal regime, that classifying DAO as a JSC is not feasible *de lege lata* neither under Turkish Law nor German Law.

2.4 Limited Companies

Limited Company ("Ltd"), a significant corporation within both Turkish and German Law, is a commercial entity established by one or more person whose capital is registered and comprised of each capital shares [Art. 573 TCC, Art. 124 TCC, § 1 GmbHG, 43, 44]. It should be highlighted that Ltd possesses a separate legal personality [Art. 124 TCC, Art. 125 TCC, § 13 GmbHG, 43, 11, 45, 46], and as a consequence, the principle of limited liability prevails.

From the DAO compatibility perspective, several vital deficiencies should be emphasized. First of all, similar to JSC, *de lege lata*; formal registration, notarization and trade registry process constitute significant barriers [7, 19]. Additionally, the limitation imposed by Turkish Law, which restricts the number of shareholders to 50 individuals [11, 43], presents a significant disadvantage. Moreover, shareholders' loyalty and non-competence obligations [Art. 613 TCC, 43, 44] which are pivotal aspects of Ltd, may give rise to substantial challenges for DAOs. Furthermore, both Turkish and German Law foresees several restrictions and formalities for share transfer which are incompatible with DAOs [Art. 593 et seq. TCC, § 15/3 GmbHG, 43, 44, 46]. Lastly, considering these factors, it remains untenable, within the existing legal framework, to classify a DAO as an LTD *de lege lata*, neither under German Law [7, 19] nor under Turkish Law.

3 A New Liability Regime Recommendation

Previous sections revealed that, numerous issues arising from the compatibility of existing company law regulations with DAOs. Therefore, a "New Code" for DAOs has been proposed [20]. Generally speaking, this New Code is dedicated to; (i) proffering resolutions to previously identified issues, (ii) rectifying deficiencies in existing regulations, (iii) proposing a harmonized and internationally applicable regulation that (iii a) extracts salient aspects of both Civil Law and Common Law regulations, (iii b) incorporates considerations of the technical dimension of the subject matter, (iii c) able to be integrated easily to national laws.

As an incompatibility with the current liability regime has been revealed, this section aims to present a new liability regime proposal for DAOs as a part of a New Code Recommendation. Thus, Chapter 4 of the New Code focuses on the "liability" of DAOs will be presented with Article 3 of the New Code which regulates the legal nature of a DAO. For this purpose, the relevant Article and Commentaries in the following paragraphs until the "Conclusion" have been quoted directly in their original form [20]. However, certain sections have been abridged, indicated by (...), while necessary explanations have been added in ().

Article 3: Legal Nature

A DAO, meets the requirements of this Code, is a sui generis legal entity which is subject to a limited liability regime, possessing a separate legal personality and legal capacity, shall be established by one or more individuals for any lawful purpose.

Commentary

The intention behind the formulation within the paragraph is to maintain briefness and clarity in definition. Instead of lengthy provisions found in many existing regulations [*v.d.* Art. 104 Marshall Islands DAO Act, Art. 48-5-104 Utah DAO Act], compact legal terms are preferred.

(...)

As previously underscored, while DAOs may share similarities with various facets of company law, they do not conform precisely to any one model. Moreover, as articulated, the intention is to leverage specific elements of several different legal forms beneficial to DAOs while maintaining requisite flexibility. Therefore, the appropriate choice is deemed to be a "sui generis legal entity", tailored to the distinctive requisites of DAOs.

Chapter 4: Liability

Article 18: Liability of Members

1. The main and sole obligation of the members is to make contributions to the DAO to redeem the DAO's tokens, unless otherwise regulated under this Code.
2. Members shall not be held personally liable for any obligation incurred by the DAO, any excess liability if the DAO's assets have been exhausted, and the wrongful act or omission of the DAO or any other member of the DAO, unless otherwise regulated under this Code.
3. In case the DAO refuses to comply with an enforceable court decision, arbitration or any alternative dispute resolution award or official order, all members who do

not vote in favour of compliance shall be liable for any monetary payments ordered in that decision, award, or order in proportion to their contribution in the DAO pursuant to the first paragraph of this Article.

4. The above paragraphs shall not affect the personal liability of a member in case of the failure event attributable to its own bad faith or gross negligence.
5. The above paragraphs shall not affect the personal liability of a member in tort for its own wrongful act or omission.

Commentary

First and foremost, it is imperative to underscore that existing DAO regulations do not provide for a comprehensive liability regime as delineated within this chapter. Presently, emerging technologies such as blockchain, DAO, and cryptocurrencies remain unbound by specific liability regimes or compensatory regulations. Nevertheless, numerous supra-national reports unequivocally advocate for the necessity of such regulatory frameworks [47]. Indeed, this Code proposes to address liability concerns in this context. Unlike the existing regulations, this provision includes provisions from the existing corporate law liability regimes that could be advantageous and are implementable to DAOs. Undoubtedly, most of these provisions have not been directly adopted but have been incorporated into DAOs by harmonization. Indeed, proposals for fault-based liability rules [47] have been contemplated across various modalities and proportions herein. This may also be clearly seen in the subsequent provisions.

This provision regulates the liability regime of members whose definition and details are articulated under Article 14 (titled "Members", defines the members and regulates their rights and obligations). The first paragraph emphasizes that, in accordance with this Code and the fundamentals of DAO, the only obligation of the member is to make contributions to the DAO to redeem the DAO's tokens. Indeed, this framework notably parallels the sole obligation principle of shareholders in traditional corporate law systems [*v.d.* Art. 480 TCC, § 54 et seq. AktG].

The second paragraph explicitly dictates that beyond the principle of sole obligation, no additional liabilities shall be incurred to the members. Matters dispersed across various paragraphs or provisions in existing DAO regulations are consolidated into a singular paragraph herein. Thus, except for the members' contribution to DAO, it is explicitly stipulated that members shall not be held liable for any obligation incurred by the DAO, any excess liability if the DAO's assets have been exhausted, and the wrongful act or omission of the DAO or any other member of the DAO. Moreover, unlike existing regulations [Art. 5 COALA Model Law for DAOs], not only the wrongful acts or omissions of any other member of the DAO but also those of the DAO itself, are encompassed herein. According to the view posited herein, considering the DAO as a legal entity, such an inclusion is deemed requisite.

The third paragraph incorporates a provision, articulated under the existing regulations [Art. 485-202 Utah DAO Act, Art. 5 COALA Model Law for DAOs] appropriately and reasonably, into this Code. However, it diverges from these regulations in two crucial aspects. Firstly, the term, "enforceable court decision, arbitration or any alternative dispute resolution award or official order" delineated in this paragraph, is preferred for more precise terminological usage, which could be more beneficial. It is imperative to note that, the term "enforceable" covers court decisions, awards, and orders. However, the enforceability shall be interpreted upon the applicable law of such decision, award, or order. It could be criticized for not preferring the phrase "final and binding" instead of "enforceable". Nevertheless, it should be kept in mind that interim decisions or interim awards could still be enforceable even they are not final and binding yet. Indeed, official orders often lack finality as they are subject to judicial review. Moreover, enforcement of them must precede any appeals process. Therefore, the more comprehensive term "enforceable" is preferred considering all the above matters. It should be reiterated that enforceability shall be contingent upon the applicable law governing the respective decision, award, or order. The second aspect that diverges from the existing DAO regulations [Art. 5 COALA Model Law for DAOs] is utilizing the term "who do not vote in favour of compliance" instead of "votes against", whose ground can be inferred from Article 10 which incorporates similar terminology preference.

The fourth paragraph stipulates the liability regime of members in case of a failure event [Art. 48-5-405 Utah DAO Act]. As expressed previously under the commentary of Article 4, neither in herein provision nor in this Code, particularly technical terms such as failure event is defined. Among several other grounds which could be inferred from the said commentary, one of the main reasons for that, it is anticipated that, pursuing a casuistical definition of each term may inadvertently lead to overly rigid regulations, potentially out of sync with evolving technological advancements and inadvertently creating loopholes. Therefore, namely by abstaining from certain definitions, the delineation of these terms is entrusted to the DAO practice, doctrine, and dispute resolution bodies.

Some views posit that, the failure event provisions bear a resemblance to the liability of the board of directors under traditional corporate law [Commentary of Art. 18 COALA Model Law for DAOs]. These provisions are designed to address instances where an individual possessing decision-making authority within a DAO leads a technical failure towards their own acts in bad faith or gross negligence resulting in the loss of members or other stakeholders. Undoubtedly, the corporate veil typically covers members for any incurred liability in case of a failure event. However, there exist circumstances where members may be found liable for acts of bad faith or gross negligence. In such a scenario, an analogy to piercing the corporate veil may arise, thereby enabling the pursuit of personal liability against the respective members. The concepts of bad faith and gross negligence shall be interpreted via accumulated corporate law discourse, it is imperative to consider specific features of the DAO universe.

The last paragraph reflects a tort liability as articulated under similar existing regulations.

Article 19: Liability of Other Stakeholders

1. Executive, legal representative or any individual vested with the authority for discretionary decisions in the interest of the DAO shall not have fiduciary duties towards each other, to the DAO, to the DAO members or to the third parties solely

on account of their role, unless otherwise explicitly stipulated by the resolution appointing them and conferring discretion upon them.

2. None of the aforementioned individuals may be personally liable for acts performed on behalf of the DAO, unless proven of bad faith or gross negligence.
3. The above paragraphs shall not affect the personal liability of any of the aforementioned individuals in case of the failure event attributable to their own bad faith or gross negligence.
4. The above paragraphs shall not affect the personal liability of any of the aforementioned individuals in tort for their own wrongful acts or omissions.

Commentary

This provision regulates the liability of the executive, legal representative or any individual vested with the authority for discretionary decisions in the interest of the DAO in a more detailed, comprehensive, and divergent manner from existing regulations. Considering DAO's decision-making process, organizational structure, and member-centric orientation, it is reasonable to not incorporate fiduciary duty [*v.d.* 48] to aforementioned individuals, who lack hierarchical superiority and discretionary prerogatives akin to those in corporate law regulations [*v.d.* Commentary of Art. 13 COALA Model Law for DAOs].

The second paragraph effectively merges the existing DAO regulations and corporate law regime, which reflects the innovative and distinctive approach introduced by this regulation. This paragraph both complies with the fiduciary duty regulation of the first paragraph and paves the way to the incorporation of "the due care of a prudent manager faithfully complying with the relevant duties" [§ 93/1 AktG, § 93/2 AktG] via its sub-sentence. More precisely, neither the first nor second paragraph imposes a fiduciary duty to the executive or similar individuals who have limited discretion in complying with the DAO principles. However, the more this discretion tends towards centralized authority akin to managers in traditional corporate law, the greater the possibility of triggering the term "unless proven of bad faith or gross negligence". Because, in that case, these individuals function akin to traditional corporate form managers, which necessitates them "to exercise the due care of a prudent manager faithfully complying with the relevant duties" [§ 93 AktG]. In other words, if a DAO keeps its decentralized structure as member-managed or smart contract-managed structure, there would be no executives reflecting the corporate law features. Therefore, this principle could not be applied in the interpretation of their duties. On the contrary, namely when there exists managerial power akin to traditional corporate law, then the interpretation of the liability regime also tends towards traditional corporate law. Henceforth, it is posited that in the event of the aforementioned scenario, despite the absence of fiduciary duty, the interpretation of "unless bad faith or gross negligence" may draw upon the AktG approach detailed earlier.

For the interpretation of the third paragraph, which stipulates the failure event liability, the preceding provision could be beneficial.

The last paragraph reflects a tort liability as articulated under similar existing regulations.

Article 20: Remedy, Procedure, and the Statute of Limitation

1. Pursuant to Article 18 and Article 19, if more than one individual is obliged to indemnify the same damage, they shall be jointly and severally liable. In that case, each shall be held liable in case of said damage attributable to their own bad faith or gross negligence.
2. None of the aforementioned individuals shall be held liable for the breaches of the law, SoD, or the principles of blockchain beyond their control.
3. Procedures for remedy, statute of limitation and other related details shall be regulated by the Contracting State in accordance with the liability regime regulated under Article 18 and Article 19.

Commentary

This provision introduces a novel regulation, which existing regulations do not incorporate. However, as stipulated before, this Code incorporates regulations based upon several phenomena of existing DAO regulations and traditional corporate law regulations, as appropriate. Therefore, liability regulations necessitate to regulate remedies. Considering all, remedy regulations based upon several aspects of Art. 759 the Swiss Code of Obligations ("OR"), Art. 553 TCC and Art. 557 TCC [28].

The first paragraph aims to merge DAO principles with Art. 557 TCC and Art. 759 OR. As it is recalled, Article 18 and Article 19 of this Code envisage a serious liability regime. In case of multiple individuals lead to liability, they shall all bear joint and several liability. However, it would be unfair to attribute such multiple-actors-liability to a sole individual, considering the potential variance in levels of bad faith or gross negligence among them. At this juncture, the second sentence of this paragraph shall be triggered and introduces differentiated solidarity [Art. 557 TCC, 11, 28]. It is imperative to remember that, the interpretation of this regulation from the DAO perspective requires benefiting from the doctrine and jurisprudence arising from the Art. 557 TCC and Art. 759 OR.

The second paragraph aims to merge DAO principles with Art. 553/3 TCC [28]. The underlying rationale is a simple yet fundamental logical inference: where there is no control over events, liability cannot be attributed. Indeed, similar approaches have been observed in discussions concerning the DAO liability regime [*v.d.* 48]. Therefore, while serious liability scenarios are regulated for the Executive, legal representatives or any individual vested with the authority for discretionary decisions and members in exceptional cases; they shall not be held liable for the breaches of the law, SoD (The "Statutes of the DAO" defined and regulated under Article 6 of the New Code. Broadly speaking, said article aims to regulate SoD as not only a foundational document but also internal relationship rules with non-exhaustive provisions), or the principles of blockchain beyond their control, pursuant to this paragraph. The establishment of such a merged-solution to the liability is not only fair but also allows to benefit from the accumulated doctrine and jurisprudence.

The last paragraph allows the Contracting States to regulate procedural law rules such as process, parties, and the timeframe within this proposed liability regime.

Indeed, it could be asserted that, existing DAO regulations do not encompass procedural law rules, let alone substantive law rules on this matter. Therefore, it is the appropriate and rational choice to delegate regulation of these matters to the Contracting States' discretion. However, it is imperative to consider the phrase "in accordance with the liability regime regulated under Article 18 and Article 19" when regulating these matters, which emphasizes that such regulations shall not eliminate the core of the provisions of this Code.

Article 21: Compulsory Liability Insurance and Insurance Fund

1. A DAO is obliged to submit proof of the compulsory liability insurance policy whose premiums, limits, values, and all other details shall be subject to the secondary legislation enacted by the Contracting State, in accordance with Article 6 of this Code.
2. An individual asserting a claim for compensation pertaining to their loss arising from Article 10 (Invalidity of Resolutions and Remedies), Article 12 (Dissolution), Article 18/2, Article 18/3, Article 19/1, Article 19/2, Article 22 (Hard Fork), and Article 23 (Restructuring) of this Code shall be applied for the aforementioned compulsory liability insurance. All procedural matters and the statute of limitations shall be subject to the secondary legislation enacted by the Contracting State, in compliance with the general principles of insurance law.
3. Any Contracting State may, at its sole discretion, enact secondary legislation to establish the insurance fund to redress the compensation not covered by the compulsory liability insurance. The financial and legal structure of this fund, the premiums paid by the DAOs, compensation limits, the statute of limitations and all other details shall be governed by that secondary legislation.

Commentary

This provision primarily regulates two concepts, namely compulsory liability insurance and the insurance fund. However, before delving into the detailed content of this provision, it is imperative to first articulate certain foundational observations and justifications.

Comprehensive explanations regarding the necessity for detailed liability regime regulations for the DAO and such novel technologies have been mentioned under the commentary of Article 18. Because of said grounds, it has been noted that this Code introduces a novel and comprehensive liability regime consisting of several provisions. Herein, compulsory liability insurance, which is an integral part of this liability regime, is regulated and will be examined. Despite fair criticism of the doctrine posits that compulsory insurance could not be deemed as the sole and comprehensive solution to liability matters [47], the proposal for such a liability system does not merely rely on the compulsory liability insurance but also includes it, which is considered one the most suitable solutions at present. Moreover, some scholars posit that, compulsory insurance constitutes one of the effective answers to remedy for the loss of the third parties [49]. Indeed, numerous existing regulations, especially those pertaining to robots, the compulsory insurance are envisaged.[3] Beyond all these, this Code introduces not only compulsory liability insurance as a remedy for that problem, but also establishes a multi-perspective liability regime system consisting of several provisions.

The following point deserves a notable emphasis. This Code recognizes the fact that existing EU regulations especially subject to robotics rely mainly on, tort liability [49, 50*cf.*]. However, here, contractual liability has been preferred for the following two reasons: (i) previously noted grounds and (ii) the comprehensive nature and current applicability of the proposed solution. Lastly, it should be considered that, at the juncture of the current corporate law realm, § 93/2 AktG stipulates that members of the management board may be subjected to liability insurance, albeit optionally.

The first paragraph stipulates that DAOs are obliged to obtain compulsory liability insurance, parallel with Article 6 (The Statutes of the DAO). The specifics of these policies, including premiums, limits, values, and all other pertinent details, are to be determined by secondary legislation enacted by the Contracting State. While several factors will be considered in determining these limits, it is noteworthy to consider § 93/2 AktG which proposes up to a minimum of 150% of the annual fixed remuneration of such executives.

The second paragraph lists the grounds for the loss, as *numerus clausus*. According to that, an individual makes a compulsory liability insurance claim pursuant to the listed *numerus clausus* articles of this Code. All procedural law matters, such as conditions for being a claimant, the authority to file claims, the opposing party, statutes of limitation, and insurance law subjects shall be determined by the Contracting State. The general principles of insurance law constitute a crucial standpoint for all Contracting States, when formulating those regulations. Several aspects regarding this paragraph merit attention. Firstly, the determination of the claimant will fundamentally rely on the provision upon which the claim is based. Secondly, the concept of loss will be clarified over time through doctrine, practice, and jurisprudence in accordance with both the realm of private law and the general principles of DAO. Lastly, referencing general principles of insurance law in this paragraph also serves to prevent double compensation, which constitutes one of the cornerstones of such principles.

The last paragraph envisages the insurance fund, which is another integral part of a novel and unique liability regime. Inspired by the EU regulations, this concept aims to redress the compensation not covered by compulsory liability insurance. The term "compensation not covered by the compulsory liability insurance" herein, comprehensively encompasses the scenario, where the absence of insurance, is based on inspired regulations[4] but also includes scenarios where the loss remains inadequately addressed while there exists an insurance policy. Similar to the preceding paragraphs, for analogous reasons, the financial and legal structure of this fund, the

[3] Civil Law Rules on Robotics European Parliament resolution of 16 February 2017 with recommendations to the Commission on Civil Law Rules on Robotics (2015/2103(INL), pr. 57.

[4] Ibid., pr.58, [47]

premiums paid by the DAOs, compensation limits, the statute of limitations, and all other details shall be governed by secondary legislation.

4 Conclusion

The liability regime constitutes one of the most crucial issues related to DAOs, which is also applicable to the Turkish and German Company Law systems. Therefore, the most common legal wrappers of German and Turkish Company Law are required to be examined.

Although prima facie and roughly classifying DAO as an ordinary partnership may seem plausible, there exist several incompatibilities. Several formalities and obligations for eGbR prevent DAOs as OP. But more importantly, one of the most vital problems is, in both Turkish and German Law, OP lacks legal personality, thereby rendering partners jointly, severally, and personally liable.

Several formal requirements and obligations prevent the classification of DAOs as joint-stock companies or limited companies. Moreover, mandatory provisions regime, formation audit, and other establishment formalities stand as important obstacles from the JSC perspective. Furthermore, the fulfilment of capital debt via tokens remains highly controversial.

From the Ltd perspective, the 50-person upper limit under Turkish Law, formal registration, notarization, and trade registry process constitute significant barriers. Moreover, shareholders' loyalty and non-competence obligations which are pivotal aspects of Ltd, may give rise to substantial challenges for DAOs. Furthermore, both Turkish and German Law foresees several restrictions and formalities for share transfer which are incompatible with DAOs.

Therefore, despite recognizing the potential for opportunity within this constraint, it remains assertable, within the existing legal regime, that classifying DAO as a JSC or Ltd is not feasible *de lege lata* neither under Turkish Law nor German Law.

In light of the abovementioned problems, a "New Code" for DAOs has been proposed and its liability regime has been introduced in this work. Briefly speaking, this New Code is dedicated to; (i) proffering resolutions to previously identified issues, (ii) rectifying deficiencies in existing regulations, (iii) proposing a harmonized and internationally applicable regulation that (iii a) extracts salient aspects of both Civil Law and Common Law regulations, (iii b) incorporates considerations of the technical dimension of the subject matter, (iii c) able to be integrated easily to national laws.

Roughly speaking, the New Code classifies DAO as a sui generis legal entity that possesses a separate legal personality and thus subject to a limited liability regime (Art. 3). Chapter 4 of the New Code specifically regulates the liability regime. However, it should be emphasized that it is part of a puzzle. The New Code has its own reasoning and systematic structure, so each component complements each other. While Art. 18 regulates the liability of members, Art. 19 stipulates the liability of the other stakeholders such as the executive, legal representative or any individual vested with the authority for discretionary decisions.

According to Art. 18, the main and sole obligation of the members is to make contributions to the DAO to redeem the DAO's tokens and they shall not be held personally liable for any obligation incurred by the DAO. However, parallel to the current DAO-centric regulations and the needs, paragraph 3 stipulates that, in case the DAO refuses to comply with an enforceable court decision, arbitration or any alternative dispute resolution award or official order, all members who do not vote in favour of compliance shall be liable, but proportion to their contribution in the DAO.

Article 19 regulates that any individual vested with the authority for discretionary decisions in the interest of the DAO shall not have fiduciary duties but, in case of proven bad faith or gross negligence, they shall be personally liable. Commentary of the said article provides detailed reasoning for that preference.

Article 20 identifies remedies, procedures, and the statute of limitation. It mainly regulates two following issues: If more than one individual is obliged to indemnify the same damage, they shall be jointly and severally liable. On the other hand, if there is no control over events, liability cannot be attributed. Indeed, similar approaches have been observed in discussions concerning the DAO liability regime.

Lastly, Art. 21 incorporates a compulsory liability insurance system and insurance fund to the DAO liability regime.

In conclusion, it is opined that, said liability regime proposal—with the other *sine qua non* components of the New Code—brings a new perspective to the DAO liability regime that benefits from the company law liability regime's accumulation of knowledge and also recognizes the ratio and needs of DAOs.

References

1. DEEPDAO Homepage, https://deepdao.io/organizations, last accessed 2025/3/3
2. Capiello, B.: Blockchain based organizations and the governance of on-chain and off-chain rules: towards autonomous (legal) orders? In: Capiello, B., Carullo, G. (eds.) Blockchains, Law and Governance, pp. 13–42. Springer (2021)
3. Jentzsch, C.: The History of the DAO and lessons learned (2016). https://Medium.Com/Slock-It-Blog/The-History-Of-The-Dao-And-Lessons-Learned-D06740f8cfa5, last accessed 2025/3/3
4. Mann, M.: Komplexe smart contracts: die decentralized autonomous organization. In: Braegelmann, T., Kaulartz, M. (eds.) Rechtshandbuch Smart Contracts, pp. 219–232. C.H. Beck (2019)
5. Sec: Report of Investigation Pursuant to Section 21(a) of The Securities Exchange Act of 1934: The DAO, Release No. 81207. (2017), https://www.sec.gov/files/litigation/investreport/34-81207.pdf, last accessed 2025/3/3.
6. Tevetoğlu, M.: Ethereum ve Akıllı Sözleşmeler. İnönü Üniversitesi Hukuk Fakültesi Dergisi **12**(1), 193–208 (2021)
7. World Economic Forum: Decentralized Autonomous Organization Toolkit (2023). https://www.weforum.org/publications/decentralized-autonomous-organization-toolkit/, last accessed 2025/3/3

8. Wright, A.: The rise of decentralized autonomous organizations: opportunities and challenges. Stanford Journal of Blockchain Law & Policy **4**(2), 152–176 (2021)
9. Sarcuni et al. v. bZx DAO et al., No. 22cv0618 BEN DEB (S.D. Cal. May 2, 2022).
10. Gatteschi, V., Lamberti, F., Demartini, C.: Technology of smart contracts. In: Di Matteo, L.A., Cannarsa, M., Poncibò, C. (eds.) The Cambridge Handbook of Smart Contracts, Blockchain Technology and Digital Platforms, pp. 37–58. Cambridge University Press, Cambridge (2019)
11. Bahtiyar, M.: Ortaklıklar Hukuku. 13th edn. Beta, İstanbul (2019)
12. Barlas, N.: Adi Ortaklık Temeline Dayalı Sözleşme İlişkileri. Vedat, İstanbul (2016)
13. Cantürk, B.C.: Franchise Sözleşmesinde Denkleştirme İstemi. Onikilevha, İstanbul (2020)
14. Moroğlu, E.: Makaleler. Onikilevha, İstanbul (2010)
15. Pulaşlı, H.: Şirketler Hukuku Genel Esaslar. 6th edn. Adalet, Ankara (2020)
16. Schäfer, C.: BGB § 705. In: Säcker, F.J., Rixecker, R., Oetker, H., Limperg, B., Schubert, C. (eds.) MÜNCHENER KOMMENTAR ZUM BÜRGERLICHEN GESETZBUCH BAND 7. 9th edn., Rn 1–380. C.H. Beck (2024).
17. Servatius, W.: Gesellschaft Bürgerlichen Rechts: GbR §§ 705–740c BGB Kommentar. C.H. Beck (2023).
18. Yavuz, C., Acar, F., Özen, B.: Borçlar Hukuku Dersleri Özel Hükümler. 14th edn. Beta (2016)
19. Mienert, B.: Dezentrale Autonome Organisationen (DAOs) und Gesellschaftsrecht. Mohr Siebeck (2022)
20. Cantürk, B.C.: The Future of Company Law: Decentralized Autonomous Organization (DAO) – The Existing Legal Wrappers and A New Form Recommendation: A Comparative Perspective from Civil Law and Common Law. Nomos (2025)
21. Döge, M.: Die 8 Wesentlichen Mopeg-Änderungen (2023), https://community.beck.de/2023/02/08/die-8-wesentlichen-mopeg-aenderungen, last accessed 2025/3/3
22. Fülbeck, T.: Mopeg: "Im Recht Der Bgb-Gesellschaft Bleibt Kein Stein Auf Dem Anderen" (2023). https://community.beck.de/2023/03/03/Mopeg-Im-Recht-Der-Bgb-Gesellschaft-Bleibt-Kein-Stein-Auf-Dem-Anderen, last accessed 2025/3/3
23. Özdin, F.: Alman, Avusturya, İsviçre ve Türk Hukuk Sistemlerinde Adi Ortaklıktan "Haklı Nedenle Çıkarma" Kurumunun Düzenlenişi ve Türk Hukukuna İlişkin Değerlendirmeler. İnönü Üniversitesi Hukuk Fakültesi Dergisi **14**(1), 1–14 (2023)
24. Röß, S.: Die Frage Der Haftungsbeschränkung Bei Der GbR Nach Dem Mopeg. Neue Zeitschrift für Gesellschaftsrecht **401**, 727–734 (2023)
25. Wertenbruch, J.: Das Mopeg – Die Reform des Rechts Der Personengesellschaften. Juristen Zeitung **3**, 78–88 (2023)
26. Arkan, S.: Ticari İşletme Hukuku. 26th edn. Banka ve Ticaret Hukuku Araştırma Enstitüsü, Ankara (2020)
27. Poroy, R., Yasaman, H.: Ticari İşletme Hukuku. 18th edn. Vedat, İstanbul (2019)
28. Poroy, R., Tekinalp, Ü., Çamoğlu, E.: Ortaklıklar Hukuku Cilt I. 14th edn. Vedat, İstanbul (2019)
29. Lafarre, A., Van Der Elst, C.: Legal Tech and blockchain for corporate governance and shareholders. In: Mak, V. (ed.) Research Handbook in Data Science and Law, pp. 153–182. Edward Elgar (2018)
30. Gerner-Beuerle, C., Schillig, M.A.: Comparative Company Law. Oxford University Press (2019)
31. Pentz, K.: Aktg § 23. In: Goette, W., Habersack, M., Kalss, S. (eds.) MÜNCHENER KOMMENTAR ZUM AKTIENGESETZ BAND 1 §§1–75 AKTG. 6th edn. Rn. 156–172. C.H. Beck (2024)
32. Seibt, C.H.: § 23 Aktg. In: Schmidt, K., Lutter, M. (eds.) AKTIENGESETZ KOMMENTAR, 5th edn., Rz. 53 ff, Otto Schmidt (2024).
33. Uhink, K.: Die Tokenisierte Namensaktie bei der Gründung einer Aktiengesellschaft. Zeitschrift für das Recht der digitalen Wirtschaft **8**, 309–313 (2021)
34. Karasu, R.: Anonim Şirketler Emredici Hükümler İlkesi. 2nd edn. Yetkin, Ankara (2015)
35. Kırca, İ., Şehirali Çelik, F.H., Manavgat, Ç.: Anonim Şirketler Hukuku Cilt 1, Banka ve Ticaret Hukuku Araştırma Enstitüsü, Ankara (2013)

36. Bilgili, F., Cengil, M.F.: Bitcoin Özelinde Kripto Paraların Ticaret Şirketlerine Sermaye Olarak Getirilmesi. Ankara Hacı Bayram Veli Üniversitesi Hukuk Fakültesi Dergisi **23**(3), 3–23 (2019)
37. Çağlayan Aksoy, P.: The applicability of property law rules for crypto assets: considerations from civil law and common law perspectives. Law Innov. Technol. **15**(1), 185–221 (2023)
38. Yatağan Özkan, Ç.: Kripto Paraların Ticaret Şirketlerine Sermaye Olarak Getirilmesine İlişkin Düşünceler. Terazi Hukuk Dergisi **202**, 69–82 (2023)
39. Lehmann, M.: Internationales Privat- Und Zivilprozessrecht. In: Omlor, S., Link, M. (eds.) KRYPTOWÄHRUNGEN UND TOKEN, pp. 173–256. Dfv (2021).
40. Omlor, S.: Allgemeines Privatrecht. In: Omlor, S., Link, M. (eds.) KRYPTOWÄHRUNGEN UND TOKEN, pp. 257–304. Dfv (2021)
41. Rizos, E.: The nature of rights upon cryptocurrencies. In: Synodinou, T.E. (ed.) Internet Law in the Digital Single Market, pp. 605–627. Springer (2021)
42. Wellenhofer, M.: Strukturanalyse Des Sacheigentums. In: Hofmann, F. (ed.) EIGENTUM IN DER DIGITALEN GESELLSCHAFT, pp. 69–88. Mohr Siebeck (2022)
43. Poroy, R., Tekinalp, Ü., Çamoğlu, E.: Ortaklıklar Hukuku Cilt II. 14th edn. Vedat, İstanbul (2019)
44. Gehrlein, M., Ekkenga, J., Stefan, S.: GmbhG Kommentar. 2nd edn. Heymanns (2015)
45. Veltins, M.: Gesellschaftsrecht. In: Gounalakis, G. (ed.) RECHTSHANDBUCH ELECTRONIC BUSINESS, pp. 1076–1100. Beck (2003)
46. Noack, U., Servatius, W., Haas, U.: GmbhG Beck'sche Kurz-Kommentare. 23rd edn. C.H. Beck (2022)
47. European Commission: Liability For Artificial Intelligence and Other Emerging Digital Technologies: Report from The Expert Group on Liability and New Technologies-New Technologies Formation (2019), https://op.europa.eu/en/publication-detail/-/publication/1c5e30be-1197-11ea-8c1f-01aa75ed71a1/language-en, last accessed 2025/3/3
48. Law Commission: Decentralised Autonomous Organisations (DAOs) Call for Evidence (2022). https://cloud-platforme218f50a4812967ba1215eaecede923f.s3.amazonaws.com/uploads/sites/30/2022/11/DAOs-Call-for-Evidence-LC.pdf, last accessed 2025/3/3.
49. Buğra, A.: Room for compulsory product liability insurance in the European Union for smart robots? In: Marano, P., Noussia, K. (eds.) Insurtech: A Legal And Regulatory View, pp. 167–197. Springer (2019)
50. Karner, E., Wendehorst, C., Koch, B.A., Geistfeld, M.: Civil Liability for Artificial Intelligence and Software, De Gruyter (2023)

UBI DAO IBI IUS?

Daniele Majorana

Abstract Technological innovations have historically reshaped legal frameworks by introducing principles that redefine the creation and application of laws. In the Middle Ages, fragmented national legal systems hindered trade, leading merchants to adopt Lex Mercatoria, a transnational commercial framework facilitating efficient dispute resolution. Similarly, the digital revolution gave rise to Lex Informatica, in which IT protocols operate as regulatory mechanisms beyond traditional legislative control. With blockchain technology, Lex Cryptographia has emerged as a self-governing system, enforcing rules through software under the brocade of "code is law". This shift challenges conventional legal jurisdictions and requires innovative legal approaches to preserve the "rule of law". In taxation, the existing models based on income and wealth are insufficient for digital economies. Instead, new frameworks must account for intangible digital assets and economic activities, ensuring that taxation aligns with territorial connections despite the borderless nature of digital wealth. To address these challenges, legislators must redefine their notion of value and strengthen indirect taxation mechanisms, particularly in data-driven economies. Interdisciplinary collaboration between legal experts, computer scientists, and policymakers is crucial for developing resilient legal systems. Investing in education and skill development is essential to ensure that legal frameworks evolve in tandem with technological advancements.

Keywords DAO · Regulation · Tax nexus · AEOI · Indirect taxation

1 Introduction

Technological innovations have historically played a pivotal role in shaping legal frameworks by introducing novel principles that transform the foundational paradigms upon which laws are conceived.

D. Majorana (✉)
Milan, Italy
e-mail: dmj@danielemajorana.com

M. Lustenberger et al. (eds.), *Decentralized Autonomous Organizations—Governance, Technology, and Legal Perspectives*, Springer Proceedings in Business and Economics,
https://doi.org/10.1007/978-3-032-03273-7_9

During the Middle Ages, when fragmented and inefficient national legal systems impeded international commerce, merchants adopted *the Lex Mercatoria*, a customary legal framework based on internationally accepted commercial practices. This transnational system created a "*common playing field*", enabling efficient dispute resolution and facilitating cross-regional trade.

A similar phenomenon emerged with the advent of the digital revolution, as Information Technology (IT) architectures and protocols gave rise to *Lex Informatica.* Unlike traditional legal systems, where legislative authority resides with national parliaments and judicial power with courts, *Lex Informatica* evolved under the guidance of technical experts and operated through automated network processes encompassing their jurisdictional domain.

This framework introduced innovative regulatory and governance mechanisms aligned with an increasingly digitised global environment.

The contemporary evolution of blockchain ecosystems has enabled protocols to operate autonomously from traditional jurisdictions, thereby establishing decentralised and automated environments that serve as the Foundation for Artificial Intelligence (AI) systems. The emergence of Distributed Ledger Technology (DLT) within this context represents another significant shift as blockchain protocols operate autonomously from conventional legal frameworks. Within this context, *Lex Cryptographia*[1] has emerged as a self-governing regulatory framework in which rules are created and enforced under the brocade of "*code is law*", epitomising an era where software serves as the foundational regulatory mechanism, transcending physical boundaries.

Given the rapid advancement of technology, it is imperative to incorporate solutions rooted in innovative approaches into contemporary legal systems rather than merely adapting traditional models. To this end, cooperation among legislators, legal scholars, and computer scientists has become essential for defining a new, resilient legal system. Such interdisciplinary cooperation ensures that legal systems evolve to address the challenges posed by technological innovation while upholding the "*rule of law*". This necessitates significant investment in education and skill development, fostering a proactive approach to identifying novel legal frameworks capable of addressing these challenges.

In fiscal matters, this entails identifying new approaches to the notion of the *ability to pay*, such as the capacity to manage intangible spaces and resources that go beyond conventional notions of income or wealth. This requires establishing a fiscal law framework capable of constructively addressing the evolving digital economy while also tackling the emerging forms of inequality stemming from unequal access to digital technologies, commonly referred to as the *digital divide.*[2]

Within this framework, tax legislators' primary challenge is to establish a new definition of value[3] that will ensure taxpayers are taxed according to their territorial

---

[1] Dell'Erba [1].

[2] Fransoni [2].

[3] Emanuele [3].

connection to a jurisdiction, even when dealing with an abstract digital manifestation of wealth characterised by a lack of territoriality (*a-territoriality*).

To this end, this essay explores the following primary research question.

"*How should countries allocate taxing rights within the DAO environment*?". To provide a comprehensive response, the analysis is structured around two key sub-questions:

1. "*How can the OECD Model guide the allocation of taxing rights over DAO transactions?*"
2. "*What technology-related considerations should inform policy decisions regarding the allocation of taxing rights over DAO transactions?*"

The methodology employed in this study is highly interdisciplinary, focusing on the technological developments of DAOs to stimulate discussions on various taxation approaches by offering reflections *de jure condendo* for scholars and regulators. It provides an overview of the technological and regulatory framework to ensure technological advancements remain consistent with constitutional principles and fundamental rights.[4] This includes an in-depth analysis of the framework provided by the OECD Model, followed by a functional examination of how the technological features of DAOs affect income qualification and the allocation of taxing rights in DAO-related transactions. Thus, it is necessary to strengthen indirect taxation through new mechanisms to capture the value stemming from data consumption.

The analysis first examines how the regulatory framework has been reformed to establish a minimum threshold of legal certainty within the new economic environment shaped by the development of Distributed Ledger Technology (DLT) (Sect. 2). Subsequently, the notion of Decentralized Autonomous Organizations (DAOs) is explored, focusing on their integration into the regulatory framework (Sect. 3). This examination begins with an analysis of the legal status of DAOs, followed by an examination of U.S. practice and jurisprudence, which have already faced some situations establishing some fixed points. This section provides more information about the EU regulatory framework to determine the existence of formal requirements that may establish a territorial connection between DAOs and EU Member Countries jurisdictions. Furthermore, this study investigates the evolution of the *tax nexus* notion with reference to DAOs (Sect. 4) and token holders (Sect. 5). Moreover, the study provides an overview of the evolution of the exchange of information (Sect. 6), the new framework of indirect taxation (Sect. 7) and some insight into the potential of DAOs as a tool for tax authorities.

Based on the evaluations provided, this study's conclusions will assess how the EU regulatory framework interacts with DAOS' economic activities and how direct and indirect taxation mechanisms can capture the value they generate.

---

[4] Article 5, EU Directive 2924/1760, Corporate Sustainability Due Diligence Directive (CSDD) while those for the "Fundamental Rights Impact Assessment for High-Risk AI Systems" are dictated by Article 27, Regulation 2024/1689 (AI Act).

2 The Evolution of the Regulatory Framework Through Technological Innovation

In traditional accounting, a ledger is a physical book or document used to record transactions and track changes in data manually. However, technological advances have enabled the digital recording of transactions in an electronic ledger that can be distributed across multiple locations or participants through a network of computers or nodes—commonly referred to as Distributed Ledger Technology (DLT).[5] The most well-known form of DLT is blockchain technology, which is a shared abstract data structure consisting of a sequential chain of cryptographically linked blocks. This structure ensures *data integrity and* preserves the chronological order of recorded transactions. Compared to other DLTs, blockchain operates on a decentralised model in which each network node retains a complete copy of the ledger, encompassing all transactions conducted by all participants.[6] Within a blockchain, transactions are verifiable and immutable without the consensus of network nodes. This technology introduces a novel governance paradigm characterised by the progressive elimination of intermediaries, which are often costly and have access to sensitive data transmitted where technological mechanisms serve as infrastructure and regulatory frameworks enabling *transparency*.[7]

Blockchain networks are generally classified as *permissioned* or *permissionless* depending on their design regarding access control, data visibility, operational restrictions, and consensus validation criteria. The key difference is that in a permissioned blockchain, access to the network and participation in the consensus process is restricted to a designated group of authorised participants. In contrast, in permissionless blockchains, any individual can access and join the network, validate transactions, and engage in the consensus process without requiring prior approval, authentication, or identity verification.[8] These networks are commonly utilised for cryptocurrencies and decentralised finance (DeFi). Prominent examples of permissionless blockchains include Bitcoin and Ethereum.

The emergence of DLT has endowed the development of "*smart contracts*", initially conceptualised by Nick Szabo as "*a set of promises, specified in digital form, including protocols within which the parties are to perform on these promises*".[9] Under this definition, the "*set of promises*" may encompass contractual clauses, legal provisions or corporate procedures, embodying the immutability and transparency

[5] Under Art. 2 of the EU Regulation 2022/858 on a pilot regime for market infrastructures based on Distributed Ledger Technology DLT is defined as: "a technology that enables the operation and use of distributed ledgers" (No. 1), while "distributed ledger" is defined as "an information repository that keeps records of transactions and that is shared across, and synchronised between, a set of DLT network nodes using a consensus mechanism".

[6] Olivieri et al. [4].

[7] Müller [5].

[8] Olivieri et al. [4].

[9] Szabo [6].

inherent to their underlying networks.[10] Furthermore, these promises are "*specified in digital form*", adhering to the "*code is law*" Brocard underpinning the blockchain revolution.[11]

3 DAO: Components and Definition

The European Law Institute defines the Decentralised Autonomous Organisation (DAO) as: "*an organisation encoded as a computer program on a blockchain, facilitated by smart contracts, operating based on votes by members holding digital tokens of their membership*".[12] This definition pinpoints the technical features while leaving substantial uncertainty regarding such entities' legal classification and status.

To address this ambiguity, it is beneficial to consider the insights provided by Vitalik Buterin,[13] the creator of the Ethereum blockchain network, the infrastructure that first enabled the development of decentralised finance (DeFi). Buterin elucidates the technological and organisational foundations of DAOs by deconstructing the acronym into its constituent components: *Decentralised Organisation* (DO) and *Autonomous* (A). The notion of a DO refers to a horizontal technological architecture in which transactions occur without a central authority, eliminating hierarchical structures for execution and post-transaction control. These operations are governed by pre-established rules, shared among participants in advance and encoded within smart contracts. The notion of A relates to the idea of an Autonomous Agent in computer science: an entity that requires human intervention only during its initialisation. Once created, it executes predefined functions independently without further human oversight. This principle parallels the operation of computer viruses,[14] which propagate autonomously across systems without ongoing human interaction. Likewise, an Autonomous Agent ceases operations upon fulfilling its designated purpose.

This innovative software architecture enables participants to interact within a decentralised and transparent environment, where each transaction is executed through smart contracts and recorded on the blockchain. The immutable nature of blockchain records ensures that DAOs eliminate the need for trust among contracting parties. As a result, DAO members rely on the automated execution of smart contracts, removing the necessity for personal relationships or concerns about the reputation of administrators or officials. By mitigating corruption and lack of transparency risks, DAOs represent a significant step towards more inclusive and democratic organisational management.[15]

---

[10] Lener and Furnari [7].

[11] Dell'Erba [1].

[12] Report of the European Law Institute [8].

[13] Buterin [9].

[14] Furnari and Villani [10].

[15] Cardoso [11].

However, despite the transparency provided by blockchain infrastructure, the anonymous participation of DAO token holders presents challenges related to compliance with anti-money laundering (AML) and tax regulations. Furthermore, while the autonomy inherent in DAOs offers significant operational advantages, it limits the flexibility associated with the "*efficient breach of contract*" theory that promotes efficiency in contract performance by allowing parties to breach a contract when unforeseen circumstances arise that could not have been anticipated during negotiation and codification.[16]

Over time, scholars[17] have systematised the variety of DAO business models that have emerged into three main categories and five principal clusters. The primary categories are Governance, Community, and Treasury. The main clusters include on-chain product and service DAOs, investment-focused DAOs, networking-focused community DAOs, off-chain product and service DAOs with a community focus, and off-chain product and service DAOs with an investor focus.[18]

Finally, to represent the phenomenon quantitatively, the current market capitalisation of the largest DAO is USD 24.2 billion.[19]

3.1 The Legal Status of DAOs

A DAO's governance authority is distributed among its members. Its decentralised technological architecture transcends traditional corporate distinctions between ownership—represented by token holders—and management, which is typically entrusted to executives. In a DAO, decision-making authority resides collectively with token holders in proportion to their governance token holdings. These decisions are then executed through automated innovative contract protocols, eliminating the need for a hierarchical chain of command characteristic of traditional corporations.

The establishment of a DAO often necessitates the creation of one or more legal entities. These entities enable digital organisations to hold Intellectual property and asset ownership, ensure the protection and enhancement of digital resource value, and sign legally binding contracts with developers, suppliers, and strategic partners.

Without formal legal recognition, there is a significant risk that relationships between DAO token holders could be classified as de facto partnerships, potentially exposing all participants to unlimited liability. To mitigate such risks, DAOs may adopt the established legal structures available in various jurisdictions, a process referred to as "*wrapping*" the DAO.

The legal structuring of DAOs, which bridge the digital blockchain environment with traditional legal frameworks, remains an evolving field that requires careful

[16] Dell'Erba [1].

[17] Ziegler and Welpe [12].

[18] Müller [5].

[19] https://coinmarketcap.com/view/dao/ (accessed 11 April 2025).

consideration of regulatory compliance, governance efficiency, and the core principles of decentralisation. While each corporate structure presents distinct advantages, the challenge is to balance legal certainty with the decentralised ethos that defines DAOs.[20] Ongoing regulatory developments will determine how much DAOs can achieve mainstream adoption while preserving their decentralised governance models.

From a corporate law perspective, three main corporate structures are available for "*wrapping*" DAOs: foundations, limited liability companies (LLCs), and business trusts (BTs)[21]:

- Foundations operate autonomously following the founding principles enshrined in their incorporation documents, maintaining operational immutability (the "solidification principle"). This autonomous character aligns with the decentralisation ethos of DAOs, which are designed to function independently of their original developers once established. However, jurisdictional requirements regarding operational flexibility and taxation vary significantly. Switzerland and the Cayman Islands are often regarded as preferred jurisdictional choices. In particular, whereas the Cayman Islands impose no income taxation on foundations,[22] the Swiss regime is more nuanced: foundations are, as a rule, subject to corporate income taxation at both federal and cantonal levels, although exemptions may be granted where they pursue public-benefit or charitable purposes.[23]
- Limited liability companies (LLCs) provide flexibility and limited liability protection for token holders. Certain jurisdictions[24] have introduced blockchain-based limited liability companies (BBLLCs), offering legal recognition for blockchain governance mechanisms while ensuring member liability protection. However, this structure necessarily introduces elements of centralisation that contrast with core DAO principles.[25] Moreover, business trusts (BTs) provide flexible legal frameworks for DAO operations, particularly in managing and distributing profits.

[20] Mienert [13].

[21] Möslein and Ostrovski [14].

[22] "Cayman Islands Foundation Companies – Tax Treatment" Harneys Legal Insights (Harneys) https://www.harneys.com/media/zphoua3y/legal-insights-cayman-islands-foundation-companies.pdf accessed 21 September 2025)

[23] Giedre Lideikyte Huber, "Philanthropy and Taxation: Swiss Legal Framework" Expert Focus 2018, Geneva (university publication) https://www.unige.ch/philanthropie/download_file/view/125/458 accessed 21 September 2025, especially Art. 56(g) LIFD/DBG and comparable cantonal norms for exemption from federal, cantonal and communal income tax for foundations with public interest / charitable purposes

[24] The DAO LLC of Wyoming (United States), the Blockchain-Based Limited Liability Company (BBLLC) of Vermont (United States), the LAO of Delaware (United States). In Europe, the Decentralized Autonomous Association—DAA (Switzerland) as well as a special form in Malta with the "innovative technology arrangement" are relevant for establishing a DINO. Additionally, the United Kingdom is currently exploring the possibility of creating a new legal framework specifically for DAOs and has initiated a Call for Evidence—Pre-consultation Phase (https://lawcom.gov.uk/project/decentralised-autonomous-organisations-daos/ (accessed 11 April 2025). Under English proposal, DAOs should be classified as a partnership (see Müller [5]).

[25] Mienert [15].

The blockchain hosting DAO smart contracts within this structure may be classified as intangible trust property. The trust deed could be integrated into the DAO protocol, and transaction processors (miners) would act as trustees.[26]

Contemporary decentralised projects typically operate through a tripartite structure comprising a non-legal entity (the DAO), a development company (DEVCO), and a foundation. Each entity serves a distinct yet complementary role in ensuring the project's long-term success and sustainability.

1. *The DAO*, functioning as a decentralised governance system based on smart contracts running on a blockchain operating without traditional legal status, the DAO.
2. *The Developer Company (DEVCO)*, typically established as a commercial entity by the project's developers, provides IT services to the DAO and the Foundation. It is responsible for implementing technical improvements, maintaining the network, and enhancing the underlying protocol.
3. *The Foundation* represents the project's non-profit dimension. It promotes the protocol globally, produces educational content, and collaborates with institutions to foster adoption.[27] Sometimes, the foundation issues and sells governance tokens to fund the project. Alternatively, a special purpose vehicle (SPV), often owned by the Foundation, may issue the tokens to separate fundraising activities from the Foundation's other responsibilities.

The interaction among these three entities is crucial for the success of decentralised projects. Through its members, the DAO drives strategic and governance decisions; the DEVCO implements technical innovations and network enhancements; and the Foundation promotes global awareness and adoption of the protocol.

Despite the benefits of this structure, the interaction between the DAO, DEVCO, and the Foundation presents several legal and regulatory challenges. These interactions may give rise to value-added tax (VAT) and transfer pricing issues. Furthermore, the Foundation or SPV must comply with local and international financial regulations when selling tokens.

3.2 DAOs in U.S. Practice and Jurisprudence

One of the first Decentralised Autonomous Organisations (DAOs) to be launched, "The DAO", developed in 2016 by Christoph Jentzsch, raised the equivalent of $150 million in Ethereum through an initial coin offering (ICO) within 15 days. "The DAO" was managed and executed by computer code on a blockchain, where decision-making occurs through a democratic vote by shareholders (who are referred

[26] Reyes [16].

[27] For example, the Ethereum Foundation, registered in Switzerland, supports the Ethereum project, while commercial companies like ConsenSys develop products and services (e.g., the MetaMask wallet) to facilitate Ethereum's adoption.

to as token holders) on an equal basis. With previously defined rules, governance is managed by a self-sufficient programme, i.e., smart contracts, without a hierarchical structure.[28]

Following its launch, the U.S. Securities and Exchange Commission (SEC) challenged "The DAO", asserting that its ICO constituted an unregistered securities issuance in breach of federal financial regulations.[29](A) Switzerland and the Cayman Islands are often regarded as preferred jurisdictional choices. In particular, whereas the Cayman Islands impose no income taxation on foundations (*), the Swiss regime is more nuanced: foundations are, as a rule, subject to corporate income taxation at both federal and cantonal levels, although exemptions may be granted where they pursue public-benefit or charitable purposes (**) (*) "Cayman Islands Foundation Companies – Tax Treatment" Harneys Legal Insights (Harneys) https://www.harneys.com/media/zphoua3y/legal-insights-cayman-islands-foundation-companies.pdf accessed 21 September 2025) (**) Giedre Lideikyte Huber, "Philanthropy and Taxation: Swiss Legal Framework" Expert Focus 2018, Geneva (university publication) https://www.unige.ch/philanthropie/download_file/view/125/458 accessed 21 September 2025, especially Art. 56(g) LIFD/DBG and comparable cantonal norms for exemption from federal, cantonal and communal income tax for foundations with public interest / charitable purposes

Later, in 2022, the Commodity Futures Trading Commission (CFTC) took action against Ooki DAO for operating as an unregistered futures commission merchant (FCM),[30] thereby breaching the Commodity Exchange Act (CEA). The CFTC classified Ooki DAO as an "*unrecognised association*", defining it as a voluntary collective organised without formal legal status yet pursuing common objectives. Based on this classification, the CFTC attributed personal liability to token holders who authorised organisational actions. Subsequently, on 8 June 2023, a federal judge[31] issued an order and default judgement, determining that Ooki DAO had operated an illegal trading platform and acted as an unregistered FCM. Following this ruling, the CFTC[32] classified Ooki DAO as a "*person*" under the CEA, thereby extending liability for statutory violations to individual token holders. This reasoning was upheld in the LIDO DAO judgement,[33] where the court classified LIDO DAO as a partnership based on substantive analysis despite the absence of formal legal recognition. Specifically, the court considered the active role of token holders in the DAO governance

---

[28] Müller [5].

[29] https://www.sec.gov/newsroom/press-releases/2017-131 (accessed 11 April 2025).

[30] In US law, a futures commission merchant (FCM) is an individual or organisation engaged in the business of soliciting or accepting orders to buy or sell futures or futures options in exchange for the payment of money (commission) or other assets from customers. MMFs are subject to the Commodity Exchange Act (CEA) and the rules and regulations issued by the Office of the Comptroller of the Currency (OCC) as well as the rules and regulations issued by the Commodity Futures Trade Commission (CFTC), the National Futures Association (NFA). In Europe, MMFs are analogous to futures market clearing members. (See Chen [17]).

[31] United States District Court Northern District of California, Case No. 3:22-cv-05416.

[32] CFTC Release Number 8715-23.

[33] United States District Court Northern District of California, Case No. 23-cv-06492-VC.

sufficient grounds for partnership classification. Consequently, even minimal governance participation could constitute "*involvement in the partnership*", potentially resulting in unlimited personal liability.

Based on the aforementioned U.S. law, there is a significant risk that relationships between DAO token holders could be deemed *de facto* partnerships without formal legal recognition. This may lead to unlimited liability for all participants. To mitigate such risks, DAOs might consider adopting established legal structures available in various jurisdictions (Wrapping DAO).

In this respect, a recent survey[34] shows that 88% of operators are interested in incorporating the DAO into a corporate vehicle precisely to limit the liability of DAO members and that, in a complementary way, the main reason for not adopting a legal screen for the DAO lies in the difficulty of finding an appropriate structure in the law.

It is worth noting that on 24 January 2023, U.S. President Donald Trump signed an executive order establishing a working group tasked to develop regulations for the cryptocurrency industry and digital assets. This initiative indicates that a new regulatory framework may soon emerge, introducing specific obligations tailored to operators in the sector, distinct from those currently applied to conventional legal framework entities.[35]

3.3 DAOs and the EU Legal System—GDPR Regulation

In the European Union, ensuring that personal data is processed fairly, for specified purposes, and based on consent or another legitimate legal basis is a fundamental right.[36] To this end, the General Data Protection Regulation (GDPR)[37] governs the processing of personal data by EU institutions, bodies, and Member States when acting within the scope of EU law. Within this framework, the GDPR serves a two-fold purpose: (*i*) facilitating the free movement of personal data across Member States while (*ii*) ensuring the protection of fundamental rights as outlined in the Charter of Fundamental Rights.

Under GDPR compliance rules, responsibility and accountability for personal data processing rest with the *data controller*, defined as "*the natural or legal person, public authority, agency, or other body which, alone or jointly with others, determines the purposes and means of the processing of personal data*".[38] The primary role of the controller is "*to determine who shall be responsible for compliance with data*

[34] BlackVogel—A Blockstand Project [18].

[35] Available at: https://www.whitehouse.gov/presidential-actions/2025/01/strengthening-american-leadership-in-digital-financial-technology/ (accessed 11 April 2025).

[36] Article 8 of the EU Charter of Fundamental Rights.

[37] EU Regulation 2016/679.

[38] Art. 4, Num. 7, EU Regulation 2016/679

protection rules and how data subjects can exercise the rights in practice".[39] By contrast, the processor is the legal or natural person processing personal data on behalf of the controller.

A functional approach is employed to assess whether a controller or processor is established in the EU and whether the establishment represents an effective and genuine exercise of activity through stable arrangements.[40] This functional approach facilitates the allocation of responsibilities based on factual influence; thus, for every data point, there must be at least one controller whom data subjects can contact to enforce their rights, regardless of the technology used—reflecting the GDPR's technology-neutrality principle.[41]

The rise of blockchain technologies complicates accountability,[42] particularly in public and permissionless blockchains, where no legal entity (such as a company or consortium) controls data processing. This leads to increasingly complex data environments.[43] In contrast, private and permissioned blockchains provide greater compliance feasibility due as identifiable legal entities determine the means and, in many cases, the purposes of processing personal data.

A functional, case-by-case analysis is recommended to identify the controller among developers, miners, and nodes for the purposes of personal data processing.[44] When a consortium establishes a legal entity, it qualifies as the data controller, given its significant control over the purposes and means of personal data processing. In the case of DAOs, a connection is established between the Distributed Ledger Technology (DLT) and the jurisdiction in which its registered office is located. Consequently, in public and permissionless blockchain environments, no single legal entity clearly qualifies as a data controller. Instead, private and permissioned blockchains[45] offer enhanced regulatory compliance due to the involvement of an identifiable legal entity (such as a company or consortium) that determines the means and, in many cases, the purposes of processing personal data.[46]

The allocation of responsibility in decentralised systems must ensure compliance with data protection rules is upheld in practice. In this context, the Court of Justice of the European Union (CJEU)[47] has ruled that a data controller "*must ensure, within the framework of its responsibilities, powers, and capabilities*", that the rights of data subjects are effectively and comprehensively upheld. This reasoning implies that

[39] Article 29 Working Party, Opinion 1/2010 on the concepts of "controller" and "processor" (WP 169) 00264/10/EN, 15.

[40] Recital 22 EU Regulation 2016/679.

[41] Recital 15 EU Regulation 2016/679.

[42] EU Data Act, Recital 57.

[43] Article 29 Working Party, Opinion 1/2010 on the concepts of "controller" and "processor" (WP 169) 00264/10/EN, 2.

[44] Finck [19].

[45] A notable example of a permissioned blockchain is Hyperledger Fabric.

[46] Finck [19].

[47] EUCJ Case 131/12 Google Spain, para 38.

controllers are only liable for GDPR compliance to the extent that they are factually capable of fulfilling their obligations.

From the Tax perspective, whereas the EU intends to tax the extraction of a country's "*digital value*" with "*digital excise taxes*", [48] precisely as if it were the extraction of mineral resources or fuels, the data controller's role and information may be pivotal. Notably, under the current framework, excise duties apply only to alcohol consumption, energy products, electricity, and tobacco products. These products, once consumed, are removed from the production cycle. In contrast, data is fungible and can be utilised in several processes, potentially resulting in multiple instances of taxation on the same data.

3.4 DAOs and the EU Legal System—DATA Act

Under the EU Data Act,[49] a smart contract[50] is a "*computer program used for the automatic execution of an agreement or part thereof using a sequence of electronic data records and ensuring their integrity and accuracy of their chronological order*". To "*make the data available*", smart contracts must comply with the following essential requirements[51]:

a. Robustness and access control: Smart contracts must be designed to incorporate access control mechanisms and a high degree of robustness to prevent functional errors and resist third-party manipulation.
b. Safe termination and termination (i.e., kill switch): Smart contracts must include mechanisms to cease the automated execution of transactions while also providing internal functions that allow for resetting or stopping operations to prevent future accidental executions.
c. Data storage and continuity: In cases where a smart contract needs to be terminated or deactivated, there must be provisions for archiving transaction data, as well as the logic and code of the smart contract, to maintain a verifiable record of past operations (so-called verifiability).
d. Access control: Smart contracts must be protected by robust governance mechanisms that regulate access control.
e. Coherence: Smart contracts must align with the terms of the data-sharing agreement they execute.

---

[48] Galimberti [20].

[49] Concerning the European Data Strategy, The EU Regulation No. 2023/2854 settles the right of access to data produced by Internet of Things (IoT) to respond to the needs of the digital economy and to eliminate obstacles to the smooth functioning of the internal data market, to establish "*a harmonized framework specifying who has the right to use data from a related product or service, under what conditions and on what basis*" (see Recital n. 3).

[50] Art. 2, Num. 39, EU Regulation No. 2023/2854.

[51] Art. 36, EU Regulation No. 2023/2854 ("Essential smart contract requirements for the execution of data sharing agreements").

Access control requirements can consistently be enforced at the smart contract layer by adding conditional statements that are satisfied only when executed by specific users or under conditions that can change over time. Governance strictly depends on the type of blockchain network. In permissioned blockchains, governance can be explicitly established at various levels, for instance, by forming a consortium, sub-networks, or private collections for transmitting sensitive data. Conversely, in the case of permissionless blockchains, governance is inherently absent at the network level due to the open and decentralised nature of such blockchains. Indeed, in a permissionless setting, governance considerations are primarily relevant for write access, as reading data is unrestricted and does not require smart contracts.[52]

3.5 DAOs and the EU Legal System—MICA Regulation

The Regulation on Markets in Crypto-Assets (MiCA)[53] marks a significant advancement in standardising crypto-asset requirements within the EU. This regulation aims to ensure uniform supervision and oversight across EU jurisdictions by establishing common standards for public crypto-asset offerings and crypto-asset service providers (CASPs).[54]

Recital 22 of the MiCA Regulation is particularly relevant to this discussion, as it excludes from its scope "*crypto-asset services provided in a fully decentralised manner, without any intermediary*". However, the regulation does not provide a precise definition of "*decentralisation*" beyond the general reference to the absence of intermediaries. For DAOs, this lack of clarity could lead to divergent interpretations and legal uncertainties, potentially complicating compliance and increasing the risk of operating within a regulatory grey area.

From a technical perspective, DAOs can be classified according to their level of autonomy[55] as *Algorithmic DAOs*, operating continuously through self-executing smart contracts without requiring member intervention, achieving the highest degree of independence. In contrast, *Participative DAOs* require periodic input from their members on operational matters, reducing their autonomy level.

It could be argued that algorithmic DAOs that exclude third-party interventions, including intermediaries, meet the decentralisation requirement under MiCA. However, regulators must assess whether the software is genuinely self-executing. This evaluation will require examining the rights associated with tokens and the organisational structure of token holders. Conversely, participative DAOs, in which

[52] Olivieri et al. [4].

[53] Regulation (EU) 2023/1114 of 31 May 2023.

[54] Pursuant to Art. 3, Num. 15), Reg. (EU) 2023/1114, a "*cryptocurrency service provider*" is defined as "*a legal person or other undertaking whose occupation or business consists in the provision of one or more cryptocurrency services to customers on a professional basis and which is authorised to provide cryptocurrency services in accordance with Article 59*".

[55] Cardoso [21].

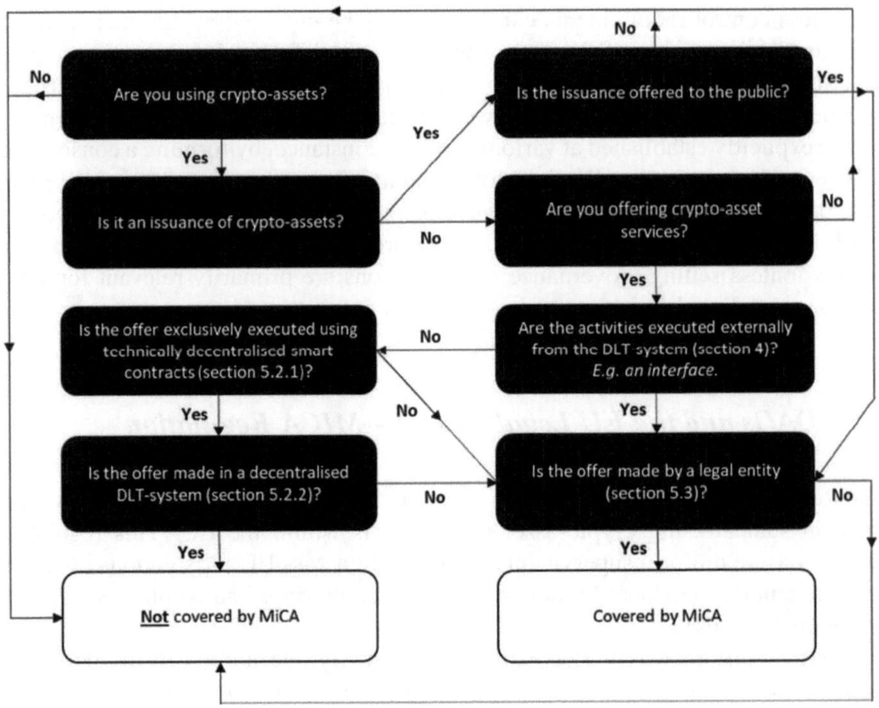

Fig. 1 Is your offer decentralised or covered by MiCA?

token holders retain decision-making authority (e.g., access to services), depart from the concept of decentralisation outlined above.

The Danish Financial Supervisory Authority (FSA) has adopted a specific approach regarding decentralisation.[56] When regulated activities are offered in a fully centralised manner, a legal entity maintains complete control over the activities, which are conducted exclusively through the company's systems without access to a conventional blockchain. In contrast, in partially decentralised operations, a legal entity still retains control over activities but offers services using partially or fully smart contracts via the application layer. Finally, a provision is considered fully decentralised only when no legal entity exercises control over the activity and transactions or rights are structured autonomously through smart contracts deployed within the application layer.

Under this framework, as illustrated in the figure below, the defining characteristic of decentralisation is the autonomous execution of transactions free from external control (Fig. 1).

[56] Finanstilsynet: Principles for the assessment of decentralisation in the markets for crypto-assets (in https://www.dfsa.dk/Media/638549094736906876/PrinciplesCryptoAssetsPDF_250624.pdf , accessed 11 April 2025).

Another critical provision of the MiCA Regulation is Recital 74, stating that "*to enable effective supervision and eliminate the possibility of circumventing or evading supervision, services for crypto-assets should only be provided by legal persons having their registered office in a Member State where they engage in substantial business activities, including the provision of services for crypto-assets*". This requirement has significant implications for DAOs seeking to provide crypto-asset services within the EU. Specifically, DAOs must adopt a recognised legal structure and establish a registered office in an EU Member State.

According to this regulation, if the DAO wishes to qualify as a cryptocurrency service provider (CASP), it must be "wrapped" in a legal structure with a registered office in an EU country to comply with MICA purposes. This regulatory requirement aligns with the tax nexus principle, granting the respective European jurisdiction the sovereignty to apply corporate tax and value-added tax (VAT) according to the relevant standards.

4 The DAO Tax Nexus

The allocation of taxing rights has long been a *vexata quaestio* of the international tax regime, dating back to the 1923 Report on Double Taxation to the Financial Committee of the League of Nations, which marked the Foundation of the international tax framework. The 1923 Report established that business income should be taxed primarily in the source country. However, its definition of "source" extended beyond the mere origin of income to include destination (i.e., market) countries. This broader interpretation aligns with the view that wealth creation encompasses all stages, from production to realisation, meaning that profit cannot exist without sales.[57]

The existence of a connecting factor between an entity and a specific jurisdiction defines the notion of "*tax nexus*", providing justification for the latter's tax sovereignty over the taxing rights. In traditional corporate structures (commonly referred to as "*brick-and-mortar*" businesses), this nexus is typically established through both formal criteria, such as the location of the registered office, and substantive criteria, such as the physical presence of offices, establishments, and employees within the jurisdiction. Therefore, based on the current international tax framework, companies are taxed in the jurisdictions where they are formally established and operate through a legal entity.[58] Furthermore, under the functional approach, allocating taxing rights among jurisdictions necessitates identifying each jurisdiction's

[57] The 1923 Report illustrated this principle through the metaphor of oranges on trees in California: wealth is generated through multiple stages, including harvesting, packaging, transportation, and final sale. The value of the oranges is realized only when they reach consumers, highlighting that each stage contributes to wealth creation and, consequently, to the allocation of taxing rights.

[58] Art. 7(1), OECD Model Tax Convention.

contribution to "economic value" through a functional analysis of enterprise activities within the "global value chain". This process is based on the "*separate entity approach*",[59] which treats each enterprise segment as an independent entity for taxation purposes. Therefore, companies generating income in other jurisdictions through local "*permanent establishments – PE*"[60] incur taxation in those foreign jurisdictions against which the company's jurisdiction of incorporation usually grants a tax credit to avoid double taxation.[61]

The OECD Model Tax Convention, which aims to prevent double taxation on income and capital, employs the concept of "corporate residence" as a fundamental principle in providing double tax treaties between different countries. However, the notion of "*place of effective management (POEM)*"[62] is crucial when addressing dual tax residence issues. In this regard, the OECD Commentary to the Model Tax Convention clarifies the "*POEM*" is the jurisdiction where "*the company, was actually managed*", [63] specifically the place where "*the most senior person or group of persons (for example a board of directors) made the key management and commercial decisions necessary for the conduct of the company's business*".[64]

Furthermore, regarding the digital economy, in 2015, the OECD introduced the concept of Significant Economic Presence (SEP),[65] which expands traditional permanent establishment principles to include foreign enterprises that, despite lacking physical presence, actively engage in economic activities within a jurisdiction through digital technologies.

Finally, in 2017, the OECD radically shifted its approach through amendments to the draft OECD Model Tax Convention and the design of the Multilateral Convention to Implement Tax Treaty Related Measures to Prevent Base Erosion and Profit Shifting (the MLI).[66] The OECD now advocates for a somewhat discretionary approach to resolving cases of dual tax residence for companies through a mutual agreement procedure (MAP) and denying treaty benefits as the preferred approach.[67]

---

[59] Art. 7(2), OECD Model Tax Convention

[60] Art. 5, OECD Model Tax Convention.

[61] Art. 23/B, OECD Model Tax Convention.

[62] Article 4(3) of the OECD Model Convention.

[63] OECD [22].

[64] OECD [23].

[65] OECD [24].

[66] The main MLI provision dealing with dual tax residence of companies can be found in article 4 paragraph 1 which provides as follows: "*Where by reason of the provisions of a Covered Tax Agreement a person other than an individual is a resident of more than one Contracting Jurisdiction, the competent authorities of the Contracting Jurisdictions shall endeavour to determine by mutual agreement the Contracting Jurisdiction of which such person shall be deemed to be a resident for the purposes of the Covered Tax Agreement, having regard to its place of effective management, the place where it is incorporated or otherwise constituted and any other relevant factors. In the absence of such agreement, such person shall not be entitled to any relief or exemption from tax provided by the Covered Tax Agreement except to the extent and in such manner as may be agreed upon by the competent authorities of the Contracting Jurisdictions*".

[67] Olika [25].

Within this regulatory framework, DAOs navigate in an unknown area of international tax law. In fact, DAOs are established globally, with their blockchain code decentralised and executed across a distributed network. In such a case, determining residency is crucial for applying international tax law and its associated regulations. Most DAOs are not organised internationally with a legal wrapper; they exist just in the digital sphere. Consequently, the lack of distinct geographical boundaries in digital spaces complicates the distribution of taxing rights among countries, raising the risk of double taxation for users within the DAO[68] or double non-taxation on gains.[69]

In addition, the inherent anonymity of DAO transactions poses significant challenges in identifying revenue-generating jurisdictions. When determining jurisdictions proves impossible, entities risk being classified as "*stateless income*" generators. This aspect renders DAOs potentially effective vehicles for tax avoidance through sophisticated planning strategies, particularly given that the OECD's Base Erosion and Profit Shifting (BEPS) initiatives still do not explicitly address DAO-specific issues and challenges.

The decentralised and fragmented nature of DAOs further complicates applying the separate entity approach. In DAOs, economic "value" generation does not occur through discrete transactions or identifiable functions within specific jurisdictions. Instead, value arises from the organisation's intrinsic characteristics—an integrated combination of software and digital infrastructure functioning as a unified entity. This renders the separate entity approach inapplicable for DAOs.

In light of these considerations, *DAOs lack the traditional features necessary to establish a tax nexus* as defined within this framework. From *a formal perspective*, DAOs do not possess a place of incorporation or a registered office due to their inherently decentralised nature. From a *substantive perspective*, instead, as DAOs typically do not require employees, physical offices, or retail locations, and therefore lack an identifiable physical presence that could establish jurisdictional tax sovereignty over their income. As a result, under the current international tax system, it is thus challenging to identify a jurisdiction with tax sovereignty over a DAO's income proceeds.

The idea behind the DAO is to automate all of the agreements necessary to coordinate a group of individuals to accomplish the work of an organisation—in other words, to replace the centralised overhead of a conventional business with code. The core technological component of a DAO—self-executing agreements and automated record-keeping—allows an organisation to function with minimal human managerial discretion, deliberation, and control. Consequently, within the DAO environment, the notion of POEM may be replaced by two core Taoist tenets for daily business operations: (1) action without deliberation and (2) alignment of that action with nature and natural laws.[70]

---

68 Cipollini [26].

69 Müller [5].

70 Shakow [27].

Furthermore, even if it were possible to establish a DAO's tax residence, its decentralised structure creates further complications. Indeed, in a DAO blockchain, it would be impossible to identify an individual with signature authority to fulfil tax compliance obligations, such as submitting tax returns or making tax payments. These obligations must be fulfilled anonymously and automatically, a requirement that current tax systems are not equipped to handle.

Finally, the MAP tool cannot be used to determine a DAO's tax residence without a reference jurisdiction.

Based on these considerations, DAOs face the same issues of entities operating in the metaverse[71]: Can a jurisdiction exercise tax sovereignty over income earned in cyberspace? To address this question, it is helpful to consider that DAOs are not the first example of entities possessing financial autonomy without legal personality—mutual funds serve as a notable precedent. From a *de jure condendo* perspective, the taxation of DAOs could be approached through a transparency-based model, similar to that of investment funds. Under this framework, income is calculated at the level of the investment fund but taxed at the level of the fund's unit holders. Accordingly, it would be necessary to determine whether a tax nexus exists for the natural persons holding DAO tokens.

Based on this approach, the Coalition of Automated Legal Applications (COALA), in its *Model Law for Decentralized Autonomous Organizations (DAO)*, proposed a taxation provision that upholds the principle of transparency.[72] It suggests that taxation should occur at the level of token holders, in proportion to their holdings, rather than at the entity level. Indeed, token holders are the only subjects who exhibit a capacity to pay in relation to the income generated by the DAO and are also the only parties clearly anchored within a tax jurisdiction.

From COALA's perspective, DAOs are not comparable to other taxable persons or entities. Similarly, no taxable nexus can be established through a permanent establishment (PE)[73] or agents, as DAOs cannot be attributed to any specific geographic location. This is because the underlying smart contracts operate exclusively in cyberspace and are maintained by a distributed network of participants.

Given this context, it may be inferred that DAOs could appropriately be treated for tax purposes as look-through entities, with taxation arguably more suitable at the level of the token holders, who would accordingly bear the responsibility for meeting their fiscal obligations. However, exclusive taxation at the token holder level may incentivise profit shifting, as token holders are generally identifiable only through pseudonymised wallet addresses that do not establish tax residency. Furthermore, token holders may relocate to low-tax jurisdictions to minimise their tax burden. Considering these challenges, establishing a coordinated framework across

---

[71] Kim [28].

[72] Coalition of Automated Legal Applications, Model Law for Decentralized Autonomous Organizations (DAOs), available at https://www.lextechinstitute.ch/wp-content/uploads/2021/06/DAO-Model-Law.pdf (accessed 9 April 2025), Art. 20.

[73] Article 5 of the OECD Model Convention.

tax jurisdictions would be appropriate to reduce opportunities for tax arbitrage.[74] This problem can be solved at the OECD level based on due diligence procedures stated in the Crypto-Asset Reporting Framework (CARF) and at the EU level in Directive DAC 8.[75]

A further challenge arises when a DAO is treated as a tax look-through entity: the in come allocated to token holders is not reported in a tax return and, therefore, has no fiscal effect.[76] This prevents income attribution through transparency mechanisms, thereby hindering token holders from fulfilling their tax obligations. As an alternative, token holders could be taxed upon the actual receipt of bonuses, dividends, or tokens and upon the realisation of capital gains derived from the sale of DAO tokens. This approach would grant token holders *tax deferral* benefits analogous to that enjoyed by shareholders of traditional corporations with respect to accrued but undistributed dividends. Going back to the case of investment funds, it is worth noting, however, that they own companies typically subject to corporate income tax, meaning that the income distributed to unit holders has already been taxed at the corporate level. By contrast, if a DAO is treated as a stateless entity, token holders may receive income that is not subject to taxation in any jurisdiction.

Under these assumptions, a sustainable solution could involve taxing token holders based on income accrued during the tax period using a mark-to-market approach.

Finally, regarding DAOs that have adopted a recognised legal structure and established a registered office in an EU member state in accordance with the MiCA Regulation, such entities are likely to operate as "shell companies", primarily holding intangible assets or cryptocurrencies. Nevertheless, due to the lack of economic substance characterising their business models, these entities can hardly be deemed tax residents in any other jurisdiction based on the effective place of management principle. Adopting the proposed directive to prevent the misuse of shell entities for tax purposes[77] could lead to the transparent taxation of such entities.

5 The Token Holder Tax Nexus

According to the OECD Model Tax Convention on Income and Capital,[78] the tax nexus of a person with jurisdiction is connected to the notion of tax residence. Tax residence is usually determined based on the "*domicile*", "*residence*", or "*place of effective management*". However, these criteria were developed with traditional

[74] Müller [5].

[75] DAC8, ANNEX III, Section III.

[76] Shakow [27].

[77] Proposal for a COUNCIL DIRECTIVE laying down rules to prevent the misuse of shell entities for tax purposes and amending Directive 2011/16/EU COM(2021) 565 final {SEC(2021) 565 final}.

[78] Art. 4, of the OECD Model Tax Convention.

physical spaces in mind and do not adequately capture the nuances of digital environments, such as the complexities introduced by VPN usage and geolocation-masking tools.

For individuals, "*domicile*" generally implies a place with a lasting connection and intention to remain, which is typically tied to physical presence and long-term residence. Nevertheless, determining domicile becomes challenging in digital environments, as users can mask or obfuscate their physical locations through VPNs and other tools. Similarly, "*residence*" often defined as the place where a person lives or stays for a significant period, is traditionally linked to physical presence.

When users spend substantial time in virtual environments without disclosing their true location, the concept of residence becomes challenging to apply. In such cases, the ability to mask one's physical presence in digital spaces undermines traditional methods for determining residence, suggesting a need for tax authorities to adopt more flexible and nuanced approaches. In this context, the due diligence procedure under the Crypto-Asset Reporting Framework (CARF)[79] and the EU Directive DAC 8[80] requires the paying agency to identify Crypto Asset Users and Controlling Persons, as well as to ascertain the relevant tax jurisdictions for reporting and exchange purposes, which may assist in solving this problem. Once tax residence is established, the OECD Double Tax Convention (DTC) can govern the transaction, thereby facilitating cross-border tax coordination with the source country and diminishing the risk of double taxation. Regarding the source jurisdiction, in the case of wrapped DAOs, consideration may be given to the jurisdiction in which the DAO has been incorporated. For income distributed to token holders via Crypto-Asset Service Providers (CASPs) acting as a paying agent, the relevant source jurisdiction is where the CASP is incorporated. However, transactions conducted directly between fully unwrapped DAOs and token holders are excluded from this jurisdictional attribution; these cases will be addressed later in this section.

5.1 The Qualification of Income Perceived by Token Holders

Blockchain technology challenges tax regulations due to its disintermediation feature. This feature allows for pseudonymity,[81] which facilitates tax avoidance.

---

[79] Crypto-Asset Reporting Framework (CARF) and Amendments to the Common Reporting Standard, Rules, Section I, OECD (2022), Paris, https://www.oecd.org/en/publications/international-standards-for-automatic-exchange-of-information-in-tax-matters_896d79d1-en.html.

[80] DAC8, ANNEX III, Section III.

[81] S. Parsons: "*Taxing Crypto-Asset Transactions*"—IBFD Doctoral Series Num. 66, paragraph 7.2.5.1.: "*A taxpayer therefore knows very little about the counterparty's identity to a transaction. The proposed measures focus on restoring taxing rights eroded by the digitalised economy in market jurisdictions. Its implementation therefore presupposes that the taxpayer is able to determine at least the location, if not the identity, of counterparties in a reliable manner (...) Pseudonymity is a central ideological and pragmatic proposition of blockchain technology. It may therefore be impossible for taxpayers to identify the market jurisdictions in which they are transacting. While*

Existing regulatory requirements, such as anti-money laundering (AML)[82] rules and the exchange of information frameworks, such as the Crypto-Asset Reporting Framework (CARF) and the EU Directive DAC 8, primarily focus on service providers.[83] However, these regulations may not cover certain transactions, such as initial coin offerings (ICOs), block rewards, fortuitous issuances and receipts, because they do not have source jurisdiction. Consequently, tax administrations may struggle to identify the transactions and tax jurisdictions involved.[84]

For transactions involving crypto-assets across tax jurisdictions, tax treaties aimed at avoiding double taxation of income or capital (Double Tax Treaties—DTTs), allocate taxing rights to specific jurisdictions. However, determining whether a payment is taxable and how and when it should be taxed ultimately depends on each jurisdiction's domestic tax regulations.

Once a transaction is deemed taxable under domestic law—typically by applying the ability-to-pay principle—it influences how international tax treaties are implemented.[85] Although the OECD *Model Tax Convention on Income and Capital* (MC)[86] does not explicitly address crypto-asset transactions, conventional tax rules can be determined by drawing analogies based on each transaction's unique facts and circumstances.

Several provisions of the OECD MC may be relevant in determining the tax treatment of crypto-asset transactions, including Article 7 on business income, Article 10 on dividends, Article 11 on interest payments, Article 12 on royalties, Article 13 on capital gains, and Article 21 on other incomes.[87]

5.2 *Initial Coin Offering (ICO)*

Fundraising through the issuance of cryptocurrencies, commonly known as Initial Coin Offerings (ICOs), has become a prevalent use case that leverages the benefits of the blockchain infrastructure.

regulatory requirements that crypto-asset exchanges obtain personal information from parties may go some way towards addressing this issue, those requirements focus primarily on the regulatory and tax compliance of the transacting party. Using the information collected to support the tax compliance of a counterparty would take these measures a significant step further. In addition, cryptoasset exchanges are not an essential element of any particular transaction, and play no role in a number of transactions, perhaps most notably those of transaction validation. Requirements imposed on exchanges may therefore at best only partially address this challenge".

[82] Directive (EU) 2018/843.

[83] See *infra* Section 5 (DAC8, ANNEX III, Section III).

[84] Baer et al. [29].

[85] "*... if a country taxes the sale of a token under its domestic law, the relevant treaty provisions, such as Article 13 on capital gains, may guide how the transaction is taxed at the cross-border level*". Cipollini [26].

[86] OECD [30].

[87] Majorana [31].

In 2019, the European Securities and Markets Authority (ESMA)[88] defined Initial Coin Offerings (ICOs). According to the ESMA, ICOs are operations wherein companies, entrepreneurs, developers, or other promoters raise capital for their projects by offering crypto assets to investors. Typically, ICOs are promoted through online platforms and social media channels, accompanied by detailed "*white papers*".[89]

Blockchain technology in ICOs enables direct *peer-to-peer* transactions between the ICO issuer and investors, resulting in significant cost savings compared to the traditional and resource-intensive process of conducting an Initial Public Offering (IPO).

Since ICO investors may reside in different jurisdictions from where the ICO is conducted, the allocation of taxing rights to income derived from ICOs should be determined under applicable tax treaties. To address this issue, it is necessary to examine the tax treaty classifications of

- Capital raised by the ICO issuers.
- Returns on invested capital for ICO investors.
- Investors earn profits through the sale of crypto assets obtained via ICOs.

5.2.1 Initial Coin Offering (ICO): Issuance of Utility or Equity Token

The MICA Regulation defines utility tokens as a: "*type of crypto-asset that is only intended to provide access to a good or a service supplied by its issuer*".[90] On the other hand, equity tokens[91] represent equity in an underlying asset, typically a company's stock. Moreover, the principle of technological neutrality [92] must be considered when determining the tax treaty classification of capital raised through

---

[88] ESMA: Advice Initial Coin Offerings and Crypto-Assets (9 January 2019), available at https://www.esma.europa.eu/document/advice-initial-coin-offerings-and-crypto-assets (accessed 13 April 2025).

[89] "*In order to ensure their protection, prospective retail holders of crypto-assets should be informed of the characteristics, functions and risks of the crypto-assets that they intend to purchase. When making an offer to the public of crypto-assets other than asset-referenced tokens or e-money tokens or when seeking admission to trading of such crypto-assets in the Union, offerors or persons seeking admission to trading should draw up, notify their competent authority and publish an information document containing mandatory disclosures ('a crypto-asset white paper')*". (Recital 24 of Regulation (EU) 2023/1114 of the European Parliament and of the Council of 31 May 2023 on markets in crypto-assets MICA). Article 6 of the same Regulation rules the "Content and form of the crypto-asset white paper".

[90] Art. 3. Num. 9), Regulation (EU) 2023/1114 of the European Parliament and of the Council of 31 May 2023 on markets in crypto assets (MICA).

[91] "Tokenized equity refers to the creation and issuance of digital tokens or "coins" that represent equity shares in a corporation or organization" (Frankenfield [32]).

[92] "Union legislative acts on financial services should be guided by the principles of 'same activities, same risks, same rules' and of technology neutrality. Therefore, crypto assets that fall under existing Union legislative acts on financial services should remain regulated under the existing regulatory framework, regardless of the technology used for their issuance or their transfer, rather than this Regulation". (Recital 9 of Regulation (EU) 2023/1114 of the European Parliament and of the Council of 31 May 2023 on markets in crypto assets).

the issuance of utility and equity tokens. This principle suggests that a financial instrument's fundamental characteristics should be considered. These should be its underlying economic substance regardless of whether it is traded and registered with a trusted intermediary or stored on a blockchain. As a result, the tax treatment of a financial instrument should not be solely influenced by its form.[93]

In general, funds raised from issuing utility tokens may be classified as business income and taxed only in the issuer's country of residence.[94] Instead, equity tokens are characterised by the right to future profit from the funded project rather than the digital asset itself. However, equity tokens do not grant investors actual ownership of the ICO issuer, such as shares.[95] Taxation of capital raised through the issuance of equity tokens may be classified as capital gains, based on the commentaries' literal interpretation,[96] which falls within the jurisdiction of the ICO issuer's residential state,[97] if any.

5.2.2 Initial Coin Offering (ICO): Issuance of Governance Token

Advanced jurisdictions in the realm of crypto-asset regulation, such as Switzerland[98] and the United States,[99] classify tokens, which allow access to a service and give a right to receive a dividend based on the economic results of the issuing company, almost exclusively as securities. Under these circumstances, some may submit that DAO's security token issued via an ICO should not be deemed "income" for the issuer under domestic tax law, given that the payment obtained from the ICO investor is counterbalanced by the issuer's responsibility to reimburse the capital to the token holder. In this scenario, there is no net increase in an ICO issuer's ability to pay or wealth. Therefore, furthering the COALA look-through approach,[100] it may not be considered taxable income, not even for the token holder.

93 Kjærsgaard [33].

94 Kjærsgaard [33].

95 Kaal and Dell'Erba [34].

96 Article 13(5) of the OECD MC classifies as capital gains: "... from the alienation of any property, other than that referred to in paragraphs 1 (immovable property), 2 (movable property), 3 (ships or aircraft) and 4 (shares or comparable interests), shall be taxable only in the Contracting State of which the alienator is a resident". In this regard, the OECD Commentary precise the words' alienation of property' are: "*used to cover in particular capital gains resulting from the sale or exchange of property and also from ... the sale of a right, the gift and even the passing of property on death*".

97 Kjærsgaard [33].

98 FINMA, *Guidelines, supra* note 53, at 5 ("If a utility token additionally or only has an investment purpose at the point of issue, FINMA will treat such tokens as securities (i.e. in the same way as asset tokens)".

99 Securities and Exchange Commission, Release No. 81207 / July 25, 2017.

100 See *supra,* Section 3.

In the EU context, particularly under the Markets in Crypto-Assets Regulation (MiCA),[101] only those tokens that confer rights akin to financial instruments explicitly excluded from MiCA should be considered outside its scope. In particular, these include shares in companies, securities equivalent to shares, partnerships or other entities, and depositary receipts representing shares, bonds, or other debt instruments.[102] For other tokens, the regulatory alternative between classifications such as tokenised financial instruments and crypto assets is not one of "*all or nothing*" in terms of investor protection. It, instead, involves a choice between two comparable regimes, each based on a disclosure document—a prospectus or a white paper—with corresponding liability resting on the issuer or offeror. The white paper closely resembles the prospectus and adequately supports offering tokens with financial characteristics.

Under this framework, the "governance" function—namely, the ability of token holders to vote on matters related to the development of the blockchain project or the distribution of crypto-assets held by a decentralised organisation—does not qualify a token as a financial instrument in itself.

As has been correctly observed, governance rights are generally not designed to generate claims to cash flows but rather to enable participation in decisions concerning the use and development of the blockchain project.[103] Accordingly, the purchaser of a governance token is not acquiring an instrument equivalent to a company share, as there is typically no direct entitlement to the profits of the underlying project, which in many cases may be entirely absent. Therefore, DAO governance tokens do not confer ownership rights in an underlying company. While such tokens may grant a form of "*membership*" in the blockchain-based platform, the purpose is not to generate future cash flows but to facilitate functional interaction with the blockchain protocol. This functional orientation starkly contrasts the economic model associated with traditional equity shares.[104] Therefore, governance tokens—viewed as utility tokens with partial investment functions—may fall within the scope of MiCA.[105] In that case, the DAO to make an ICO of governance token should be a legal person within the EU[106] (*wrapped DAO*), thus integrating the formal tax nexus with the jurisdiction of incorporation of the legal entity. Therefore, DAO governance tokens issued via an ICO should be deemed "income" for the issuer (an EU taxpayer) and not for the token holder.

---

[101] Regulation (EU) 2023/1114 OF 31 May 2023.

[102] Securities referenced in Article 4(1)(44) of MiFID II.

[103] "*These governance tokens likely will help keep the smart contract developers in check by preventing them from taking actions that would go against the smart contract's users. At the same time, holders of the governance tokens can take ready action to account for regulatory requirements, should they arise, or complex technical or organizational issues that may emerge over time*". Wright [35].

[104] Hacker et al. [36].

[105] Patti [37].

[106] Art. 4 (1), let. a), Regulation (EU) 2023/1114 OF 31 May 2023.

5.2.3 ICO Investors' Return from Tokens

For investors in the Initial Coin Offering (ICO) market, it is worth contemplating whether returns on equity tokens should be classified as dividends according to Article 10 of the OECD Model Convention (MC). The MC defines dividends as "*income from shares, jouissance shares or jouissance rights, mining shares, founders' shares or other rights, not being debt-claims, participating in profits, as well as income from other corporate rights which is subjected to the same taxation treatment as income from shares by the laws of the State of which the company making the distribution is a resident*".

Income must be paid by a "*company*" to qualify as dividends, which is defined in Article 3(1)(a) of the OECD MC as "*anybody corporate or any entity that is treated as a body corporate for tax purposes*". If the issuer of tokens can be considered a company, then the dividend notion may apply. According to the commentaries on the OECD MC, the key requirement for classifying income as dividends is whether the investor "*effectively shares the risks run by the company, i.e., when repayment depends largely on the success or otherwise of the enterprise's business*".[107] Therefore, if an investor participates in current profits and any potential liquidation proceeds, it can be argued that such instruments share entrepreneurial risk.

In light of the above, the return on investment in equity or governance tokens should not be classified as dividends but as other income[108] taxed in the recipient's country of residence (i.e., the ICO investor), regardless of where the income is earned.

5.3 ICO Investors' Capital Gains from the Sale of Tokens

The profits derived from the sale of tokens can be classified as capital gains[109] under Article 13(5) of the OECD Model, which implies that they will only be taxed in the recipient's jurisdiction.

5.4 Token Issued for the Remuneration of the Employee

According to Article 15 of the OECD Model Convention (MC), employment income comprises monetary and non-monetary benefits, including crypto-asset token receipts from employment.[110] The OECD Commentary on Article 15 emphasises the importance of establishing a causal relationship between employment and income received, particularly in determining the source state of such income.

---

[107] OECD MC Art. 10, Paragraph 3, num. 25.

[108] Article 21 of the OECD MC.

[109] Article 13(5) of the OECD Model.

[110] OECD MC Art. 15—Paragraph 1-2.1.

As already pointed out, a DAO must be wrapped in a legal entity to enter in an employment contract. Therefore, the jurisdiction of the source coincides with the jurisdiction of the registered office of the latter legal entity.[111]

For the principal, the employee's income should be recognised at the market value of the tokens awarded when the services are provided, adhering to the principles of a barter transaction. Employees are not required to recognise additional income in cases where there is a change in the token value between the time the services are provided and the payment date, provided that the number of tokens received represents the actual substance of the agreement. No additional tokens were granted or forfeited. Any change in value will have tax implications upon realisation, based on the difference between the market value on the transfer date and the market value on the date the services were provided.

Moreover, if tokens are transferred with restrictions on disposal or retained by the principal until certain conditions are met, principles applied to restricted employee stock options may be relevant. However, because the model conventions do not address timing considerations, domestic legislation should state when employment income is taxed, reflecting the market value of the tokens on that date rather than the date and value at which the tokens were granted. This approach aims to achieve fairness for transactions that have similar purposes.[112]

6 DAO and Exchange of Information

For anti-money laundering (AML) compliance,[113] the regulatory framework encompasses both virtual currency exchange service providers and wallet service providers facilitating virtual-to-fiat currency conversions. This framework enables competent authorities to monitor virtual currency usage via obligated entities. To mitigate anonymity risks, national financial intelligence units must be capable of associating virtual currency addresses with the identities of currency owners. With this aim, the European Banking Authority (EBA) has recently updated specific risk factors for crypto-assets and crypto-asset service providers (CASPs), establishing both simplified and enhanced customer *due diligence* measures.[114]

Financial intermediaries managing overseas assets on behalf of clients must report holdings to the relevant tax authorities under two primary frameworks: the Foreign Account Tax Compliance Act (FATCA) for U.S. taxpayers and the Common Reporting Standard (CRS) for residents of other OECD countries.

[111] See *supra*, section 2.1.

[112] S. Parsons, Work Quoted, paragraph 5.4.3.2

[113] Xiong, X.—Huth, M.—Knottenbelt, W.: REGKYC: Supporting Privacy and Compliance Enforcement for KYC in Blockchains. In https://eprint.iacr.org/2025/579 (accessed 14 april 2025).

[114] Guideline 21, EBA/GL/2024/01 of 16 January 2024 and DAC8, Annex III, Section III.

FATCA aims to prevent tax evasion by U.S. taxpayers holding financial assets in non-U.S. Foreign Financial Institutions (FFIs).[115] These institutions must identify U.S. persons owning financial assets and report them to the Internal Revenue Service (IRS) through their jurisdictional tax authority. Non-compliant FFIs face a 30% withholding tax on payments made to U.S. clients and counterparties.

Notably, crypto-assets, including DAO-issued tokens, are currently excluded from FATCA's list of reportable accounts and assets.[116] From a U.S. regulatory perspective, the IRS classifies cryptocurrencies as intangible assets rather than currencies.[117] However, while a similar exclusion applies under the Foreign Bank and Financial Account Reporting (FBAR)[118] regime, crypto-assets held in hybrid accounts containing both legal (fiat) currencies and crypto-assets remain subject to reporting requirements. This nuanced approach exemplifies the evolving nature of the regulatory landscape, with potential reforms anticipated under the current U.S. administration.

Again, the executive order that U.S. President Donald Trump signed on 23 January may change this regulatory framework.

The CRS, developed by the OECD in 2014, establishes protocols for the automatic exchange of information (AEOI) regarding financial accounts between global tax authorities. It enhances cooperation and minimises opportunities for offshore tax evasion by requiring financial institutions—such as depository institutions, custodial institutions, investment entities, and specified insurance companies—to adhere to strict due diligence and reporting rules.

While the CRS applies to traditional financial assets and legal (fiat) currencies, crypto assets are outside its scope. Furthermore, crypto assets may be held directly by individuals in cold wallets or through crypto asset exchanges that do not have

---

[115] U.S. Internal Revenue Code (IRC) § 1471- D(4).

[116] Reportable accounts/assets include financial accounts maintained by a foreign financial institution and include the following foreign financial assets if they are held for investment purposes and not in an account maintained by a financial institution- Shares or securities issued by an entity that is not a U.S. person, including shares or securities issued by an entity established under the laws of the United States.- Any equity interest in a foreign entity.- Any financial instrument or contract that has an issuer or counterparty that is not a U.S. person, including a financial contract issued by, or an entity organised under the laws of, a U.S. possession. (U.S. Treasury Regulations -26 CFR § 1.1471-5(b)).

[117] IRS Notice 2014-21 (First official IRS guidance on cryptocurrency)—Issued: March 25, 2014

[118] U.S. persons maintain overseas financial accounts for a variety of legitimate reasons, including convenience and access. They must file Reports of Foreign Bank and Financial Accounts (FBAR) because foreign financial institutions may not be subject to the same reporting requirements as domestic financial institutions. The FBAR is also a tool used by the U.S. government to identify persons who may be using foreign financial accounts to circumvent U.S. law. The government can use FBAR information to identify or trace funds used for illicit purposes or to identify unreported income maintained or generated abroad. (available at https://www.irs.gov/newsroom/how-to-report-foreign-bank-and-financial-accounts#:~:text=The%20FBAR%20is%20also%20a,income%20maintained%20or%20generated%20abroad , accessed 14 April 2025)

reporting obligations under the CRS, thereby limiting tax administrations' visibility into tax-relevant transactions involving or holding crypto assets.[119]

To address this regulatory gap, in August 2022, the OECD's Committee on Fiscal Affairs approved the Crypto-Asset Reporting Framework (CARF),[120] which aimed to provide standard guidelines for due diligence rules and procedures, stated "... *for the automatic exchange of tax-relevant information on Crypto-Assets and has been developed to address the rapid development and growth of the Crypto-Asset market and to ensure that recent gains in global tax transparency are not gradually eroded*".[121]

Following CARF's approval, the European Commission[122] undertook to update the scope of the Administrative Cooperation Directive (DAC) to mitigate tax avoidance risks associated with crypto-assets and their users. This initiative led to the eighth amendment to the DAC regime (DAC8),[123] approved on 17 October 2023 and set to take effect from 1 January 2026, which extends reporting obligations to all crypto-asset service providers (CASPs) regarding transactions conducted by their EU-based customers.[124] This measure enhances the ability of EU tax authorities to monitor and verify crypto-asset revenues and their tax implications.[125]

DAC8 aligns with the tax transparency objectives of the CARF recommendations and builds upon the regulatory taxonomy established by the Markets in Crypto-assets Regulation (MiCA) by introducing obligations for "*...reporting and automatic exchange of information in the detail required for direct tax purposes*".[126] Notably, DAC8's scope extends beyond OECD CARF standards to include non-EU operators with EU-based users. To access the EU market, these operators must register in a Member State and comply with the prescribed reporting rules. The DAC 8 information exchange operates through a two-step process. Firstly, service providers report their users' specific cryptocurrency transactions to the tax authorities. Secondly, tax authorities across Member States exchange this information, which includes cross-border transactions,[127] to enhance regulatory oversight and tax compliance.

---

[119] OECD [38].

[120] OECD [38].

[121] OECD [39].

[122] European Commission, Communication from the Commission to the European Parliament and the Council—An action plan for fair and simple taxation to support the recovery strategy, Brussels, 15.7.2020 COM(2020) 312 final.

[123] Council Directive (EU) 2023/2226 of 17 October 2023 amending Directive 2011/16/EU on administrative procedures, cooperation in the field of taxation.

[124] European Commission. (2022). Proposal for a Council Directive amending Directive 2011/16/EU on administrative procedures. cooperation in the field of taxation, COM(2022) 707 final.

[125] European Commission. (2022). *Executive Summary Of The Impact Assessment Report*: *Initiative to strengthen existing rules and broaden the framework for exchange of information in the field of taxation to include crypto-assets*, (2022) 402 final. 1.

[126] Gorissen et al. [40].

[127] European Commission. (2022). *Impact Assessment Report: Initiative to strengthen existing rules and broaden the framework for exchange of information in the area of taxation to include crypto-assets*, SWD(2022) 401 final. 8.

Moreover, DAC8 ensures that such information can be used for purposes other than direct taxation, such as assessing, administering, and enforcing value-added tax (VAT), other indirect taxes, customs duties, anti-money laundering, and countering the financing of terrorism.[128]

For the sake of completeness, it should be noted that *peer-to-peer (or person to person)*.[129] transactions between self-hosted wallets and decentralised exchanges (DEXs) fall outside the scope of the DAC8 rules, as they are not included in the definition of a reportable transaction.[130]

Specifically, a DEX, rather than being a centralised entity that matches orders and holds custody of funds, operates through a set of smart contracts that facilitate direct, peer-to-peer cryptocurrency swaps.[131]

As a result, transactions involving Decentralized Autonomous Organizations (DAOs) may fall outside the scope of DAC8. Nevertheless, for anti-money laundering (AML) purposes, originator and beneficiary information of a transaction must be exchanged between crypto-asset service providers (CASPs), or between a CASP and a self-hosted wallet, for transactions exceeding USD 1,000. This requirement aims to ensure the traceability of virtual asset transfers under the so-called "*travel rule*".[132]

7 DAO and Indirect Taxation

In general, the supply of goods and services that are (i) provided for consideration and (ii) delivered by an entrepreneur or self-employed person are subject to Value Added Tax (VAT).[133] Based on this subjective legal assumption, fully decentralised algorithmic DAOs are excluded from VAT liability, as they do not qualify as businesses or self-employed individuals.

However, if a DAO qualifies as a CASP providing services for cryptocurrencies within the EU market, is required to establish a corporate structure in a member state

[128] DAC8, Art. 1 (7)(a).

[129] Art. 14, section 5 and 16, section 2 of Regulation (EU) 2023/1113 of 31 May 2023 on information accompanying transfers and certain crypto-assets—TFR.

[130] DAC8, Annex, III, Section IV, C(4).

[131] https://blog.uniswap.org/what-is-a-decentralized-exchange (accessed 11 April 2025).

[132] In 2019, the Financial Action Task Force (FATF) expanded its anti-money laundering and counter-terrorist financing (AML/CFT) measures to encompass virtual assets and virtual asset service providers (VASPs), the measure known as Recommendation 16 (the Travel Rule). To prevent criminal and terrorist exploitation of the virtual asset sector Recommendation 16 serves as a set of rules VASPs must follow when conducting virtual asset transfers. According to Recommendation 16, VASPs must collect, verify and exchange specific customer information before a virtual asset transfer can occur. Moreover, it guides how VASPs are to transact with self-hosted wallets (See FATF [41]). Art. 14, Section 5 and 16, Section 2 of Regulation (EU) 2023/1113 of 31 May 2023 on information accompanying transfers and certain crypto-assets—TFR) has implemented the FATF Travel Rule Within the EU.

[133] Art. 1, Presidential Decree No. 633/72.

under MICA Regulation, thus creating a tax nexus with that jurisdiction, which then acquires tax sovereignty over gains derived from this business. Consequently, the question arises as to whether the services provided by a DAO fall within the scope of VAT and, if so, what VAT rate is applicable and which invoicing method should be adopted.

Regarding tokens, the VAT treatment of crypto-assets requires a case-by-case assessment, considering their economic function or use, in line with the "technology neutrality" principle established by the MiCA Regulation.[134]

This principle extends to VAT considerations, requiring an evaluation of each transaction to ascertain its true nature, practical function, and actual utilisation, irrespective of the label assigned by the issuer for commercial purposes.[135] In this regard, the clarifications provided by the Court of Justice of the European Union (CJEU).[136] in the *Hedqvist* judgement remain authoritative. Accordingly, when the sole purpose of a crypto-activity is to serve as a means of payment, cryptocurrency transactions qualify as VAT-exempt.[137] Thus, the following financial transactions, when conducted for consideration, are VAT-exempt[138]:

- The exchange between traditional and virtual currencies, as well as exchanges between virtual currencies.
- Mining activities involving virtual currencies, where remuneration is received through fees charged by the miner.
- Fees for digital wallet services.
- Staking activities.

Consistent with the functional approach outlined above, these exemptions pertain to tokens that primarily function as a means of payment or virtual currency. Additionally, the exemption framework extends to security tokens that serve as investment instruments, such as shares, bonds, and other securities, along with their associated service.[139]

Utility tokens also require a case-by-case assessment to determine whether they serve as vouchers rather than payment instruments.

From a residual perspective, it is useful to highlight the VAT notion of "*Electronically supplied services*" which include "*services which are delivered over the Internet or an electronic network and the nature of which renders their supply essentially automated and involving minimal human intervention, and impossible to*

---

[134] Recital No. 9, Reg. (EU) 2023/1114.

[135] Revenue Agency, Circular No. 30/2023, para. 3.7.1.

[136] Judgment 22 October 2015, C-264/14 (Hedqvist case).

[137] Article 135(1)(e) of Directive 2006/112/EC.

[138] VAT Committee in *Guidelines resulting from the 120th meeting of 28 March 2022–1045*, paragraphs 3 and 4.

[139] Article 10(1)(4), Presidential Decree No. 633/72. In this regard, the ECJ (Judgment 19 July 2012, C-44/11, Deutsche Bank case) excluded from the scope of the exemption the services of "*safekeeping and administration of securities as well as the individual portfolio management service*", which therefore remain subject to VAT at the ordinary rate.

ensure in the absence of information technology".[140] Consequently, the provision of "Electronically supplied services" for consideration by a "wrapped DAO" established in the EU is tax-relevant for VAT purposes. Generally, the supply of services between businesses (B2B services) is, in principle, taxed at the customer's place of establishment. In contrast, services supplied to private individuals (B2C services) are taxed at the supplier's place of establishment.[141]

Conversely, the provision of "*Electronically supplied services*" by an unwrapped DAO is not relevant for VAT purposes. In this regard, it is useful to reference the German case law on VAT liability for renting virtual land in the Metaverse. In August 2019, the Regional Fiscal Court in Cologne issued a judgement stating that renting virtual land is taxable for VAT purposes.[142] However, in November 2021, on appeal, the Federal Finance Court of Germany (Bundesfinanzhof [BFH])[143] fundamentally deviated from this decision, stating that anything within a game lies outside the real world and the economic sphere where VAT applies. The BFH's judgement may lead to the conclusion that everything occurring in the virtual game world is not subject to VAT. Let us refer to it as the "*what happens in Vegas, stays in Vegas*" approach.[144] Accordingly, the same reasoning should be applied to unwrapped DAOs.

8 DAO as a Tool for Tax Authorities

In a decentralised, crypto asset-based economy, DAOs could play a pivotal role in serving as a technical umbrella for integrating national tax authorities, taxpayers, and intermediaries into a cooperative, cross-border tax platform. This would facilitate tax collection through a transaction-based mechanism enabled by smart contracts. These contracts ensure automatic execution and could support the imposition of indirect taxes, such as value-added tax and transfer pricing rules, which depend on the verifiable, cross-border transmission of tax-relevant data. This approach aligns with the DAO's foundational principle of community governance and resonates with the OECD's horizontal monitoring framework, promoting cooperative rather than authoritarian tax enforcement.

Smart contracts could automate tax payments directly at the transactional level, enhancing efficiency and compliance. However, successful implementation hinges on the availability of accurate underlying data and a robust technical infrastructure.

To calculate taxes effectively, a dual on-chain/off-chain architecture is required. Blockchain would provide immutable documentation of transaction data, ensuring

[140] Art. 7, par.1, Council Implementing Regulation (EU) No 282/2011 of 15 March 2011 laying down implementing measures for Directive 2006/112/EC on the common system of value added tax (recast) (OJ L 77, 23.3.2011, p. 1).

[141] Art. 1, Directive (UE) 2017/2455.

[142] Bundesfinanzhof [42].

[143] Bundesfinanzhof [43].

[144] Majorana [44].

data integrity and transparency, while tax computation would occur off-chain using artificial intelligence (AI).

Although the adoption of such a system would entail substantial implementation and maintenance costs, it offers long-term cost-efficiency by addressing the current fragmentation in tax systems. A standardised, cross-border digital infrastructure would reduce administrative burdens and enhance the capacity to combat tax evasion. Thus, the integration of DAOs, blockchain, and AI presents a promising framework for modernising international tax collection in the digital economy.[145]

9 Conclusions

Lex Cryptographia facilitates the creation of autonomous and decentralised digital entities, which U.S. case law has classified as "unrecognised associations". These entities may exhibit a degree of financial autonomy but lack legal personality. As a consequence of this classification, governance token holders entitled to vote may bear unlimited liability.

From a tax perspective, a DAO is typically regarded as a stateless entity unless it is incorporated into a special purpose vehicle (SPV) to satisfy regulatory obligations associated with its operations (e.g., when functioning as a Crypto-Asset Service Provider, or CASP). In such cases, the sole connecting factor for determining the entity's tax residence is the formal criterion, whereby the SPV is deemed resident in the jurisdiction in which it is incorporated and under the legal framework pursuant to which it was established.

Moreover, the purely digital nature of a DAO's operations fails to meet the substantive requirements outlined by the OECD for defining the Effective Place of Management (EPoM)—a concept traditionally applicable to physical, brick-and-mortar enterprises. Nor is recourse to the Mutual Agreement Procedure (MAP) sufficient to resolve the fiscal ambiguity surrounding DAOs. Given these challenges, and in the absence of specific regulation, unwrapped DAOs may currently operate as mechanisms that facilitate tax avoidance.

To mitigate this risk, the Coalition of Automated Legal Applications (COALA), through its *Model Law for Decentralised Autonomous Organisations (DAO)*, proposed a taxation provision that upholds the principle of transparency. This provision mirrors the treatment of investment funds, which possess financial autonomy without legal personality—a status already recognised within the tax domain and, therefore, potentially suitable for adoption in the context of DAOs. Under this approach, taxation would be imposed primarily at the level of the token holder, proportionate to their token holdings, rather than at the entity level.

Unlike investment funds, however, DAOs are not just recognised as tax entities and cannot determine income to be allocated distributable to token holders. Consequently, token holders may be taxed upon the actual receipt of bonuses, dividends, or tokens

[145] Müller [5].

and upon the realisation of capital gains from the sale of DAO tokens. This framework affords token holders a tax deferral benefit akin to that shareholders enjoy concerning accrued but undistributed dividends.

Importantly, while companies owned by investment funds are subject to corporate tax—implying that income distributed to fund unit holders has already been taxed at source—DAOs considered stateless entities may avoid such taxation. Consequently, income received by token holders might not be liable to corporate tax in any jurisdiction. Under this premise, a sustainable approach would involve taxing token holders on income accrued during the tax period, determined through a mark-to-market method based on the market value of the tokens.

Based on the observations presented in this essay, it can be concluded that for DAOs that have adopted a corporate structure (i.e., wrapped DAOs), the current OECD-developed framework of international taxation remains applicable to the allocation of taxing rights. Instead, the OECD framework does not apply to fully decentralised DAOS, as the absence of a source jurisdiction precludes the emergence of double taxation concerns. As a result, the taxation of income flows received by token holders falls within the purview of domestic tax law in the jurisdiction of the token holder's residence.

It may be argued that the anonymity of token holders renders such an approach impractical. However, obligations arising under the Anti-Money Laundering Directives (AML) and the Directive on Administrative Cooperation (DAC8), which apply to exchanges and CASPs, enable the identification of token holders for tax purposes.

Furthermore, DAOs could serve as instruments for tax authorities to automate tax collection at the transactional level, thereby enhancing compliance and administrative efficiency. However, the effectiveness of such an approach would depend on the availability of accurate underlying data and the establishment of a robust blockchain infrastructure, with tax computation occurring off-chain through artificial intelligence (AI).

From the indirect taxation perspective, the actual consumption of data within the Distributed Ledger Technology (DLT) ecosystem—quantified and processed by data controllers under the GDPR regulatory framework—could serve as the basis for a "digital excise tax". In this context, the data controller could act as the designated tax representative.

Accordingly, the time is ripe for DAOs to transition from the informal framework of *Lex Cryptographia* to a formal regulatory structure that ensures a level playing field for all stakeholders. In this regard, the recent Letta Report on European competitiveness[146] has advocated the creation of a "28th jurisdiction": an EU-wide legal framework tailored to young and innovative enterprises. This framework would enable such entities to operate under a harmonised set of EU rules, circumventing the complexities of 27 disparate legal regimes—marking a significant regulatory

---

[146] E. Letta, *Much more than a market*, April 2024.

milestone. A parallel proposal for a 28th legal regime aimed at streamlining regulatory compliance and lowering the cost of failure—including in areas such as corporate, insolvency, labour, and tax law—has recently been adopted by the European Commission.[147]

References

1. Dell'Erba, M.: Demystifying technology. Do smart contracts require a new legal framework? Regulatory fragmentation, self-regulation, public regulation. Available at SSRN: https://ssrn.com/abstract=3228445 or http://dx.doi.or, 17 May 2018
2. Fransoni, G.: Fisco internazionale, servono idee nuove e non vecchi modelli, in Il Sole 24 ore, 11 February 2025
3. Emanuele, V.: The value creation principle: delving into the past to understand its future role in the international tax reform. Intertax **53**(3), 267–283 (2025)
4. Olivieri, L., Pasetto, L., Negrini, L., Ferrara, P.: European Union data act and blockchain technology: challenges and new directions, Proceeding 6th Distributed Ledger Technologies Workshop (DLT 2024), Turin, Italy, 14–15 May 2024
5. Müller, R.: Tax challenges and potential opportunities arising from decentralized autonomous organizations, IBFD Bulletin for International Taxation, November 2024
6. Szabo, N.: Smart contracts: building blocks for digital markets. https://www.fon.hum.uva.nl/rob/Courses/InformationInSpeech/CDROM/Literature/LOTwinterschool2006/szabo.best.vwh.net/smart_contracts_2.html (1996). Accessed 11 April 2025
7. Lener, R., Furnari, S.: Organisational models to the test of new technologies. First reflections on DAO and general principles of business law, Atti XII Convegno dell'Associazione Italiana dei Professori Universitari di Diritto Commerciale Orizzonti del Diritto Commerciale, Rome, 17–18 September 2021
8. Report of the European Law Institute: ELI Principles on Blockchain Technology, Smart Contracts and Consumer Protection, ISBN: 978-3-9505318-1-7 (Project Number: P-2018-17) (2023)
9. Buterin, V.: DAOs, DACs, DAs and more: an incomplete terminology guide. Available at https://blog.ethereum.org/2014/05/06/daos-dacs-das-and-more-an-incomplete-terminology-guide, 6 May 2014. Accessed 11 April 2025
10. Furnari, S., Villani, C.: Regulation of financial protocol DAOs. Addressing the problems of decentralisation and ai governance. Available at SSRN https://ssrn.com/abstract=5023440 or https://doi.org/10.2139/ssrn.5023440, 15 November 2024
11. Cardoso, A.G.: Decentralized autonomous organizations—DAOs: the convergence of technology, law, governance, and behavioral economics, MIT Computational Law Report. https://law.mit.edu/pub/decentralizedautonomousorganizations. Available at SSRN https://ssrn.com/abstract=4699165, 20 November 2023
12. Ziegler, C., Welpe, I.: A taxonomy of decentralized autonomous organizations, ICIS 2022 Proceedings 1. Available at https://aisel.aisnet.org/icis2022/blockchain/blockchain/1/ (2022). Accessed 11 April 2025
13. Mienert, B.: Limited liability as applied to DAOs. In: Perestrelo de Oliveira, M., Garcia Rolo, A., Siebeck, E.M.: Decentralised autonomous organisation (DAO) Regulation principles and perspectives for the future (2024). https://doi.org/10.1628/978-3-16-163701-8
14. Möslein, F., Ostrovski, D.: Legal personality of decentralised autonomous organisations (DAOs): privilege or necessity? In: Perestrelo de Oliveira, M., Garcia Rolo, A., Siebeck, M.E.

[147] EU Commission, *A Competitiveness Compass for the EU*, Brussels, 29.1.2025 COM(2025) 30 final.

(eds.) Decentralised autonomous organisation (DAO) Regulation principles and perspectives for the future (2024). https://doi.org/10.1628/978-3-16-163701-8
15. Mienert, B.: How can a decentralized autonomous organization (DAO) be legally structured? In Legal Revolutionary Journal LRZ. Available at SSRN https://ssrn.com/abstract=3992329 or https://doi.org/10.2139/ssrn.3992329 1 December 2021
16. Reyes, C.: If rockefeller were a coder 2. 87 Geo. Wash, in L. Rev., 2019, 373. Available at SSRN: https://ssrn.com/abstract=3082915 or https://doi.org/10.2139/ssrn.3082915 5 December 2017
17. Chen, J.: Future commission merchant (FCM): definition, role, registration, available at https://www.investopedia.com/terms/f/fcm.asp, 22 August 2024. Accessed 11 April 2025.
18. BlackVogel—a blockstand project: DAOs and the Legal Wrapper Dilemma. The voices of the industry. Available at: https://www.blackvogel.com/advancingdaostandarization-blockstand, January 2025. Accessed 11 April 2025
19. Finck, M.: Blockchain and the general data protection regulation (par. 4.3.2). EPRS | European Parliamentary Research Service, PE 634.445—July 2019.
20. Galimberti, A.: Nuove accise digitali per tassare le big tech e reagire agli Usa. In "Il Sole 24 Ore", 6 April 2025
21. Cardoso, A.G.: Decentralized autonomous organizations—DAOs: The convergence of technology, law, governance, and behavioral economics. Available at SSRN: https://ssrn.com/abstract=4341884 or https://doi.org/10.2139/ssrn.4341884, 15 September 2022
22. OECD: Model Tax Convention on Income and on Capital: OECD (2017), Model Tax Convention on Income and on Capital: Condensed Version 2017. OECD Publishing (2017). https://doi.org/10.1787/mtc_cond-2017-en-CommentaryonArt.4(21)
23. OECD: Model Tax Convention on Income and on Capital: Condensed Version 2017. OECD Publishing (2017). https://doi.org/10.1787/mtc_cond-2017-en-CommentaryonArt.29(149)
24. OECD: Addressing the Tax Challenges of the Digital Economy, BEPS—Action 1–2015 Final Report, OECD/G20 Base Erosion and Profit Shifting Project. OECD Publishing, Paris (2015). https://doi.org/10.1787/9789264241046-en
25. Olika, D.: The tiebreaker rule for tax residence of companies under the MLI: A critique of the tiebreaker rule for tax residence of companies under the MLI. Revista Técnica Tributaria **1**(140), 135–153. Available at SSRN: https://ssrn.com/abstract=4436011 or https://doi.org/10.2139/ssrn.4436011, 31 March 2023
26. Cipollini, C.: Virtual real estate in the metaverse: how should countries allocate taxing rights? In World Tax J. **17**(1) https://doi.org/10.59403/259j6nb(2025)
27. Shakow, D.J.: The tao of the DAO: taxing an entity that lives on a blockchain. In Tax Notes, U of Penn, Inst for Law & Econ Research Paper No. 18–23. Available at SSRN https://ssrn.com/abstract=3247155, 13 August 2018
28. Kim, Y.R.: Taxing the Metaverse, 112, Georgetown Law Journal 787 (2024), Cardozo Legal Studies Research Paper No.724. Available at SSRN https://ssrn.Com/Abstract=4549974, 23 August 2023
29. Baer, K., de Mooij, R., Hebous, S., Keen, M.: "Taxing cryptocurrencies". IMF Working Paper—Fiscal Affairs Department, June 2023
30. OECD: Model Tax Convention on Income and on Capital 2017 (full version). OECD Publishing, Paris (2019). https://doi.org/10.1787/g2g972ee-en
31. Majorana, D.: Italian and cross-border tax regulatory framework. In: Hilpold, P., Hörtnagl-Seidner, V. (eds.) Besteuerung von Kryptowerten EU, Österreich, Italien. (Facultas) (2024). ISBN 978-3-7089-2501-1
32. Frankenfield, J.: What is tokenized equity? how tokenized stock works, and example. Available at https://www.investopedia.com/terms/t/tokenized-equity.asp#:~:text=Key%20Takeaways,and%20transfer%20of%20digital%20tokens. Accessed 7 July 2023
33. Kjærsgaard, L.F.: Blockchain technology and the allocation of taxing rights to payments related to initial coin offerings. Intertax **48**(10), 879–903 (2020)
34. Kaal, W.A., Dell'Erba, M.: Initial coin offerings: emerging practices, risk factors, and red flags, U. of St. Thomas (Minnesota) Legal studies research paper No. 17–18, p. 2. Available at https://papers.ssrn.com/sol3/papers.cfm?abstract_id=3067615 (2018). Accessed 7 July 2023

35. Wright, A.: The rise of decentralized autonomous organizations: opportunities and challenges. Stanford J. Blockchain Law Pol. Available at https://stanford-jblp.pubpub.org/pub/rise-of-daos/release/1, 30 June 2021. Accessed 9 April 2025
36. Hacker, P., Thomale, C.: Crypto-securities regulation: ICOs, token sales and cryptocurrencies under EU financial law. European Company Financial Law Rev. **5**, 645–696. Available at SSRN https://ssrn.com/abstract=3075820or https://doi.org/10.2139/ssrn.3075820 (2018), 22 November 2017
37. Patti, F.P.: The European MiCA regulation: a new era for initial coin offerings. Georgetown J. Int. Law, Forthcoming, Bocconi Legal Studies Research Paper No. 4810910, Available at SSRN https://ssrn.com/abstract=4810910 or https://doi.org/10.2139/ssrn.4810910, 23 April 2024
38. OECD: Crypto-asset reporting framework and amendments to the common reporting standard, OECD, Paris, p. 3. Available at https://www.oecd.org/en/publications/international-standards-for-automatic-exchange-of-information-in-tax-matters_896d79d1-en.html (2022). Accessed 11 April 2025
39. OECD: International Standards for Automatic Exchange of Information in Tax Matters: Crypto-Asset Reporting Framework and 2023 Update to the Common Reporting Standard. OECD Publishing, Paris (2023). https://doi.org/10.1787/896d79d1-en
40. Gorissen, T.M.L., Uslu, Y.: Investing in crypto-assets: council adoption of DAC8. Finance and capital markets 24 (3) (2023). Available at SSRN https://ssrn.com/abstract=5164404or https://doi.org/10.59403/1xj7qr4.
41. FATF: Targeted upate on implementation of the FATF standards on virtual Assets/VASPs, FATF, Paris, France. https://www.fatf-gafi.org/content/fatf-gafi/en/publications/Fatfrecommendations/targeted-update-virtual-assets-vasps-2024.html (2024). Accessed 11 April 2025
42. Bundesfinanzhof: ECLI:DE:FGK:2019:0813.8K1565.18.00. https://nrwe.justiz.nrw.de/fgs/koeln/j2019/8_K_1565_18_Urteil_20190813.html,13 August 2019. Accessed 11 April 2025
43. Bundesfinanzhof: ECLI:DE:BFH:2021:U.181121.VR38/19. https://www.bundesfinanzhof.de/de/entscheidung/entscheidungen-online/detail/STRE202210041/, 18 November 2021. Accessed 11 April 2025
44. Majorana, D.: The Metaverse: why, where and what to tax. Available at SSRN: https://ssrn.com/abstract=4834837 or https://doi.org/10.2139/ssrn.4834837,, 20 May 2023

Correction to: Decentralized Autonomous Organizations: Is a New Liability Regime Possible? Current Landscape of German and Turkish Company Law and a New Liability Regime Recommendation

Barış C. Cantürk

Correction to:
Chapter 8 in: M. Lustenberger et al. (eds.), *Decentralized Autonomous Organizations—Governance, Technology, and Legal Perspectives*, Springer Proceedings in Business and Economics, https://doi.org/10.1007/978-3-032-03273-7_8

The original version of the paper starting on 135 was revised. An acknowledgement has been added. The original article was corrected accordingly.

The updated version of this chapter can be found at
https://doi.org/10.1007/978-3-032-03273-7_8

M. Lustenberger et al. (eds.), *Decentralized Autonomous Organizations—Governance, Technology, and Legal Perspectives*, Springer Proceedings in Business and Economics,
https://doi.org/10.1007/978-3-032-03273-7_10

MIX
Papier aus verantwortungsvollen Quellen
Paper from responsible sources
FSC® C105338
FSC
www.fsc.org

If you have any concerns about our products,
you can contact us on
ProductSafety@springernature.com

In case Publisher is established outside the EU,
the EU authorized representative is:
Springer Nature Customer Service Center GmbH
Europaplatz 3, 69115 Heidelberg, Germany

Printed by Libri Plureos GmbH
in Hamburg, Germany